T0210662

Tacit Engagement

Satinder P. Gill

Tacit Engagement

Beyond Interaction

 Springer

Satinder P. Gill
Centre for Music and Science
University of Cambridge
Cambridge, UK

ISBN 978-3-319-36792-7   ISBN 978-3-319-21620-1 (eBook)
DOI 10.1007/978-3-319-21620-1

Springer Cham Heidelberg New York Dordrecht London
© Springer International Publishing Switzerland 2015
Softcover re-print of the Hardcover 1st edition 2015

Cover artist: Josie Camus, 1979–2014

Printed on acid-free paper

Springer International Publishing AG Switzerland is part of Springer Science+Business Media (www.springer.com)

Preface

Over the years, whenever I have been asked about what I do, I find myself telling complex stories of people and ideas and projects, and the stories can seem to be about different things, yet they are all connected for me and have a clear thread. In writing this book I present the whole picture.

My story begins in my teenage years growing up with a father, Karamjit S Gill (Founding Editor of *AI & Society*), who was passionate about how technology can be used to help people who are disadvantaged and marginalised in society. He created two amazing national and European funded projects, one for children with learning difficulties, Computer Aided Animated Arts Theatre (CAAAT) at the University of Brighton, UK, and the other for minority women in Brighton (PAROSI – which means neighbour in Hindi), both based on fundamental principles of enabling the disadvantaged to engage in society and for society to engage with them, as equals. Where others may have conducted their projects in the buildings and institutions of disabled children, my father brought the children to the university and hired unemployed artists, teachers and musicians, to work with his computer science and AI students to develop technologies with the teachers and parents of the disabled children. A goal was to give access to the child in a way they had not had until now, to connect with others and without prejudice. His commitment and those who shared it sowed the seeds for how I think about the purpose of technology.

When I turned 17, my father took me to my first AI conference, in fact it was the first AI conference in Europe, in Orsay. I sat with Hans Berlinger whilst he patiently tried to explain to me what chess programmes do and listened to Kowalski speaking about Prolog. I witnessed a heated exchange between Shanks and Kowalski in the conference hall about the values of representing our knowledge in scripts versus logic. Although I did not understand the particulars about the field, this was a curious world concerned with how we process information and perceive ourselves as cognitive beings.

As a teenager I also came to know the AI group at Sussex where Maggie Boden and Aaron Sloman were leading figures, and she has always been supportive and encouraged me over the years to develop my ideas and is a lovely and remarkable person.

My own research life has its origins in one Christmas vacation during my final year at Keele University (where I was studying PPE). I came home to Brighton that year to find two Swedish visitors, Bo Goranzon and Ingela Josefson, in our living room. They had come to meet my father and spoke of a concept they called tacit knowledge. We talked about aesthetics (my special subject in philosophy), which I learnt was a part of tacit knowledge, and of issues around culture and dialogue. I explained how growing up in two cultures one can lie in between both and not fully be in either and how I was aware of this through the movements of mine and others' voice and gestures that could sometimes cause the information we were speaking to become missed.

After graduation I became an apprentice on the study of tacit knowledge with Bo and Ingela at the Swedish Centre for Working Life (which no longer exists) in Stockholm. It was a reflective experience and a privilege to work with such committed and deep thinkers. The pleasures of being an apprentice involved spending time with Kjell Johannessen and Tore Nordenstam at the University of Bergen, the home of Wittgenstein's archives. Kjell and Tore, both professors in philosophy, set me to reading Polanyi's *The Tacit Dimension* and Wittgenstein's *Philosophical Investigations*. I found Bergen incredibly beautiful and enjoyed some of the best fish cooked by Kjell and his partner which I still remember today. But most of all, I remember both Kjell and Tore's kindness to spend time to teach me about philosophers and thinkers who I am still trying to understand better today.

Being an apprentice also involved participating in Board meetings of a major Scandinavian conference on Language, Culture and Artificial Intelligence (1988), which was to garner the experience of applying knowledge-based technologies in all spheres of society. It would address issues arising for working life, skills and the future. I did not understand the Swedish spoken but found the meetings insightful for understanding how decisions are made – they take time and consider all points of view, but once made, the decision stands. How decisions are made was to become a focus of my later research.

I loved the spirit and direct warmth of the Scandinavians and will never forget the head of the trade unions grabbing my hand and running alongside the water to reach a meeting in time, not something an English man would do.

As part of my conference responsibilities, I travelled in Europe bringing together scholars working in the area of human-centred systems for a workshop which would form part of the conference. I had met them all at the various *AI & Society* conferences my father had organised whilst I was growing up, but now I was to meet them in a different capacity. In Bremen I stayed with Felix Rauner's family in a beautiful house that he had literally built with his own hands and was introduced to the concept of social shaping of technology. This was slightly different from the participatory approach of Pelle Ehn whom I was to learn about soon after, as it focused on the personality, wellbeing and learning capacities of people. How we relate to technology is unpredictable, so no outcome to any design can be predetermined. Instead what is important is that a person can experience self-transcendence and self-renewal and not be stressed. Furthermore, in designing technology with a person, their total personality needs to be considered, not just the functional situation of the particular work task, i.e. a whole person is a wage earner, a citizen, a private person, a parent, a child, a consumer, etc., always faced with conflicting interests with their own self. Much of what Felix and his colleagues at Bremen University spoke about is being lamented today as we hear about the mechanistic approach to workers, with the quantified measurement of work, health, and education, and rising levels of stress in daily life. We increasingly separate the person from their whole system and thereby fragment the organisational and community systems they work and live in. Aside from the research, as a culture Germany felt more hierarchical than Sweden, but decisions were highly inclusive of those who would be affected and might be affected by them.

From here I travelled onto Italy, where in the beautiful old university town of Urbino, Massimo Negrotti disagreed with the Swede's use of the term dialogue for anything other than communion with God, and for all earthly matters the word 'communication' was considered more suitable. Massimo's work was and is on understanding the nature of the artificial, on what happens when we reproduce from nature (naturoids) and then engage with the artificial reproduction. His work is about fundamental concepts that are important for us now as we deal with the consequences of the artificial in many aspects of our daily life.

In Denmark, I learnt about the experimental prototyping approach to designing technologies from Lauge Rassmussen at Lyngby University. By experiment they did not mean 'scientific method', but rather about how we examine our world out of curiosity and to fulfil our needs, a continuous confrontation between our experience and social concepts. An experiment is a means by which we learn. They did use the expression dialogue, and its process was just as important as the results of the design it was creating. The other expression was 'user cooperation', which meant mutual corrections by participants. Lauge and his family lived by a beautiful lake, and I enjoyed the warm-hearted atmosphere of their home and kind personality of the Danish that I have encountered in other Danes since.

Back in Sweden I saw my mentors' passion to value the qualities of creativity, of skill, reflection, and dialogue. Bo created the Dialogue Seminar which is running strong today and brings together scholars, artists and performance artists, to go deeply into the relation between knowledge and dialogue. So much of the focus on dialogue nowadays is reduced to communication that as an idea assumes we must converge on sameness, a common ground. Yet this idea of a common ground needs to accommodate the complex conflicts both within us and between us that can coexist in simultaneity. Reflection is part of dialogue. Bo's passion came from what he saw happening in working life from the effects of knowledge-based technologies; as a mathematician, he observed mathematicians beginning to doubt their own judgements. His questions were about the effects of engaging with the certainty of abstracted and rule-based data and the measurement of practice.

Ingela is a linguist, and her work with nurses made me aware of the power of forms of expression for shaping how we think, how we practise and how we perceive ourselves. With nurses, she was developing a language born out of their daily practice, and this was at a time when nursing in Sweden was becoming 'professionalised' with the 'scientific language' of medicine and nursing degrees. The status given to scientific speaking over practical knowledge was interesting but worrying too, given that 'care' is a critical part of nursing someone who is ill.

As part of my apprenticeship, I edited a collection of the works of their group as a book, which was published in 1988 for the conference itself. In these writings I came to see the importance of the body in knowing, of reflection, of taking the time needed and of being in dialogue with oneself and others, as a continuous process in order to form tacit knowledge and perform as an expert. Their discussion on skills and tacit knowledge was to influence how I studied the processes of tacit and explicit knowledge in dialogue itself.

Upon leaving the Swedish Centre for Working Life, I embarked on a Ph.D. with Ajit Narayan, a philosopher of logic at Exeter University, and in that first year I presented a paper based on my Scandinavian experience at the British Computer Society Expert Systems conference. Bob Muller was chairing my session and later invited me to join a workshop retreat organised by his company where they were creating a new identity of their people, as consultants. I would track the process of how they went about this and study the various ways in which tacit knowledge was being expressed. I had an amazing week with these highly skilled and senior corporate managers, watching them do role plays, produce cartoons, create performances, etc., all in a mission to perform as an authentic 'consultant'. I write about one of these sessions in Chap. 4.

Bob's kindness and support for a young person was astonishing, and he gave me wise advice as well. It was deeply sad to hear of his passing. The experience he gave me was a catalyst for leaving the field of computer science to continue my Ph.D. in experimental psychology at the University of Cambridge under Debra Bekerian, a formidable applied psychologist working on autobiographical memory. She understood the relation between the tacit and the explicit in dialogue and viewed this from the context of autobiographical memory. I learnt a great deal from her and owe her so much for her support. Despite being a brilliant statistician, she took on a student who wished to do a qualitative Ph.D. She was known for beginning her talks with reams of statistics and then putting them aside to focus on the psychology. Cambridge was to be one of the most wonderful periods in my life with amazing mentors whom I have kept in touch with, and whenever I have become lost on my research path, I have been able to seek advice from them. I will never forget my interview with the head of the department, Nick Mackintosh, who patiently listened to all the reasons I gave as to why I could not, in principle, conduct experiments to study the tacit dimension, but we did agree on basic principles, and he wished me good luck. I was fortunate that he had a background in philosophy and classics, as well as experimental psychology, which must be why he was able to be so open to this naïve student questioning the methods of analysis intrinsic to the discipline.

Mentor and psychologist David Good, who has always kindly listened and provided a common sense grounded perspective, placed me in the field at EuroParc. Here, I met Elizabeth Churchill and Paul Dourish and the smiling face of Tom Moran. Both Elizabeth and Paul have gone on to become tour de forces in the field of human computer interaction, and Elizabeth is now a member of the *AI & Society* Advisory Board. Also, whilst I was at EuroParc, I spoke with Judy Olson for advice on studying the processes of activity in design teams. Inspired, I decided to study the life course of a piece of data in dialogue, in my case the dialogues of the design team I was tracking, and I selected 'topics' to play the role of data.

Within the university, one person who was an anchor to the study of the tacit was the historian of science Simon Schaffer. Simon was generous in giving time to speak about the tacit and the explicit, over a lunch or drink in the Eagle pub, and when it came to my Ph.D. viva, he kindly gave me a mock one in preparation. Matthew Jones, working on knowledge and management, read the dissertation and painstakingly pointed out where I needed to be more clear. Hugh Mellor, head of philosophy, gave his approval of my grounded view of knowledge, which was a relief, and in the spring of 1995 Geoffrey Lloyd, the renowned classicist, and Master of my college, Darwin, described what I was doing as 'betwixt and in-between'. I have made his words the title of my last chapter.

My Ph.D. examination viva was almost entirely about how to prepare my dissertation for publication. I had been warned by my examiners that if I did not publish my Ph.D. soon afterwards, the chances were that I never would. I did not heed these warnings, and it has taken me 20 years to finally write up some of that work into this book.

Throughout my journey ever since those teenage years, there is an inspiring thinker who has had a profound influence. When Mike Cooley speaks you are transported with his poetic oratory on the complex issues of knowledge and skill and technology. Mike was a brilliant engineer who designed the wings of Concord, and his unflagging humanity and questioning of the mechanisation and quantification of the human being and human skill constantly reminds one that this must never be forgotten. I first met Mike at my father's *AI & Society* conferences, and he became one of the founding members of the journal and chairs its Advisory Board.

Mike was close to the engineer Howard Rosenbrock who said that engineering was more of an art than a science and that in saying this he was elevating it. He argued that it was never possible for the explicit to have meaning without a tacit dimension and that there are many paths one can take and which path you take depends on your purpose; hence, it is a moral choice. Technology is not neutral.

Another inspiring and humanistic thinker has been David Smith, University of Wales, Newport, whose passion and care about the social impacts of technology and critical intellect make one pause and think again. David has been involved in the discussions on *AI & Society* since I was a child and is one of the founding members of the journal.

Following the Ph.D. I went to work on a project at Lancaster University on aesthetics and landscape architecture where I witnessed an interesting problem of breakdown in sharing the tacit knowledge of seeing colours in a distributed apprenticeship setting. It was a pivotal moment in my research, to understand what it is about sharing the same physical space and moving together that enables us to share something tacit. Dede Boden, a leader of the project, had asked me about whether the ways the architects moved together as they were speaking could be interesting to look into. At the time I did not make the connection, with what I was to later realise was a profound insight, with my reflections about the breakdown, and was to recall it many years later.

I arrived in Japan in 1997 to take up a postdoc position as a research scientist with NTT's (Nippon Telegraph and Telecommunications) Basic Research Labs. The lab consisted of 100 researchers from around Japan and the globe, studying a range of sciences. For me, this was a creative period of free thinking out of the box with no disciplinary boundaries of what is and is not possible to think. It was an astonishing place. I had heard that the head of any Japanese organisation is its still centre, and this seemed true of the lab's Director, Ishii san. In the Cognitive Science group, I was taken under the wing of Hisao Nojima, a brilliant thinker who wanted me to understand Japanese culture. I remember my first meeting with him, where I thought that his silence meant I needed to ask a more interesting question, in a Socratic-type dialogue. At some point he gently said, 'Satinder, the meeting finished ten minutes ago'.

I was now in a culture where I had no clue how to read the body and voice of my colleagues, and I was reminded of my interest in how the movement of the body and voice can lead to information becoming missed.

Yet, this was not my first time to Japan, but it was the first time to experience it on my own. In 1991, Masuda-sensai of Tokyo University and Yoshiro Sato from NTT Data had hosted me at the EU-Japan conference on Anthropocentric Systems and Technologies. Masuda-sensai sadly passed away; he was a gentleman and scholar. Sato-san and I keep in touch, via the magic of Facebook. And family friends, the reflective practitioner Takao Nuki and his wife Masumi, became my home from home during the 3 years I was in Japan.

Whilst at NTT, I was sent by my group for a period to the ATR (Advanced Telecommunications Research) labs in Nara. Nojima and the team prepared me on how I should bow and what I should say on arriving there and told me that I would be representing my group. This was a huge responsibility that I took seriously. Now, if NTT was a free thinking space, ATR's Media Lab felt like floating in the clouds of free thought. In Yasuhiro Katagiri I had a group leader who thought nothing of my wandering over to speak with the artists in another division, who were producing astonishing interactive art works. I was particularly drawn to the artist Koiso's neurobaby. It was a strange feeling to be pulled emotionally by the sounds of a cartoon baby, which was represented by just a few lines moving on a large screen, responding to my voice. I got anxious when it began to cry and I could not stop it. As an artist, Koiso was approaching the interface as intuitive. At that time she was already working on the idea of interactive poetry.

But it was my work with ATR scientists, Katagiri and Atsushi Shimojima, that was to set me on the path that eventually brought me to music and helped me to continue the investigation about the breakdown in seeing colours. It was at ATR in that intensive month of August 1997 that I formed the theory of Body Moves with their guidance and critical feedback, helping me to get clarity on how the body can mediate knowledge. I was to continue the analysis and bring it to fruition with my NTT colleague and mentor on dialogue analysis, Masahito Kawamori, to whom I am indebted.

Would it be well received outside the free thinking bubble of NTT and ATR though? In 1999 I presented the Body Moves idea at a conference in San Francisco, organised by the pragmatist Jacob Mey. I was very nervous as I was aware the concept was completely unconventional. To my astonishment, Jacob liked it and published it in the journal *RASK*, as well as incorporating it into his second edition of *Pragmatics*. His support encouraged me to continue.

At that same conference I met Timo Saari who was setting up a new institute in Helsinki with Seija Kulkki, a brilliant economist. They are both very special people. At the heart of their institute lay a research interest in tacit knowledge, inspired by their mentor, the management scientist, Nonaka. I was to join their Centre for Knowledge and Innovation Research (CKIR), located in the beautiful city of Helsinki, soon after meeting them and found myself based at Stanford University's Centre for the Study of Language and Information to undertake research on dialogue and tacit knowledge.

During that US visit in 1999, I had briefly visited Stanford University (not knowing I would soon be based there) and presented the Body Moves to Herb Clark's seminar group. Herb is a leading scholar in psycholinguistics, and his theory of grounding is a foundation for many studying human interaction and conversation. It was an emotional moment, and Herb was to become an important mentor and supporter. I will never forget his generosity and kindness.

I also said hello to Terry Winograd whom I knew through my father, and it was lovely to meet him. On arriving at CLSI in the spring of 2000, I went to see him to discuss what experiments I might be doing, and to my surprise he offered me his Interactive Workspaces lab as a home to carry them out in. Terry's approach to designing technology was a revelation for me. He was open to ideas and encouraged an exploratory approach, which reminded me of an artist at work with materials, and it was designed with human purpose. The atmosphere was one of a craft workshop with lots of positive energy.

One day whilst I was in the lab, Terry walked in with Sha Xin-Wei and briefly introduced us as he felt we would have much to share. It was to be a very important introduction. I spent many a long discussion with Xin-Wei at Stanford, and there never seemed to be enough time to talk about all the interesting ideas around knowledge, the tacit, performance, dialogue, etc., and our collaboration began and continues. Later I was to invite him to join the *AI & Society* Journal of which he is now a North American editor along with the artist Victoria Vesna.

I knew of Victoria through her work with the *AI & Society* Journal and her friendship with my father and family. We finally met in 2000 when Victoria invited me to speak at her MediaArts international seminar at UCLA. I was touched by her calm, her warmth and her clarity, and remain fascinated by the way she addresses our relationship with technology and our understanding of science, through artistic engagement.

Whilst at Stanford, I took the opportunity to meet with the philosopher on tacit knowledge and skill, Hubert Dreyfus, in Berkeley, whose work I have always admired. Hubert is an authority on Heidegger and Merleau Ponty, and I first met him at the Stockholm conference in 1988 and again at a conference organised by Massimo Negrotti in Italy during my Ph.D. years.

On returning to the UK in 2003, I attended a conference on AI in Leeds where I heard the music psychologist Ian Cross, from the University of Cambridge, give a talk in which he spoke about the limits of our perception of a beat. I knew I needed to work with him to take my work further and address the temporal dimension of tacit knowing, of 'knowing when'. If I was to be helped to investigate this further, that knowledge was going to come from either music or dance. Ian had created a Centre for Music and Science in the Music Faculty at the University of Cambridge in 2001, and with the arrival of the linguist Sarah Hawkins in 2010, it has grown to become a world centre for research on music psychology and the relationship between music and language. I owe much to Ian for his inspirational work and for giving me a home at the CMS. He has made it possible for me to write this book.

I must also thank Alan Blackwell and the Rainbow Group at the Computing Lab for an inspiring spell as a Visiting Scholar at the Computing Lab in 2009. Alan is passionate about conducting and supporting interdisciplinary research across the arts and sciences. On the matter of art (including literature), I have always been drawn to it for reflections about the tacit. Both aesthetics and ethics lie in the realm of the tacit, and I found both to be important in the mediation of knowledge in embodied engagement. In 2004 I took a senior fellowship at Middlesex University where I set up a Body Interface seminar to explore the relation between the arts and technology. The university has a creative performance arts group called ResCen which has fellows attached to it who are practitioners, and it was there that I met the dancer and choreographer, Ghislaine Boddington. Ghislaine's body-data-lab has become an important part of the British scene on art and science/technology. My head of research, Collin Tully, understood my interest and supported my exploration of the art/science world. I travelled to Brussels to speak at media arts and arts and society events organised by Alok Nandi, including the fun Pechakucha, and experienced a vibrant energy of ideas from a vast spectrum of professions and practice. Alok is a soft spoken thinker with a sharp and eclectic creativity and humane.

Xin-Wei introduced me to Maja Kuzmanovic, the co-founder of the FoAM lab in Brussels, and visiting her and her group in Brussels was enlightening. In some way they remind me of Terry's interactive workspaces lab, a crafts workshop, where there is a positive spirit about what is possible, grounded in social purpose. Where Terry's lab had been working within areas of professional expertise, Maja's lab is working at possible futures for our societies. I would say that this is the common ethos of the people I speak about in the last chapter of this book.

Whilst at Middlesex, I participated in an EU proposal on presence and technology, where I met Caroline Nevejan. This was a special meeting, and we talked and did not wish to stop talking. Caroline is a profound person with a warmth and care that is precious. She has a great generosity of spirit and a brilliant perception of what it means to be present with others as an ethical matter. We have become good friends.

This book is my way of saying thank you to the people who have inspired me. I have many friends to thank for their support and care and encouragement. I give deep thanks to friends and colleagues who have helped me gain clarity in the writing of this book, especially Mike Cooley, David Smith, Caroline Nevejan, Sha Xin-Wei,

Maja Kuzmanovic and Jane Liddle-King. I also thank Ian Cross, Debra Bekerian, Jacob Mey, Masahito Kawamori, Yasuhiro Katagiri, Herb Clark, Jan Borchers, Terry Winograd, David Good, Simon Schaffer, Bo Goranzon, and posthumously Bob Muller, for their support at various phases of the research that informs this book. I must also thank Beverley Ford, the editorial director of Computer Science, UK at Springer, for her unfailing support and encouragement to write this book and complete it. She has been patient and always positive. And last, but very very far from least, writing this book would never have been possible without the tremendous support of my parents, Karamjit and Ajit, and my brothers, Harinder and Rajinder, who have kept me going.

Cambridge, UK   Satinder P. Gill
April 2015

Contents

Chapter 1
Tacit Engagement

Abstract What does it mean for an interface to be interactive and mediating? What would 'interface' mean outside of technology? Where does the interface lie in the human system? Can the interface be located in tacit knowing? These are the questions this chapter addresses. It revisits the concepts of the last 30 years in relation to concepts that guide innovations now, exploring the landscape of ideas that have come to shape the concepts of 'interface' and 'mediation' and concepts of how we relate to each other and share knowledge.

1.1 Introduction

In this book, a consideration of *interface* as being located in *dialogue, performance,* and the *tacit dimension of knowledge* within the human system, is explored in order to expand possibilities for what it could then mean as technology. It is proposed that for an interface to support how we relate to each other, it would need to support the bandwidth of human sense-making, that is, our personal act of knowing.

Distributed interaction via various forms of technology is often referred to as mediated communication. What does it mean to mediate? What is the difference in the processes of mediation when we are engaged in embodied co-present interaction, and when we are communicating via electronic means? What then is the relation between mediation and interface? What does 'interface' mean? It can mean *technology*, but could we say we interface each other when we meet in the street, play with our children, conduct meetings at work, give a successful presentation, dance together, and diagnose a patient's health condition? 'We interface' would then have something to do with how we play and make sense of each other, handle ambiguities, identify problems, negotiate differences, empathise, and make skilled judgements. All these involve a *personal act of knowing*, that is *tacit* (Polanyi 1966) and necessarily embodied.

The world we now inhabit is filled with computer based technologies that interface our relations with each other, our thinking through problems, making decisions, and making consumer choices. The devices we use in everyday life at home and in the workplace are mostly a variation on the trilogy of the screen, keyboard, and mouse. Some changes are taking place with wearables (e.g. fashion 'smart' glasses, health monitoring devices), implants (cyborgs), smart technologies embedded in artifacts in the house (fridges, cookers, lights, etc.), and robots (functional and social). Mobile tools may be said to chart a movement away from a mechanical paradigm towards a biological model manifested on several levels, from the micro scale 'smart' materials capable of registering and responding to external stimuli, to larger network formations between people, objects, spaces, and landscapes (RAD lab, Toronto University). In public spaces artists experiment with installations embedded in buildings or objects in the environment to create a different sense of our relations with our environment and perceptions of each other (Gaver 2001, RCA). Artists and their installations explore how communication technologies affect collective behavior and how perceptions of identity shift in relation to scientific innovation (Victoria Vesna, e.g. Vesna 2012).

As our understanding of human sociality and cognition has evolved, so have our ideas about what technology needs to be able to do and its role in our everyday lives. Conceptions of interface have evolved from the early days of the punch card, to using text (e.g. 'wizard of oz' agent, Eliza), speech (computational linguistics), gesture (e.g. embodied agents, artificial life, robotics and emotions), movement (e.g. robots, sensory art interfaces, microsoft kinect), and emotion detection (affective computing, facial recognition), and neuroscience (neural control). Along the way designers and researchers have drawn upon findings in the fields of language understanding, psychology, gesture, art and aesthetics, multi-sensory interaction, performance arts, and neuroscience, amongst others.

At the present moment in our societies explicit knowledge is a great force driving the design of technology interfaces, providing us with an abundance of data through online shopping sites, social media sites, health care data bases, institutional data bases, banking data bases, online dictionaries and 'information' resources such as Wikipedia, etc. The culmination of this force of the explicit is 'big data', vast sets of real time transactional data too large to be manipulated in a normal desktop computing environment, and the semantic web. All this is removed from our person and our tacit knowledge, with the human functioning as a *user* of technology.

At the same, we are witnessing an opposing force, to focus on the human in the interface by designing for emotional expression and response, physical contact, tangibility, movement, presence, and human values, to find ways to collapse the boundary between human and machine and afford alternative possibilities that could be human centred. Yet in this opposing drive to locate the human, the force of the explicit and the transactional becomes foregrounded when we try to define particular movements and senses of the body as functions (gesture and movement interfaces, sensory perception), specify causal links between gestures and emotions (to both detect these in humans and to express them in a multimodal interface), and separate the tangible body from the person. If we fragment and reconstruct our corporeality and define ourselves as users, we will continue to miss the human *personal act of knowing*.

Recent collaborations between the arts, performance arts, and sciences, offer possibilities outside the user interface paradigm with explorations of materiality, time, imagination, aesthetic pleasure, and human relations, that may allow for the personal act of knowing. For example the work of Sha Xin-Wei (2013) and the

Topological Media Lab[1] based on the premise that *matter* is dynamic, temporal, and imbued with history, drives an "investigation to understand distributed, field based activity and materiality in rehearsed as well as unrehearsed situations in the presence of responsive media…". Another example is Ghislaine Boddington's work with body-data-space[2] which creates visions of the future human body and its real time relationship to the shifts in society and technology. Caroline Nevejan's work, Witnessing You (2012) investigates how we negotiate trust, truth, and presence in networked life. The arts by their nature express the *relational*, whilst the concept of user expresses the *transactional*.

The concept of user is tied to the concept of machine (Chap. 2) and entails the quantification and measurement of human capacities leading to misconceptions around 'knowledge' and 'expertise' (Chap. 3), all of which fail in the context of our performance in work and in our shared lives (Chap. 4). The challenge of the relational (Chap. 5) is to balance purpose, ethics, aesthetics, and quality of life (human and of nature), and is addressed by those working on the edges of the meeting of art, science, technology and society.

This opening chapter revisits the concepts of the last 30 years in relation to concept that guide innovations now, exploring the landscape of ideas that have come to shape the concepts of 'interface' and 'mediation' and concepts of how we relate to each other and share knowledge.

1.2 Interaction Interface: Background

One of the early designs of human and machine interaction was based on a model of a psychiatric interview. Eliza was a computer program for the study of natural language communication, and real patients would confide in the 'psychiatrist'. Joseph Weizenbaum (1976) at MIT chose this context as "it is one of the few dyadic…..communication situations in which one of the participating pair is free to assume the pose of knowing almost nothing of the real world. If, for example, one were to tell a psychiatrist "I went for a long boat ride" and he responded "Tell me about boats", one would not assume that he knew nothing about boats, but that he had some purpose in so directing the subsequent conversation. It is important to note that this assumption is one made by the speaker. Whether it is realistic or not is an altogether separate question. In any case, it has a crucial *psychological utility* in that it serves the speaker to maintain his sense of being heard and understood. The speaker further defends his impression (which even in real life may be illusory) by attributing to his conversational partner all sorts of background knowledge, insights and reasoning ability. But again, these are the *speaker's* contribution to the conversation" (Weizenbaum 1966: 35–36).

---

[1] http://topologicalmedialab.net/
[2] http://www.bodydataspace.net/

Eliza is an early *conversational agent*. Since then the field of computational linguistics has evolved with research on natural language to include the complexities of speech performance. The analysis of patterns in human behaviour where gestures and speech work as a multi-modal system has lead to the creation of *embodied* conversational agents (ECA). These are 'computer generated cartoon like characters that demonstrate many of the same properties as humans in face-to-face conversation, including the ability to produce and respond to verbal and nonverbal communication' (Cassell et al. 2000). Where Eliza used text, the embodied agents are graphics displaying 'visual features of a conversation in the same way that the face and hands do in face-to-face conversation among humans'. An early example is Rea, the 'estate agent' created by Justine Cassell and the team at MIT, and the first prototype is based on a Eliza type program, where Rea's responses mimic the "user's" last utterance. Rea's goal is to describe the features of a house 'that fit the user's requirements while also responding to the user's verbal and non-verbal input that may lead in new directions. When the user makes cues typically associated with turn-taking behaviour such as gesturing, Rea *allows herself* to be interrupted, and then takes the turn again when *she is able. She is able* to initiate conversational repair when *she misunderstands* what the user says and can generate voice and gesture output'. Embodied conversational characters are considered to be the logical extension of the metaphor of human-computer interaction as a conversation, where embodiment needs to be based on an understanding of conversational function, rather than an additive – and ad hoc – model of the relationship between nonverbal modalities and verbal conversational behaviours (Cassell et al. ref). Currently, Cassell heads the Articulab, whose mission is to study human interaction as an input into computational systems which will then be used to better understand human interaction. It is believed that this will improve and support human capabilities, for example of children with Autism and children of African-American background. Cassell emphasizes that the ECA is a virtual peer.

In some ways, the ECA project is a continuation of the Expert Systems project of which Eliza is part. Where Eliza focused on the illusory capacity of the human user, ECAs seek to be a reproduction of social behaviour. ECAs and social robots are both projects that seek to simulate humans. Such simulations may be considered as *naturoids* (Negrotti 2012). The production of naturoids is a distinct class of technological activity. They will always be the result of a reduction of the complexity of the natural object (in this case the human being), due to an unavoidable multiple selection strategy (e.g. the selection of the particulars, such as gestures, head nods, and particular posture changes, that correlate with certain acts of speech). Furthermore, reproduction implies that naturoids take on their own complexity resulting in the transfiguration of the natural *exemplars* and their performances. The paradox is that the more the reproduction is improved and developed, the further it moves away its natural counterpart. Naturoids will affect our relationships with technology and nature (and each other, other humans) but in ways that are beyond our predictive capabilities (Negrotti op. cit).

Eliza and Rea may be said to represent a dualist and modernist concept of interface, where the user of a system and the computer conduct interaction at primarily a transactional level of communication, that is, on the transfer of information carried with intentions towards goals; even though ECAs include the design of features of human interaction that are primarily relational, such as head nods, eyebrow raises, and shifts in posture. The more dominant models of interface are located primarily at the *transactional* level of communication. This can be seen in one major field of interactive technology called Computer Supported Cooperative Working (CSCW), or social computing (Dourish 2004), that is methodologically rooted in the social sciences, and seeks to support and promote collaborative or cooperative human social behaviours. In general, cooperative interactions are represented in CSCW theory in terms of how they directly affect the achievement of the goals of the collaboration (Schmidt 2011) through the transfer and sharing of information. The work on gesture in interaction within the design of interactive interfaces has largely focused on gestures that are content-oriented or transactional. These are gestures that have a direct effect on the goals of the interactive task, such as touching, swiping etc. in jointly using electronic smartboards or in navigating smart tabletop interfaces (e.g. Zemel et al. 2008), or in relating bits of information on say a drawing by 'binding' them via a speaker's simultaneous hand gestures referring to them (Oleksik et al. 2010).

In contrast to the work on Embodied Conversational Agents, "expressive" gestures that do not directly affect the content of the interaction, such as smiling, eyebrow flash, nodding, and that are associated with the relational dimension of interaction, have received little attention in CSCW (Balaam et al. 2011) or the design of Tangible and Embedded Interfaces (TEI). Balaam et al. have produced one of the few studies in CSCW on the relational aspects such as synchrony and other non-verbal features of interaction.

At large in Human Computer Interaction (HCI) there is a growing interest in temporality and bodily interaction, notably in the work of the Mobile Life lab at Stockholm University which is exploring how the body and temporality can inform the design of various forms of interfaces.

Within communication analysis, there has been work on non-goal-directed behavior in speech (Coupland et al. 1992) and in body movement (Gill et al. 2000) that identifies interactive features that support successful cooperation. These features, characterised as phatic or relational, are primarily concerned with setting up and sustaining social relationships by establishing and maintaining the communication situation. The relational is primary in the performance arts of dance and music (Cross 2012), and in art, and in everyday interaction it is expressed in how our bodies and vocal sounds move together (Hall 1983) as collective acts that increase contact between people and allow for empathy and shared understanding (Gill 2007).

If one considers the case of *musical* interaction, this is about the relational dimension (Cross 2012). Interactive music serves many different communicative functions in different societies, but one that appears common across cultures is that of setting up and maintaining social relationships, '*engendering a sense of social solidarity*' (Turino 2008). Recent research suggests that music may enhance the empathic capacities of participants (Rabinowich et al. 2012), which supports the premise that it has a *relational* or *phatic* function as an interactive medium (Cross op. cit).

This dimension of social interaction has been increasingly recognised as essential for successful communication in language (Coupland et al. op. cit.; Gill et al. op. cit.). It is also imbued with memory rather than simply being ephemeral interaction (Rogers 1998; Gill 2002). The relational dimension of communication could be said to "scaffold" or "frame" the temporal unfolding exchange and sharing of ideas.

The temporal and the emotional aspects of the relational are beginning to be addressed within the field of Tangible and Embedded Interfaces with respect to the "physicality" of touch and movement in interaction. Though most research has tended to focus on a single user's experience (e.g. Wolf et al. 2011), some designs consider multiple users, for example on the experience of intimacy through the cooperative manipulation of sound (e.g. Muller et al. 2011). The sensory immediacy of tangibility, combined with real-time connectivity, allows for the sharing of experience that is essential for "being with others" (Nagargoje et al. 2012). In Naragoje et al., interactive yoga mats have been designed for a distributed setting to allow people to experience the real time actions of each other at any time through visualisations that are visible on the mat. These include avatars representing each person in the network, and colours that vary with the intensity of another's activity, and pulses to show when at least one person is exercising at the same time. The premise is that we are more motivated to keep up the exercise and be successful in completing it when we experience exercising with others, by noticing them and being noticed.

Paradoxically, although music is 'proto-social', the design of music technology interfaces has tended towards individual-interface interaction, e.g. to conduct or to improvise. In recent years, musicians are increasingly engaging with other performance arts such as dance, and extending the possibilities of what collaborative musical performance could be as they create symbiotic movement-sound-notation interfaces that are responsive in real time. For example, Fluxis Tree,[3] which is an interactive sculpture for dancers using data from sensors to help generate notation live, which is then played by a cellist.

Both transactional and relational dimensions of interaction make use of verbal and gestural signals, and are grounded in processes that are cognitive *and* affective, but the relational dimension primarily serves to facilitate the maintenance of interaction to support its success. When the interaction is mediated by technology, the success of the interaction will depend on the extent to which the technology is sensitive to cues of both transactional and relational dimensions, cues that both underpin and manage cooperation. Hence there is a need to understand the ways in which the computational mediation of interaction can take account of both aspects. The designers of ECAs are seeking to do this, however their goal is to simulate the human and the interactions are primarily about transactional goals to transfer information.

One project that has sought to create a mediating interface for primarily relational interaction is called Touching Sound (Aaron et al. 2013). This is the development of a shared musical instrument to address how to support synchronisation in time and facilitate the capacity to cooperate with another person. The aim of

---

[3]A collaboration between musician Richard Hoadley, dancer/choreographer Jane Turner, and Cellist/composer Cheryl-Frances Hoad, Anglia Ruskin, 2012–2013).

such an instrument is to be tangible and pleasurable, requiring at least two people to play by touching it with their hands to create musical sounds, and to serve as a complement to the current instruments and methods used by music therapists. It is envisaged as something that, in the future, could be used by families and friends to engage with those they love and seek to support. Within music therapy (Magee et al. 2011) technology has tended to be designed without the specific clinical context in mind, leading to a misfit between the technology and its situated use. Touching sound has been informed from its outset by music therapy, understanding its practices and experiential knowledge of the therapist. At the heart of music therapy is experiencing each other through sound and movement. The tangibility of the shared musical instrument is crucial for the cooperative experience, but this requires an understanding of how the tangibility of continuous body movement and sound shapes cooperative interaction.

The project extends the development of interactive technologies that facilitate collaborative or cooperative behaviour by understanding real-time, relational aspects of interaction to inform the design of applications to facilitate this behaviour. Touching Sound may be said to locate the interface within the human temporal system, addressing how the temporal dimension of the *personal act of knowing* is a crucial part of how we make sense of each other and are able to be intersubjective. In addition to *knowing how* and *knowing what* about something, we also need to *know when* to do something.

The consideration of *real-time* needs to be located within the personal act of knowing. Once it is quantified outside the experience and embedded into systems to regulate behavior, then it becomes part of the explicit paradigm and outside the natural human system, and may in turn adversely affect it. Hall (op. cit.) draws our attention to the *principle of extension transference* by Alfred Korzybski which holds that any extension not only can but usually does eventually take the place of the process which has been extended. This is explained with the example of the clock. "We have taken our own biological clocks, moved them outside ourselves, and then treated the extensions as though they represented the only reality. In fact it is the tension between the internal clocks and the clock on the wall that causes so much of the stress in today's world. We have now constructed an entire complex system of schedules, manners, and expectations to which we are trying to adjust ourselves, when in reality, it should be the other way round…. Because of Extension transference, the schedule is the reality and the people and their needs are not considered." (Hall op. cit. p. 131). This is something to bear in mind when making any human phenomena explicit, and particularly where the intention is to simulate and automate, whereby the human experience itself becomes a construct of the artificial, a naturoid.

Within the context of Human Computer Interaction (HCI), Dourish (2004) provides a historical background to the idea of interaction, which is defined as 'the means by which work is accomplished dynamically and in context'. He takes us through the new models of interaction design, particularly of *tangible* and *social computing*, as evidenced in the projects from *CSCW* and Tangible interfaces cited above. These have the 'same underlying principles, of exploiting 'our familiarity with the everyday world, social interaction or physical artifacts." They draw on the 'ways we experience the everyday world, through directly interacting with it', and hold that 'we act in the world by exploring the opportunities for action that it provides to us…'. These new models of interaction design oppose 'naïve cognitivism' where the mind is the seat of consciousness and rational decision making, that can be operated upon to form plans of action, that Dourish calls 'a disembodied brain'. A disembodied brain could not experience the world in the same way we do because our experience of the world is intimately tied to ways *we act in it*. Physically, our experiences cannot be separated from the reality of our bodily presence in the world, and this applies to our nature as social beings which is based on ways in which we act and our interaction in real time, all the time. Hence we act in the world by exploring its physical affordances, and we jointly construct our social actions. Embodiment, for Dourish, has a participatory status; it is about the fact that *things are embedded in the world* and the ways in which their reality depends on being embedded. It follows that interaction is intimately connected with the settings in which it occurs, and the study of it includes an understanding of the role of the environment be it physical, social, or organizational, of real users in real settings doing real work. Various methods from the social and anthropological sciences have been applied to uncover details of work for interactive systems to support that world. This idea of identifying features of the human system to better match technology for a better user experience shares a fundamental ethos with that of the Embodied conversational agent.

Dourish (op. cit.) seeks to ground the conception and development of interactive technologies in the philosophical ideas that have underpinned embodiment through twentieth century thought, in particular phenomenology. This is 'concerned with how we perceive, experience, and act in the world around us'. Dourish highlights Husserl's idea of *preontological apprehension* of the world: 'perception begins with what is experienced, rather than beginning with what is expected'. Phenomenology's concern with action and understanding heavily influenced the work of Afred Schutz and Garfinkel two of the most influential methodologists of interaction technologies. Schutz (1932, 1962) produced phenomenological tools for understanding social action and practice and drew on Heidegger and Weber, whilst Garfinkel (1967) produced an ethnomethodology for understanding the experience of the participants in the social system as they perceive it, as expressed in what and how they speak, and drew on Schutz and on Wittgenstein's work on language.

> Tangible computing draws on embodiment by recognizing the physical embedding of action in the world, whilst social computing draws on embodiment by recognizing its social embedding in the systems of meaning. Founded on the same preontological apprehension of the world, that identifies the physical, social world, and most particularly the interface at which we encounter it, as the site of meaning. (Dourish, op. cit.)

He is critical of ubiquitous computing, the invisible interface, that implies that computation is no longer located in a place and the interface is spread in information appliances. Conventional models of screen, keyboard windows, sliders, buttons, menus etc. do not apply and would interfere with the structure of the environment and activity. This invisible interface (Weiser 1994) was a great goal of user-centred design (Norman and Draper 1986), out of the way between the user and technology. This poses problems for interaction design where interaction is seen in a larger social and cultural frame, wherein interactive artifacts need to be designed within it, and design expresses a system of values that it communicates. Interaction Design involves 'considering the message that the design should communicate and how this relates to the task at hand and to the details of the design'. The design perspective shifts from user 'interface' to user 'experience'. 'But you cannot be engaged with something that's invisible.' 'In everyday physical environment *objects* never disappear, even when we do act through them; they are continually present in the ways in which they mediate activity. Heidegger's hammer does not become invisible when he uses it, rather it withdraws into a larger frame of activity but is critically present in the way in which I can act through it, feel through it. An invisible artifact, one that does not impinge on my world at all, is not a tool I can use effectively for *anything*. *Invisible interface is too simplistic. It misidentifies the problem, demonises the interface, abandons the idea that interface might mediate use action. In fact, this mediation is critical but we need the resources to control it'*. Dourish argues that the Embodied Interface provides a conceptual tool for understanding how the interface might move into the background without disappearing altogether and claims that *technology and practice cannot be separated from each other, are co-extensive and will co-evolve.* ECAs make this claim too. He calls this *appropriation*.

Tangible computing is physical and symbolic, as it gives physical form to digital information. For Dourish, TC is about Embodied Interaction: action (physical) and meaning (symbolic). Action produces and draws upon meaning, and meaning both gives rise to and arises from action. A physical artifact incorporated into a practice takes on symbolic value, hence tangible computing is the physical realization of symbolic reality.

The limitation of the concept of interface within the above picture of embodied interaction is that it assumes it is located in objects that *mediate use action.* Although it is argued that this involves a fundamental shift from user interface to user experience, ultimately interaction design is about designing user interfaces for user experience, where user experience is 'action'. ''Tangible computing draws on embodiment by recognizing the *physical embedding of action* in the world, whilst social computing draws on embodiment by recognizing its *social embedding in the systems of meaning.* They are founded on the same preontological apprehension of the world, that identifies the physical, social world, and the *interface* at which we encounter it, as *the site of meaning.*' (ibid) The embodied interaction frame of tangible and social computing is focused on the use of objects or things framed as experience rather than a depersonalised transaction. And in order to achieve this, how we experience the world is analysed using *scientific* methods of empirical evidence, recording speech, movement, and the patterns that constitute social and cultural practices, in order to bring this information into building technologies that 'better match how humans do things and perceive things', to improve the utility of the object. The embodied conversational agent would fit this frame.

I would however, suggest that the Tangible Bits project by Ishii at the MIT Media Lab goes beyond a picture of the world as consisting of objects and things, and rather considers the world as bits and computations that are realized in the physical and sensory world. It still has the picture of use, but not of mediating things. This would be the difference between this desire to collapse the interface and those approaches to tangible computing that lie in the scope of social computing of objects to *mediate use action*.

In summary, the primary function of interactive technologies has been to facilitate transactional interaction to meet certain goals. This has been driven by the dominance of textual and symbolic interaction representing language and conversation. A fundamental belief seems to be that one can design technologies to better fit human needs if one understands the situated context of the experiencing user and then embed this knowledge in the technology, which is then tested with the user. This necessarily involves the reductionist paradox of the principle of selection (Negrotti op. cit.), and if one believes that humans and technologies necessarily evolve in a symbiotic relationship of this kind, then do we have methods for understanding the consequences of the artificial system on the human system in order to avoid the principle of transference (Hall 1983)? The early conception of human-machine symbiosis of the human centred movement of the 1970s through 1990s, also rooted in phenomenology and hermeneutics, addressed these fundamental issues of the computation of the human system, and although technologies may have altered in shape and form, the essential concept of the interface whether invisible, available, or backgrounded, seems to have remained unchanged. The convergence of the arts, performance arts, with science and technology explores how our understanding of science, and our relationship with the world and others can be experienced as aesthetic, emotional, trusting, sensory, and imaginary, but is their use of computation and conception of interface fundamentally different? The examples of Sha's Topological Media Lab, and the Touching Sound project, suggests that it is possible for computation to be mediated with a *human interface* (wizard of Oz and relational) rather than via a machine interface (automated and transactional). In her work on distributed interaction, Nevejan (2007) found a human *social mediator* to be essential for mediating *here and now* presence. She calls the process the 'embodied social interface'. For example, if she is conducting a discussion via say skype with a group located somewhere else, a colleague who knows her will mediate her interaction with the group. This and related ideas will be discussed further in the next section that investigates the distributed setting and the nature of human presence.

1.3   Distributed Interaction: Presence

Whilst working in Japan, I had a colleague in my lab group who always seemed to understand what I was trying to say, and could finish off my incomplete sentences. Many of us experience this connection in our lives with others, both in contexts of work and personal lives. It has a reassuring quality that allows us to have comfortable moments of stillness and quiet, as well as of movement; of something shared. In our increasingly distributed lives of work and where members of a family live in different places and loved ones travel afar, a number of us are using technologies such as Skype to talk and keep in touch and feel connected. The Skype interface does not replace the co-present physical experience of being with someone, but it allows you to feel a sense of presence until you next meet. As one friend said, nothing can replace how she feels when she and her child hold each other. However, this difference between touch and seeing, between embodied experience and disembodied experience, created some difficulty for the Japanese colleague of mine when he had to participate in video-conference meetings in English. He struggled to understand what was being 'said'. Whilst reflecting out loud one day about this, it emerged that his Japanese colleagues, who had a good command of English compared to his somewhat broken English, did not seem to have the kind of difficulties he experienced. For this cross-cultural experience, the video conference seemed to have reduced the bandwidth of communication to that of 'words' and 'grammatical fluency', of semantic and linguistic structure which lies at the transactional level of communicating information. It had not offered my colleague the cues of co-present embodied space that he uses to be with another person, to speak and think with them and make sense of what they say. Winograd and Flores, in their seminal work on interactive technologies (1986), drew attention to the phenomenon that the structure in communication 'becomes visible only when there is some kind of breakdown' (p. 68). The video-conference situation suggests that it created a gap in the communication at the relational level,[4] which in turn affected the comprehension of utterances at the semantic level. In our face-to-face everyday communications, the meanings of words can sometimes get missed or misunderstood because a gesture may have became too loud, or a voice was too quiet, an intonation ungrasped, a movement mistimed, etc. and we may ask 'how do I know that I have understood, and that I have been understood?'. It is proposed that sharing a physical space allows us to experience this *social uncertainty* and enables us to manage it. When the bandwidth of this complexity is reduced there seems to be a gap in communication that makes it difficult to 'make sense' of what is 'said'. In this case, the *interface* of the video-conference did not *mediate* the communication.

For an interface to support how we relate to each other, it would need to support the *bandwidth of human sense-making*, i.e. it would need to support our personal act of knowing.

Rhythm has an important role to play in our sense-making. In daily face-to-face communications, we are connected in rhythm and synchrony at multiple levels ranging from the moment-by-moment continuity of timed syllables to emergent body and vocal rhythms of pragmatic sense-making. Our human capacity to synchronize with each other may be essential for our survival as social beings. Moving

---

[4] Cross (2012) considers the primacy of the relational level in musical interaction in contrast to the primacy of the transactional level in speech interaction. The relational level is akin to how we connect when making music together, where the concept of a sender and receiver is not applicable, as participants are such at the very same time. The expression 'relational' is used by researchers working on the design of interactive robots (Breazeal and Picard 2009) and interactive technologies, where 'relational interaction' is concerned with relationships.

our bodies and voices together in time embodies a potent pragmatic purpose that of being together. In this synchrony of self with other, witnessing and being present become part of each other. There is growing research into how rhythm and synchrony operate in embodied face-to-face interaction and this provides parameters for investigating the relations and differences in how we connect and are socially present in the embodied and distributed settings, and understanding the effect of one setting upon the other.

1.4   Presence: Sharing a Space of Communication

What is happening when we share a physical space of communication, a space of *engagement* (Gill et al. 2000)? If you are standing in a field, and another person enters it from the far side, even though you cannot see the details of each other's face or other features, the moment you both become aware of each other's existence you become co-present and share that space. We naturally orient our bodies to express how we seek to connect with each other (Kendon 1990),[5] whether this involves standing in a circle and chatting, or standing at an angle, or directly facing each other, sitting next to each other, and so on. How we *shape* our presence affects how we can make sense of each other. The processes of sense-making through body movements, gestures, vocal sounds, speech, and stillness, is akin to an unfolding dance (Hall 1983). Our embodied co-presence is a *precondition to such understanding*.

It has been shown to be possible to simulate such presence in virtual reality. An example of postural orientation and unfolding a dance in a virtual space is that of an avatar-based 3D virtual community, OnLive Traveler10[6] that used voice based emotive head avatars in online 3D virtual environments of their own creation. This community evolved expressively rich conventions of gesture for their interpersonal relationship needs and ran this artificial theatre space as part of their daily lives. In Di Paola's demonstration of OnLive Traveler at Stanford, we had a chance to interact (via DiPaola's avatar) with the community members. Moving an avatar too close upon entering the environment to another avatar, and not responding in time when either spoken to, typed to, and gestured to, was considered inappropriate behavior. This showed how we can project onto the virtual space and engage with cues of proximity, of gestural nuances, of social performance cues of courtesy, offence, emotion, with people who can simulate these.

---

[5] Kendon provides a detailed analysis of social posturing and orientation in a variety of physical environments, be this inside buildings or outdoors in public spaces, and how this shapes our communication with each other.

[6] http://www.dipaola.org/steve/vworlds.html. Di Paola (2001) and his former colleagues had developed this avatar-based 3D virtual community that emulates many natural social metaphors and extended and adapted many of these metaphors as its very tight-nit community of users evolved over the years.

Ultimately the OnLive Traveler community was a closed and protective world: it takes a long time for new people to understand how to engage with the group and learn to follow highly specific gestures and agreed upon social performance cues that have been developed over time. In face-to-face life we are more fluid and able to adapt to others coming in to our communities and able to adapt within other communities that we move into: we *co-adapt* both in our body and in our vocal speech patterns without codifying them.

Distributed interactions via various forms of technology, including the virtual theatre space above, is often referred to as mediated communication or computer mediated communication. What is mediation in human communication? What does it mean to mediate? And what is the difference in the processes of mediation when we are engaged in embodied co-present interaction, and when we are communicating via electronic means? A recent comic sketch performed by actors, of a video conference call that is transposed to a face-to-face meeting setting, highlights the differences in an amusing way and shows how disruptive and unnatural the conference call is. This online video sketch has been shared by thousands of viewers on popular social networking sites such as facebook.[7]

The growth of social networks such as Facebook and protest networks such as AVAAZ and the UK's own 38 Degrees, at local, national, and global levels, shows that we clearly feel connected, and feel a part of real life events happening around the world. How far is this perception due to having a direct personal link with someone whom you know and is in that network, for example, when a friend recommends you join a network or sends you an email linking you to a protest issue that they seek your support on. Is it primarily this online mediation that makes the virtual experience feel real, and how sustainable is a purely virtual relationship (someone you have never met in person) or how is its function different to that of the embodied co-present relationship?

The online traveler community have never met in real life. The world they inhabit is purely virtual and abstracted from the everyday social contexts, hence it is a fragile world that is dependent on specific rules of interaction. This social group, however, was able to find a common ground of gesture, voice, and text interactions.

What about individual to individual virtual interactions that do not have this social frame for referencing meaning. People sometimes find that when they eventually meet the person they have been communicating online with, they find them to be quite different to what they expected. In Presence and the Design of Trust (2007) Nevejan explains this as being due to the combination of *attribution, synchronization*, and *adaptation* by us with the partial presence of the other that is mediated online, and how this differs from this combination to the whole presence that uses *all the senses and cognitive and emotional structures In Real Life*. She gives an example of Jane who meets Max through a mailing list. They fall in love. After 4 months, Jane finds out Max is a girl. Their love becomes intellectual and they become more deeply connected. Four years on, Max is dominating Jane's life from thousands of miles away. In year 5, Max gives her a phone number to call. It turns

---

[7] http://mashable.com/2014/01/23/conference-call-in-real-life/

out from the voice, that Max is in fact a boy. Jane realises that she prefers Max to be male and have a romantic relationship, which continues to develop over the phone and via the internet. Finally, she finds herself too overwhelmed by the control Max has over her and decides to meet him In Real Life. After just a few days, she finds she does not love him or even like him. The power of her attribution to his partial mediated online presence was driven by her own need for love.

Turkle's work shows that people project themselves onto this virtual world and live in a self referential system, and this can lead to being lonely together (Turkle 2011) even whilst in the same physical space. Even in the case of Skype there is the possibility to hide truths and maintain a degree of detachment that is not possible in the face to face presence, as the whole presence is not witnessed. Nevejan proposes that the presence of others influences how we *orchestrate* our own presence, as in her example of Jane. She takes us back to Walter Benjamin's discussion on how we relate to an original painting in comparison to say a photographed reproduction, as on a postcard or a large print. The *original*, through its *aura*, carries its own meaning perceived by all the senses and understood in the context of its tradition. Nevejan considers this aura of the original as the aura of *natural* presence and the reproduction as the mediated presence. Natural presence loses its aura and its tradition, its historical context, when mediated by technology. Further, mediated presence gives us a *partial perception* of a person. Here, she draws on Benjamin's reflections on the medium of film and the perception of the actor by the audience, compared to the case of theatre. In film, the machine defines the audiences' attitude towards the filmed actor; it tests. In editing the film, all the fragments come together and offer a new reality that was not perceivable before, which Benjamin suggests is its attraction. Partial perception is appealing to us: sometimes speaking on the phone can resolve issues that may be harder in real life that demands the application of the all the senses and cognitive and emotional structures of face to face embodied experience. Hence it is perhaps not surprising that we accept the partial presence of others online.

Research in Mediated Presence is concerned 'with how to transmit elements of human presence by way of technology as well as possible', i.e. 'technology does transmit real data about a person and the better this is done, the better the sense of presence that can evolve.' This idea of transmission, data, and elements of a person, bounds and limits the conception of technology and interface.

Nevejan's YUTPA framework (2007, 2009) explicates how trust requires both witnessing and being witnessed, and that this possibility differs according to the degree of distance one has from the presence of others via various forms of technology. Her argument is that we are able to accept the partial presence of another person(s) by balancing four dimensions (time, space, action, relation) through a process of attribution, synchronisation and adaptation. Differences in time and space, and also in how we relate and what possible actions we can take, affect the trade-offs we make for presence and trust. For Nevejan, the distinction between You and not–You, founded in Buber's I-Thou, is fundamental to whether we consider mediated communication as mere 'information' or as communication with someone whom we are in a relationship with. For example, I can send an email, but my friend receiving it may not reply immediately and may have thoughts contrary to what they compose in their reply. In a physically embodied co-present conversation with my friend, I am able to sense and experience his/her responses whilst being simultaneously witnessed by them. In Skype, the nuances of one's thoughts expressed in the subtlety of a gesture, a movement, a glance, an imperceptible sway of the body, can be hidden from each other as it is difficult to *see* these. In the same physical space, we can *experience* these nuances. This very complexity can itself give rise to misunderstandings, however it offers us the possibility to become aware of them as well, and the chance to find resolutions to them.

1.5   Core Concept: Mediation

Interaction technologies are often referred to as mediating communication, mediating presence, and mediating use action. Yet what does mediation mean and how does it work in the context of how one person connects and makes sense with another?

Generally speaking, mediation has a range of meanings, of which the most common ones that come to mind are that it is a medium of transmission of some information or some thing, or that a person is a mediator, acting as a go between to help to resolve a dispute between two or more people or groups or organisations or countries. In the West, the idea of a go between has a Latin route (*mediation, mediation*) meaning intercession or intervention, for example, the intercession of Christ between God and man. In Anglo-Norman and Middle French it evolves along this idea to mean an intermediary between God and man (thirteenth century, *mediación* and *mediation*) and also *division in two*, and this latter meaning is how a computer interface is ordinarily perceived as being. By the fourteenth century, the now common idea of a go between emerges, with people being assigned qualities as *mediators* who have agency to intercede on behalf of someone to either appease the other person or party, or settle a dispute, which by the eighteenth and nineteenth centuries includes getting warring parties to stop fighting and make peace, a role that is essential in our modern times. During the early twentieth century 'mediation' also takes on a legal form of attempting to settle a dispute without going to court, through negotiations conducted by a *neutral* intermediary. Mediating has become a professional practice carried out by individuals, institutions, and nations.

Other meanings are also pertinent for exploring the meaning of interface and of tacit knowing in human life. Mediation itself can denote agency or action that is intermediary, rather than a person or an entity being an intermediary, and this will be explored further in Polanyi's idea of the structure of tacit knowing. Mediation can also denote instrumentality where an *intermediate* agent (something that comes or occurs in between) is a medium of transmission. Hence, technology is sometimes assigned instrumental agency. In the case of my Japanese colleague, technology failed in being a medium for tacit knowing.

For someone or some thing or some act to be mediate is different from it being *immediate*. For example, the sociologist Basil Berstein (1958, p. 163), considered words as 'mediate' or indirect expression, whereas gesture, facial expression, bodily movement, and vocal prosody and volume, were immediate or direct expression. Research on gesture has shown that certain gestures can 'mediate' as language (Ekman and Friesen 1969; Kendon 2004), whilst certain gestures (beats) and bodily movements (kinesics) are immediate. In the design of ECAs certain speech related gestures of the artificial agent could be said to mediate the transactional level of the communication. However, if these gestures lie outside one's culture, they might not be either mediately or immediately comprehensible, at least not as they are intended.

In psychology, 'mediated association' denotes the indirect linking (of ideas, etc.) through unconscious or unnoticed intermediaries (Atherton and Washburn 1912), and this bears a relation to the idea of tacit knowing (Polanyi 1966), who discusses shock syllables, which are the association made between certain syllables and receiving an electric shock, without later being consciously aware of making this association. In philosophy, law, and in science, the inference or testimony i.e. logic and evidence is a form of mediated knowledge. Set in contrast to this, is Polanyi's mediational structure of tacit knowing that does not involve inference or evidence to validate it; if I look at a wood, I have an awareness of the trees that form it but I am not looking at each individual tree in order to see the wood. I attend from the trees to attend to the wood.

There is one sense of mediate used in science, where it can mean to be the medium for, or means of bringing about a force or a reaction, etc., and that does have a bearing on the meditational structure of tacit knowing as a force for emergence or discovery. Polanyi himself speaks of this, with reference to Bergson's elan vital (Bergson 1911). Lastly, and perhaps importantly, mediate can mean to lie or occupy the space *between* or *betwixt* two things, two times, etc., and to be transitional *between*.

The point of covering these various meanings of the concept of mediation is to both consider what it means to say that technology is a medium of transmission, of communicating something, as in the field of social computing (Dourish op. cit.), and they may bear on an understanding of interface where the locus is a personal act of knowing, extending beyond the relationship between 'use of something' and 'meaning'.

How we relate to others and understand them is variously referred to as Dialogue, Communication, Conversation, Interaction, and Engagement, and sometimes these terms are used interchangeably. However, each has its own history and each undergoes a shift in the twentieth century with the rise of science and computation as a methodology to study mind, behavior, and culture.

Their differing histories of meaning may be helpful for understanding why the usage of some terms are more prevalent than others in the various disciplines that inform and shape technology and our relationship with it, and will help in understanding what might be the conditions for an interface in the human system.

1.6 Core Concept: Dialogue in Human Relations

In everyday speech in English, we use the word 'dialogue' interchangeably with communication to refer to interaction between people, between human and machine, and between interconnected systems in general. However, the word Dialogue has a history that differs from that of 'communication'. It has been imbued with the quality of 'authenticity' (Gadamer 1960), and distinct from the idea of communication that has come to connote information transfer. Dialogue can hold differences both within the thoughts of a person and between people, and unlike information transfer does not need to have agreement as an end goal (Goranzon 1988). Often, there is an ideological element in the way the term dialogue is used, where it means 'understanding', 'communality' and 'honesty', with demands for clear articulation. For the Swedish Dialogue Seminar (Florin et al. 1991; Ratkic 2009), dialogue requires a degree of scepticism, whereby disagreement is one of its conditions. "Dialogue involves reflecting and opening oneself to criticism of one's own assumptions. It is the concept that expresses the dynamics of knowledge. The purpose of dialogue is to set knowledge in motion, to stop it fossilising in empty forms." (Goranzon, op. cit.).

Theories and methods to understand the nature of Dialogue are a response to rationalism and the reductionist view of language, knowledge, and experience that emerged with theories of cognition as Cartesian. Cartesian theory separates the mind from the body, and the mind becomes the source and engine of human knowledge. For the Dialogue Seminar, 'Dialogue' has 'historically been the means of clarifying issues within a community of human beings, and as a basic component of their reality', and has been the subject of pictorial as well as dramatic and literary works, for example Plato's Socratic dialogues. Philosophies of dialogue find their form in the twentieth century and deal with the dichotomy constructed between subjectivity and objectivity, evident by the turn of the nineteenth century, and a tension between the unity and fragmentation of knowledge, concerns addressed by philosophers such as Husserl (1931), Merleau-Ponty (1945), Heidegger (1927), Gadamer (1960), Martin Buber (1923), and Ludwig Wittgenstein (1953). In general the focus of dialogue is reciprocity, with its mutual dependence on I/You or I/Other relations.

The concept of dialogue allows for the shared experience of having comfortable moments of stillness and quiet with another person(s). It is more than the exchange of words. Martin Buber (1923) described dialogue as a reciprocal conversation ... an effective means of on-going communication rather than as a purposive attempt to reach some conclusion or to express some viewpoint(s). Buber's use of the word communication is in its pre-cognitive sense, as meaning to share and be in fellowship.

To 'dialogue' can mean both to converse with someone else and also oneself, and be transfigurative as in this example given in the OED from the seventeenth century, about smoking, 'where men dialogue with their noses, and their communication is smoke'. This meaning of 'dialogue' as being about connecting, sharing (without necessarily speaking) and reflecting, underlies the Swedish Dialogue Seminar's response to rationalism and reductionism and Buber's idea that dialogue is more than the exchange of words.

The concept of communication however, has a differing etymology which goes further back to Anglo Norman and Middle French denoting interpersonal relations, and by the fifteenth century comes to describe social intercourse i.e. fellowship, mutual participation, and sharing in something. The etymology of communication[8] includes the imparting of ideas, consultation, discussion, a piece of information, an act of sharing goods and property, and largely indicates a more functional and transactional quality than either Dialogue or Engagement that lean towards the relational. This may, in part, help in understanding why this word has been preferred over Dialogue within cognitivist and pragmatic approaches to computer based technologies.

The etymology of 'interaction' has at its core the idea of *reciprocal action*, i.e. the action or influence of persons or things on each other, and the earliest quotation of its usage in the English language dates to 1832, which is quite recent.[9]

In the twentieth century, the word communication sees a significant shift in its meaning, largely influenced by models of human cognition, with its core idea being that information is transmitted from a sender (speaker) to a receiver (listener) *through signals*.[10] This has been criticised for its fragmented view of language by modern scholars, notably Clark (1996) who emphasised the joint quality of language with a theory of Joint Action, and one could say that its Latin meaning of *community of ground* has found a modern meaning in the theory of Common Ground (Clark and Brennan 1991). This is now one of the foremost theories of language.

By the turn of the twenty-first century, there is a significant shift taking place with the word interaction being used in preference to communication, a move away from the prior focus on language by designers and researchers seeking to focus on the actions of people and machines in both the design of human-machine relations and machines that facilitate such interaction between humans, i.e. interactive technologies.[11] Embodiment is becoming a core concern in their design with a revisiting

---

[8] It is a fact of having something in common with another person or thing (late thirteenth or early fourteenth century in Old French), a communion rite (early fourteenth century or earlier in Anglo-Norman), (in anatomy) fact of being connected by a physical link (1314), connection, a passage (from one place to another) (a1374). It denotes, handing over (a1377 or earlier in Anglo-Norman), discussion (a1377 or earlier in Anglo-Norman), meeting, coming together (fifteenth century or earlier in Anglo-Norman), piece of information (a1420), action of sharing (goods, property), joining together to do business (1437). Its etymon, classical Latin, is commūnicātiōn-, commūnicātiō, an action of sharing or imparting, community of ground, (in rhetoric) consultation with one's audience or adversary. In post-classical Latin it means membership in the Christian society (late second century in Tertullian), participation in Holy Communion (third century), imparting (of ideas) (from thirteenth century in British sources), interchange of properties (between the two natures of Christ) (early fourteenth century in a British source), a connection, a link (1363 in Chauliac), consultation, and discussion (from fourteenth century in British sources).

[9] The Latin preposition and adverb, inter which means 'between, among, amid, in between, in the midst' becomes a prefix in the English language between the fifteenth and seventeenth centuries, and the verb 'action' derives from French where its meaning 'to set in motion, to move' arises in the sixteenth century.

[10] Shannon and Weaver (1949).

[11] See Dourish (op. cit.) for a thorough account of this shift and its historical and philosophical context.

and adaptation of twentieth century phenomenology such as that of Heidegger, Husserl, and Merleau Ponty (Dourish 2004).

Such phenomenology has been the driving force of earlier twentieth century design movements around computer technology in Europe, namely of Participatory Design in Scandinavia (Ehn 1988), and the early Human-Centred Systems movement (Cooley 1987; Rosenbrock 1996; Gill 1996; Rauner et. al. 1987, 1988 (on social shaping)) in the UK and Germany. These were holistic approaches to technology and social and learning systems, deeply rooted in philosophical and cultural approaches to thinking about the purpose of technology in human life. However these design movements were perceived to have an anti-rationalism and anti-cognitivist agenda and were slow to be taken up in countries such as the UK and the USA whilst the cognitivist agenda was dominant. As this shifted, the idea of 'Human Centred' was taken up by groups in the design community in the UK, and has now become part of mainstream design discourse.

In contrast to the ideas of 'participatory' and 'human centred', the idea of 'Interaction' has been perceived as neutral and systemic, and has become a design methodology that is encompassing a range of methods that span ideas about tangibility, emotion, and movement, for designing robotics, gaming, virtual networks, interactive art, and social media. In its neutral focus on actions, interaction has shed its sense of 'reciprocality', a crucial element of joint action. The challenges it faces in addressing the social dimension is opening up a need to consider the body as a source of knowledge (Dourish op. cit. on the phenomenology of embodied interaction) and reposition interaction as reciprocal and intersubjective.

Engagement, like Dialogue, does not necessarily mean to be in, or reach, agreement, nor to have that as the goal, rather it is about purposive and committed relations. Examples include, for example, making a pledge, a formal promise, an agreement, an undertaking, a covenant, and it can be as basic as making an appointment with another person. Engagement can carry moral and even legal obligation. The expression is often used to mean attachment and being entangled, and this includes a fight, battle, or any conflict. To engage can also mean to persuade (from French engager to invite), to attract, and to attach. The etymology is largely around the use of language and social conventions, with moral and ethical undertones. Recently, the idea of engagement has been explored in terms of an embodied space of commitment (Gill 2000) in order to understand how we express the nature of our engagement in our relations with others through our bodies.

In marked contrast to the above terms for human relations, the etymology of conversation goes back to twelfth century French and is used in English in the fourteenth century. Its meaning is rooted in being in a place and with a group of people, or in communities, and can be about how one conducts oneself in that place or group. Early behaviourist work on how humans relate considers how people conduct themselves in social settings (Sacks 1984). The verb *to converse* also originates in twelfth century French where it means to pass one's life, live, or dwell in or with. The transfer of this meaning from 'live with' to 'talk with' is recent in both French (exchange words with) and English, and it is primarily understood as the latter in English, whilst in French both meanings are current. By the seventeenth century conversation is used to mean 'a familiar interchange of thoughts, discourse, talk',[12] and by the twentieth century it is used interchangeably with the word 'discourse', and becomes a focus of empirical analysis in the discipline of conversation analysis (refs, Sacks op. cit., Sacks et al. 1974; Heritage 1984, etc.). Conversational analysis is an important method in the study of language and in the social sciences, and the structure of a turn in conversation is the dominant structure for the empirical analysis of human relations.

In summary, the expressions used to convey how we relate to others cover a rich spectrum of meanings, from mutuality, friendship, community, and reciprocality, through to the sharing and transfer of information. Technology has tended towards the latter part of the spectrum that satisfies a utilitarian vision of a human user of things. The shift that is now underfoot is revisiting the former part of the spectrum, of human mutual relations with others, to understand how we connect and are present for each other at a personal level.

1.7   Foundational Ideas

The origins of the terms, interaction, dialogue, communication, engagement, and conversation, have in common a commitment to relate to others. Some have been reshaped by cognitivism or rationalism[13] (knowledge of the world is independent of the human body and emotion), and utilitarianism[14] (where reality can be objectively codified as 'data'). In response to both rationalism and utilitarianism, concepts of dialogue and interaction have been re-articulated to focus attention back on to mutuality, reciprocal relations, the importance of social uncertainty, empathy, ethics, action, emotion, and the human body. The philosophical and theoretical foundations for this change can be largely attributed to the force of the philosophical works of Husserl (1931), Merleau Ponty (1845), Martin Buber (1923), Heidegger (1927), Gadamer (1960), Ludwig Wittgenstein (1953), Michael Polanyi (1966, 1969), and thinkers such as Whitehead (1978) and Bergson (1911). These thinkers revolutionised how we think about ourselves as human beings. They questioned how we think about our selves in relation to our environment and others in it, how we learn, how we make sense of our reality, and how being bodies shapes our perceptions and our understanding. Husserl developed a philosophy of human perception that is largely cognitive and based around the self, lifeworld, upon which judgements about the world are egocentric, such as assuming the other will behave as oneself would; intersubjective empathic experience. He believed that objects in the world exist independently of one's perception of them, i.e. they are transcendent of our consciousness, and this includes the empirical 'I'. Whilst holding a subject object dis-

---

[12] OED.

[13] Descartes, Kant, and Husserl – either cut out the footnote, or say something about these thinkers as per rationalism.

[14] Hume on utilitarianism.

tinction, he did away with inference as a method of perceiving things about other people and objects. Merleau Ponty shifted the locus of human perception from the mind to the body, and did away with the subject object distinction by ascribing the body with skills and capacities that shape our awareness of the world by engaging in it. Martin Buber, deeply spiritual, believed that we can experience unity with another person when we make ourselves completely available and able to receive them as we would God, and he calls this, 'I Thou'. Any distance or detachment from others reduces our relationships to I-It, which ultimately allows us to perceive another person as an object. Only in I-Thou can you experience true dialogue and understanding. Heidegger considers the other in relation to self as the 'who', the group from whom one does not stand out, and that constitutes one's culture, where culture is not the sum of its members but an ontological phenomenon. Hence my actions are 'what one does', absorbed from my culture. Gadamer's philosophy is about practical understanding and wisdom that one gains through dialogue. We exist in dialogue with each other, through which we come to understand our own self and others, and realise our limitations and possibilities. Wittgenstein famously said that we could never understand a Lion even if we spoke Lion, as we do not share the embodied experiences, emotions, and cultural practices of the Lion's world. He located language within embodied cultural practices, i.e. experience. Polanyi collapses the body and mind into one, where thought, perception, action, is possible due to neural processes. He developed the idea of tacit knowing, which is the way we are aware of our neuronal processes in terms of perceived objects. This has a mediational structure, hence we know more than we can say. Tacit knowing lies in experience and is a personal way of knowing.

How we relate with others has been conceived as intersubjective, as unity or objective, as bounded by cultural norms, as self-understanding and practical wisdom, as culturally embodied, and personal. These philosophies of being are not all comfortably aligned with each other, but each provides important ideas to inform the discussion in this book on the relational level of human engagement and the tacit dimension of human knowing as being a personal act. Below is a brief description of the ideas that are providing a background to this discussion and informing it.

1.7.1 Husserl (1859–1938)

Husserl formed the expression 'intersubjective' (*Cartesian Meditations 1931*) to describe our experience of relating ourselves as objectively existing subjects with an objective spatio-temporal world and other experiencing subjects within it. Intersubjectivity exists within *acts* of empathy, hence intersubjective experience is empathic experience. By empathic experience he means *consciously attributing intentional acts to others* by placing ourselves in their shoes.[15] His drew on Brentano's work (1874) for his idea of intentionality (Husserl was Brentano's stu-

---

[15] Stanford Encyclopedia of Philosophy, Husserl, 2013.

dent), and modified it (Morrison 1970). For Brentano the world appears to us in mental and physical phenomena. The mental phenomena are grasped through inner perception through *intentional inexistence* (consciousness of something) by introspection and reflection. Outer perception involves the bodily sense organs by which we grasp physical phenomena. As we can only have a possible view of a three dimensional object and never perceive its wholeness, outer perception could deceive us. Inner perception, which can be grasped in its wholeness in the mind, is the only reliable form of perception.

Husserl modifies Brentano's idea of intentionally. Not all mental phenomena are acts and thereby intentional, and he replaces the term mental phenomena with *intentional lived experience (intentionale Erlebnisse)*, hence consciousness is a lived experience. He also distinguishes between the mental experience and the object of the experience, whereby the latter is *transcendent* of consciousness, i.e. it remains as that entity over time independent of it being perceived. The objects of experience include the *empirical I*, and I is also a mental experience. Like Brentano, Husserl held that consciousness involves thoughts, feelings and actions about things in the world. In order for us to have intersubjective experience, we have to have a belief that a being that looks and behaves more or less like oneself i.e., displays traits similar to oneself, will perceive things from an *egocentric* viewpoint similar to one's own ("here", "over there", "to my left", "in front of me", etc.), i.e. I would roughly look upon things the way the other person does if I were in her shoes and perceived them from her perspective. This belief allows one to ascribe intentional acts to others immediately or "appresentatively", without using inference. So this belief must be fundamental to my belief-system, and part of a pregiven (and generally unreflected) intentional background or "lifeworld" (1954 cf. Crisis), against which my practice of act-ascriptions makes sense, and in terms of which they are justified. Husserl's notion of lifeworld can roughly be thought of (1) in terms of belief and (2) in terms of socially, culturally or evolutionarily established (but abstract) sense or meaning.

For Husserl, phenomenology is a rigorous human science that investigates the way that knowledge comes into being and the assumptions upon which all human understandings are grounded.

1.7.2   Merleau Ponty (1908–1961)

Merleau Ponty's phenomenology (*Phenomenology of Perception 1945*) is about the *intentional* constitution of the body and its role in perceptual experience. His ideas about intersubjectivity differ from Husserl's for whom the body "appears as a kind of phenomenological anomaly, posing awkward questions for the metaphysical and epistemological distinctions that Husserl ...... largely takes for granted" (Carman 1999). For Husserl my body is neither internal to my consciousness nor external to me in the environment (i.e. the body cannot see or touch itself as it can other objects, since it cannot step back and, as it were, hold itself at arm's length). The body is "a thing 'inserted' between the rest of the material world and the 'subjective' sphere" (*Id II*, 161). Hence it is cognitive attitudes rather than bodily skills that bridge an intentional (consciousness of something) gap between mind and world, and he seeks to ground bodily self-awareness in our sense of touch. For example, when a hand touches an object it perceives the tactility of the surface of the object as well as its own tactility. In this sense, the touching body knows itself through touching things in the world. This double sense of touch is complicated by the ability of the body to move towards touching and as it touches, thus taking an active role in the sensing process. The body perceives itself through its intentionality towards things in the world. Merleau-Ponty, in contrast, bases his phenomenology on an account of bodily intentionality and the challenge it poses to any adequate concept of mind. Embodiment raises questions about the mental as a distinct phenomenal region mediating our *intentional orientation* in the world. For Merleau-Ponty thought and sensation occur against a background of perceptual activity that is understood in bodily terms, by *engaging* in it. The body undercuts the supposed dichotomy between consciousness and objective reality: "the distinction between subject and object is blurred in my body."

> my body has a grip on the world when my perception and action defines a perceptual ground, a basis of my life, a general milieu for the coexistence of my body and the world. (Phenomenology of Perception: 289–90)[16]

For Merleau-Ponty, our bodies constantly self-correct, that is, they adjust their orientation in the environment and this constitutes the perceptual background against which discrete sensory particulars and judgements can occur e.g. as we walk, sit, grasp objects, and avoid bumping into things, etc. In contrast to Descartes 'I think', the body is an ensemble of lived meanings that moves to its equilibrium. Perception is therefore neither a purely mental nor purely physiological state. He speaks of the body schema, which is not an image of the body, i.e. not an object of awareness, but rather the bodily skills and capacities that shape our awareness of objects. Our bodies are skilled in making adjustments to have a grip on the world, so a posture feels right, and the position we lie in our beds feels comfortable for us to sleep, etc. Bodily orientation has a kind of 'normativity' and it constitutes a form of intentionality that is more primitive than the application of concepts.

1.7.3 Martin Buber (1878–1965)

Buber wrote a short philosophy essay, *Ich und Du* (*I and Thou*) *in* 1923 about the difference between experiencing the world of things (I and It) and experiencing *relations* with others (I and Thou). He said that we tend to view objects and people by their functions, for example when doctors examine us for specific maladies, they

---

[16] From chapter, 'sensation, judgement, and the phenomenal field' in the Merleau Ponty Reader, CUP:

view us as organisms and not as individuals. Scientists can learn a great deal about our world by observing, measuring, and examining. For Buber, such processes are I-It relationships. We often view people as such, where rather than making ourselves completely available to them, we observe them or keep part of ourselves outside the relationship. We do so either to protect our vulnerabilities or to get them to respond in some preconceived way, to get something from them. In contrast to such I-It relationships, it is possible to place ourselves completely into a relationship, to truly understand and "be there" with another person, without masks, pretenses, even without words. Such a moment of *relating* is called "I-Thou." Each person comes to such a *relationship* without preconditions. Such a bond enlarges each person, and each person responds by trying to enhance the other person. The result is true dialogue and true sharing.

I-Thou relationships are not constant or static. People move in and out of I-Thou and I-It moments. Ironically, attempts to achieve an I-Thou moment will fail because the process of trying to create an I-Thou relationship objectifies it and makes it I-It. Even describing the moment objectifies it and makes it an I-It. The most Buber can do in describing this process is to encourage us to be available to the possibility of I-Thou moments. When you have it, you know it. Buber maintains that it is also possible to have an I-Thou relationship with the world and the objects in it as well. Art, music, poetry are all possible media for such responses in which true dialogue can take place.

Buber then moves from this existential description of personal relating to the religious experience. For Buber, God is the Eternal Thou. By trying to prove God's existence or define God, the rationalist philosophers automatically established an I-It relationship. We cannot define God; we cannot set up preconditions for the relationship. We simply have to be available, open to the relationship with the Eternal Thou.

1.7.4   Heidegger (1889–1976)

One of the key concepts in *Heidegger's* philosophy (*Being and Time 1927*) is dasein, which is about being-in the world. This entails that the world itself is part of the fundamental constitution of what it means to be human. It is about an experience of openedness where one's being and that of the world are largely not distinguished. This can include artifacts or tools as they reveal themselves to us. In this way, his idea of dasein questions the subject-object distinction. Being-with denotes a shared horizon. Heidegger does not deal specifically with the body and there has been criticism of this, however, his work on technological existence reveals our fragile interconnectedness with things and does indirectly hint at the mediating role of the body in our experience with handling technology. A concept that is closer to our relations with others is 'being-with' (mit-sein): "By 'Others' we do not mean everyone else but me – those over against whom the 'I' stands out. They are rather those from whom, for the most part, one does not distinguish oneself – those among whom one is too… By reason of this *with-like* Being-in-the-world, the world is always the one that I share with Others".

(*Being and Time* 26: 154–5). Dreyfus (1990) explains this as follows: each society seems to have its own sense of what counts as an appropriate distance to stand from someone during verbal communication, and this varies depending on whether the other person is a lover, a friend, a colleague, or a business acquaintance, and on whether communication is taking place in noisy or quiet circumstances. Such standing-distance practices are of course normative, in that they involve a sense of what one should and shouldn't do. And the norms in question are culturally specific. So what this example illustrates is that the phenomenon of the Others, the 'who' of everyday Dasein, the group from whom for the most part I do not stand out, is my culture, understood not as the sum of all its members, but as an ontological phenomenon in its own right. This explains the following striking remark.

> The 'who' is not this one, not that one, not oneself, not some people, and not the sum of them all. The 'who' is the neuter, the 'they'. (*Being and Time* 27: 164)

Another way to capture this idea is to say that what I do is determined largely by 'what one does', and 'what one does' is something that I absorb in various ways from my culture. Dreyfus (1990) prefers to translate *das Man* not as 'the "they"', but as 'the "one"'. For Heidegger our relations to others is a threat to our authenticity rather than a resource for becoming authentic, and Gadamer, his student, was critical that Heidegger conceded to account for 'being-with' but did not spend time to develop this. In contrast, Dreyfus argues for an ontological interpretation which accounts for others as part of a shared habitus. The primary focus of Heidegger's work is on 'being-in'.

1.7.5 Gadamer (1900–2002)

Gadamer's roots are in Aristotelian philosophy, with a focus on practical understanding through dialogue (*Truth and Method 1960*). His primary focus is linguistic, and not the body. The concept of the 'other' is central in Gadamer's work as we exist in conversation or in dialogue with one another and it is through conversations that we come to realize our limitations. Dialogue is an irreplaceable means for self-understanding enabling us to gain insights about ourselves that we would not be able to attain any other way. All judgments are based on prejudgments and to be critically reflective is to question not only our judgments but also our prejudgments which are best drawn out through dialogue; in dialogue we come to see how others might judge differently, and this difference make us conscious of our prejudgments. For this reason he says that we should always enter into dialogue with the presumption that our interlocutor has something to teach us about the subject matter. The second argument is that in dialogue we become aware of a different perspective and sometimes acquire new knowledge about our own views. We can often find ourselves at a loss for words on a topic we thought we knew, sometimes we surprise ourselves with our eloquence on talking about ideas that we might not have even known we had. In dialogue we test our understanding and likewise reveal our limitations in understanding. Dialogue is also the way we best embody our awareness of our finitude. This is influenced by Aristotelian philosophy wherein certain beliefs are only fully realized when they are lived, i.e. self-understanding necessitates practical understanding of what this means. Practical wisdom comes from acting, so the practical wisdom about the nature of our limitations comes from acting according to our natures in such a way as to reflect awareness of our limitations.

1.7.6   Wittgenstein (1889–1951)

Published after his death, in writings on *Philosophical Investigations* (*1953*), Wittgenstein said that we could never understand a Lion even if we spoke Lion, as we do not share the embodied experiences, emotions, and cultural practices of the Lion's world. Language is more than words and structured utterances. Language is social, rooted in culture, and has a pragmatic character. Wittgenstein used the metaphor of a tool box for speech (Gill 2000, p. 118) for performing/acting in different situations for every purpose.

> Review the multiplicity of language-games in the following examples, and in others: Giving orders and obeying them – Describing the appearance of an object or giving its measurements – Constructing an object from a description (a drawing) – Reporting an event – Speculating about an event – Forming and testing a hypothesis – Presenting the results of an experiment in tables and diagrams – Making up a story; and reading it – Play-acting – Singing catches – Guessing riddles – Making a joke: telling it – Solving a problem in practical arithmetic – Translating from one language to another – Asking, thanking, cursing, greeting, praying. (PI, Macmillan, 1953, no. 23)

This predates the idea of speech acts by Searle that emerges three decades later. For Wittgenstein language is a form of physical as well as social activity, where cognitivity involves both thought and action in the form of *language games*. Furthermore language works when there is agreement in these *forms of life*:

> It is what human beings say that is true and false: and they agree in the language they use. This is not agreement in opinions but in forms of life. If language is to be a means of communication, there must be agreement not only in definitions but also (queer as this may sound) in judgements. (PI, nos. 241–242).

1.7.7   Summary

In summary, perception (knowledge) is not a matter of making inferences about the world and others, but about how we relate to them as reflexive (intersubjective), as embodied (conscious body), in dialogue (self-awareness and understanding), in unity (I-Thou), and as cultural beings (language is embodied in culture). These thinkers are concerned with the process of being in the world, not with goal oriented interaction. They share a quest to overcome the limitations of the historical separation of body and mind that can be traced back to the Ancient Greeks, Socrates and Plato, for whom truth about oneself and the world can only be found by applying the mind (argument, rationality) without the disturbance of the sensory body, the emotions, and the conventions of society and culture. Rationality and empiricism have been the drivers of Western 'progress' and modernity, where communication became usurped by the model of signal transmission and knowledge conceived as fundamentally Cartesian. By the end of the nineteenth century through the early twentieth century, there is a growing counter movement of ideas that gains force during the twentieth century. Husserl, Merleau Ponty, Gadamer, Buber, Heidegger, and Wittgenstein, bring the spiritual, the body, culture, and the emotions into the conception of knowledge. They provide us with ontologies to understand and investigate how we relate to one another in everyday life and in face-to-face reality. What role does mediation play in how we relate to one another? Can we say we mediate when we perceive the world and others in it? Can we say we mediate when we are in dialogue with someone? Can we mediate in an I-Thou relationship? In order to understand what mediation in the context of human relations might mean, I consider Polanyi's theory of tacit knowing, a personal act of knowing, which has a meditational structure.

1.8 Mediation and Tacit Knowing

1.8.1 Polanyi: Mediational Structure of Knowledge

Polanyi's (1891–1976) work on human perception (*The Tacit Dimension 1966*) brought the body into human cognition and can be said to have annulled the Cartesian divide. Merleau Ponty had begun the process by assigning *intentionality* to the body, whereby the body is a source of knowledge about the world: "the distinction between subject and object is blurred in my body." For Polanyi, the brain is body: "Tacit knowing is the way in which we are aware of neural processes in terms of perceived objects" (Polanyi 1962).[17] Hence 'we can know more than we can tell', an expression he is often cited for. Polanyi is concerned to show that the aim of exact science to establish a strictly detached, objective knowledge, is fundamentally misleading because tacit thought forms an indispensable part of all knowledge. This idea of tacit knowing is based within a discussion which starts with questions about how we can recognise a face, or any object or phenomenon, and leads into questions about knowledge acquisition. He is interested in how we pass on to others knowledge which we ourselves cannot fully describe. He cites the use of practical classes, and the act of pointing to things to connect words to things, as methods of passing on such knowledge. This act of pointing leaves something out which we cannot tell, and for its meaning to be understood the other person must discover that which we

---

[17] The structure of consciousness Brain vol, 88 1965 part iv pp 779–810.

have not been able to communicate. The discussion draws upon Gestalt psychology (Ellis 1938; Henle 1961) and the idea of shaping or integrating experience in the process of knowledge acquisition. Here we are introduced to two aspects of knowing: 'knowing how' and 'knowing that'[18] (Ryle 1949). The former denotes practical knowledge (Goranzon 1992) and the latter theoretical knowledge. This may be seen as a restatement of the classical Greek distinction between 'techne' (art or craft) and 'episteme' (knowledge). The concepts of integration, awareness, interiorization or indwelling form the core of his theory of tacit knowledge and explain the interdependence of the theoretical and practical aspects of knowing. For example, Polanyi argues that mathematical theory can only be learned by practicing its application. We can only understand that which is explicit if we can relate to it through practice. Gill (2000) gives a nice example, of explaining to his son that he will only learn to swim by swimming.

Through the use of various examples, Polanyi identifies four aspects of tacit knowing: the functional, the phenomenal, the semantic, and the ontological. The functional aspect is his basic model of the structure of tacit knowing which he uses throughout his argument. He explains it as follows. In recognising a face, we are aware of its features, yet we are unable to identify all those features. The ability to recognise the face occurs through a functional relationship between what he calls 'two terms of tacit knowing'. The first, proximal, term is the features, and the second, distal, term is the face. 'We know the first term only by relying on our awareness of it for attending to the second. It is the proximal term of which we have a knowledge that we may not be able to tell'.[19] He calls this the 'functional structure of tacit knowing'.[20] We come to know the richer and more comprehensive dimensions of our common experience by focusing (focal awareness) on or attending to their meaning from or through the less complex particulars (subsidiary awareness of subsidiary functions) of which they are composed. And what is focal in one context may become subsidiary in another and vice versa. We rely on some things in order to focus on others; we attend from some things to others. This dimensional and vectorial construing of experience allows for what Gill (2000, p. 33) calls a 'mediational' understanding of the structure of reality.

Polanyi sees a direct relationship between our bodies and the external world, for example in the way we see things, in his discussion on perception as an instance of tacit knowing. He cites physiologists who maintained that the way we see an object is determined by our awareness of certain efforts inside our body which we ourselves cannot feel. These efforts inside our body include the activity of neural traces in the cortex of the nervous system. His focus on the relationship between our bodily processes and the external world has been of interest to discussions on the nature of craftsmanship skills, such as engineering (Cooley 1987). Polanyi talks of the transformation of the tool into a sentient extension of our body, an idea inspired by

---

[18] G. Ryle (1949) The Concept of Mind.
[19] Polanyi, op. cit. p. 10.
[20] ibid. p. 10.

Samuel Butler[21]; 'When we make a thing (e.g. a tool) function as the proximal term of tacit knowing, we incorporate it in our body and extend our body to include it, so that we come to dwell in it'.

The process by which we tacitly know is through indwelling, the *phenomenal* aspect. It is not by looking at things, but by dwelling in them, that we understand their *joint meaning*. This relates back to the point that we can only understand a mathematical theory if we can relate ourselves to it in practising it. We can only understand something if we are within it and understand its practice. We cannot look at the parts and have an understanding of the whole. If we try to focus on the particulars, we can destroy our conception of an entity. For example, if a pianist whilst playing starts focusing on the movements of her fingers, she will be paralysed. However, if she focuses again on her music, she will be able to play again. With this distance the particulars will come back to life and recover their meaning and their comprehensive relationship. Thinking of the parts, rather than of the whole, as the real entity, is a misconception. 'We do not work from the parts to the whole, but rather from the whole to the parts. . the parts constitute the whole *ontologically* speaking, but our comprehension of parts as parts depends upon our first grasping some meaningful whole. The notion of part only makes sense in relation to the whole of which it is a part. ... parts do not float around as independent units.' (Knowing and Being 1969).

Polanyi does not think, however, that a knowledge of the parts is of no use in the understanding of the whole. For example, he contrasts someone who knows how to use a machine without fully knowing how it works, with an engineer who, he says, has a deeper understanding of its construction and operation. He states, however, that a knowledge of the parts cannot replace its tacit counterpart. For example, the skill of a driver cannot be replaced by the teaching of the theory of the motorcar.

Polanyi talks of the personal dimension of knowing.[22] He considers how a scientist can see a problem. He argues that all knowledge is of the same kind as the knowledge of seeing and working with a problem. To hold such knowledge is to be committed to a conviction that there is something there to be discovered. This experience cannot be represented by any exact theory. It is a personal act of knowing.

To summarise, Polanyi's discussion on how we know something to be something is explained through his model of tacit knowing which has a particular structure of going from particulars to the entity, which does not involve the explicit identification of these particulars. This structure may be seen as a *meditational* structure of knowledge. His theory of indwelling and interiorization claims that we can only understand that which is explicit if we can relate to it through practice. Knowing has a personal dimension.

---

[21] Samuel Butler wrote at the end of nineteenth century through to the turn of twentieth century, about the body as tool, the embodied transformation of objects in the world as tools, and the embodied comprehension of other living beings.

[22] Polanyi has developed his theory of personal knowing in his work, Personal Knowledge: Towards a Post Critical Philosophy (1958).

1.8.2   Mediation in Human Relations

If one were to apply this meditational structure to human relations, what would we need to consider? In this context, we will consider various levels of mediation. One is awareness of how another person is perceiving and responding to oneself, by our attending *from particulars* such as a gesture, a movement, a tone of voice, etc., the kinds of knowledge we have and assume the other to have, and our roles in relation to each other, *to the meaning or understanding* we have of the combination of these particulars that constitute this understanding. Another level of mediation is the enabling kind that is made up of the first kind, and that we are more familiar with speaking about, to bridge the discrepancies in our awareness where we match the particulars that are relevant for us to mutually attend to a shared awareness or meaning, i.e. to comprehend the nature of a problem. The latter form of mediation does not occur every moment we communicate – it occurs at particular moments with the purpose to make visible the root of the discrepancies in our states of knowing about something, and thereby make it possible to resolve them (it). Without mediation at either of these levels, engagement and dialogue is problematic, and in human interaction this is experienced as a distance of one's self from another, of miscommunication, of tension, and at the extreme level, isolation. Mediation and engagement are conceptually and experientially part of each other in human interaction, where the heightened form of mediated engagement is 'mutuality', a kind of agreement, even if it is to agree to disagree. Examples of these forms of mediation in human relations will be considered in Chaps. 3 and 4, with examples of various settings, such as people giving presentations, having group meetings, sketching together, dancing, and making music.

Mediation and successful communication is considered here to involve empathy, which has an aesthetic quality. Imagine you are viewing a work of art, you experience the work as a whole yet you have an awareness that it is composed of the brush strokes, dots of paint, textures of paint, and colours. Together, these particulars enable you to see the picture and experience an aesthetic pleasure it may give. These particulars, marks on the page, form patterns of recognizable human forms, nature, artifacts, and a narrative, i.e. they give us a mediated quality of meaning and affect. Polanyi went further to say that we attend from the particulars of a work of art to attend to the aesthetics of the artist who created it. Within human interaction, such particulars include the forms of expression, the gesture stroke, the intonation of the voice, the rhythm of the movement, that together form perceptual patterns of a personality, the role of the person in that moment, a style of communicating, their rhythm, and a kind of knowing. The mediated quality of each person's meaning by another person, lies in the equivalence of the compatibilities of these particulars, these 'marks on the page' or 'brush strokes', of the interaction. This enables us to experience empathy,[23] akin to the aesthetic emotion of aesthetic pleasure, which is necessarily part of human mediation, and thereby knowledge transfer.

If the representations of the tacit lie outside one's experience, then they become what some have termed, propositional or explicit knowledge. In human communication this could be a word, a phrase, a gesture, a movement, a tone of voice, a rhythm. They become either meaningless for the participant or cannot be interpreted or used, or responded to, by him/her in accordance to the background of understanding and practices against which they have been expressed, leading to misunderstanding. The understanding of the representation of the tacit dimension of another's action, is expressed in the skilled performance with the other, be this to agree, disagree, negotiate, acknowledge, or simply, to act at the same moment with the other (simultaneously).

In the 'Tacit Dimension', Polanyi describes a relation between emergence and comprehension as existing when 'an action creates new comprehensive entities'. In the process of arriving at shared understanding, we create new comprehensive entities that 'include, apart from our own performance, both the performance of other persons and these persons themselves' (op. cit. p. 49). This is an important point. In much research on interaction we lose sight of the person as we focus on the particulars of their speech and gesture and movement patterns.

Mediation is considered here as part of the process of the transfer and formation of tacit knowing in human dialogue. It is a pivotal moment that can facilitate a shift from a state of confusion or ignorance or inability to seeing how one may relate with another, to that of being able to understand the other. Mediation enables learning to occur as we come to realise the nature of the problem we are having in our communication with each other (Gadamer ibid). It is not necessarily the case that this understanding means we will be best of friends, and in fact it may mean we will never be friends, but it does mean that there is a resolution in our shared awareness of the discrepancy.

A consideration of 'interface' as being located in 'dialogue', 'performance', and the tacit dimension of knowledge, may expand our conception of what constitutes the relation between the physical, emotional, and cognitive dimensions of human connectivity. Interaction may be seen as the resonance of structures in communica-

---

[23] In this work, empathy is the compatibility and ability to generate shared understanding, with respect to a particular combination of compatibilities. Compatibility is the equivalence of x and y where x and y are, for example, forms of expression (linguistic, gestural) and forms of temporal coordination (synchronisation, entrainment). Empathy involves compatibility across a combination of compatibilities such as roles, dimension of knowledge, forms of expression, personality, style, etc. Empathy is necessarily personal and involves emotion. Empathy is, therefore, the ability to share or generate understanding. Empathy is distinct from sympathy. Empathy is often spoken of in the context of art where it is defined (cf. Oxford Dictionary) as 'the power of projecting one's personality onto (and so fully comprehending) the object of contemplation'. Aesthetic emotion is regarded as having an empathetic character. Being empathetic: 'the richer the personality, ... the more empathetic understanding of others it will be capable of'; person's who come from a similar background can be said to have a certain empathetic understanding of each other's personalities; in order to empathise with someone, one has to 'feel with' him/her before one can identify his/her elusive patterns of emotional response. Empathy can involve emotion at an abstract level, i.e. relating to art, as well as the kinds of emotions involved in understanding someone's personality. This discussion indicates that the emotion involved in understanding in dialogue does not mean having the same emotion or sharing the same emotions as the other person. This may be more suitably termed 'sympathy'.

tion operating at multiple dimensions. As our understanding of the world and others and ourselves is corporeal, the body may be seen as a mediating interface for social understanding, but not as an object or as a function. To develop this discussion further, the next chapter will consider the history of ideas underlying the dominance of the transactional level of interaction in interface design, and underlying the rise of the tacit, the personal and relational dimensions of knowledge and interaction.

References

Aaron, S., Barnard, P., Cross, I., Gill, S. P., Himberg, T., Hoadley, R., Odell-Miller, H., & Toulson, R. (2013). Touching sound: Vulnerability and synchronicity. In *Proceedings of the CHI2013 workshop on designing for and with vulnerable people*. http://di.ncl.ac.uk/vulnerability/files/2013/02/Aaron_DFWVP2013.pdf

Atherton, M. V., & Washburn, M. F. (1912). Mediate associations studied by the method of inhibiting associations. *American Journal of Psychology, 23*, 101–109.

Balaam, M., Fitzpatrick, G., Good, J., & Harris, E. (2011). Enhancing interactional synchrony with an ambient display. In *Proceedings of CHI 2011*, ACM.

Bergson. (1911). *Creative evolution* (trans: Mitchell, A.). New York: Dover.

Bernstein, B. (1958). Some sociological determinants of perception: An enquiry into sub-cultural differences. *British Journal of Sociology (London), 9*(1), 159–174.

Brentano, F. ([1874]/1973). *Psychology from an empirical standpoint* (trans: Rancurello, A. C., Terrell, D. B., & McAlister, D. B.) London: Routledge and Kegan Paul (English Edition).

Brezeal, C., & Picard, R. (2009). The role of emotion-inspired abilities in relational robots. In R. Parasuraman & M. Rizzo (Eds.), *Neuroergonomics the Brian at work*. Oxford: Oxford University Press.

Buber, M. (1923). *I and Thou*. English Edition. 1958. (trans: Smith, R.G.). New York: Charles Scribner's Sons.

Carman, T. (1999). The body in Husserl and Merleau Ponty. *Philosophical Topics, 27*, 1.

Cassell, J., Sullivan, J., Prevost, S., & Churchill, E. (2000). *Embodied conversational agents*. Cambridge, MA: MIT Press.

Clark, H. H. (1996). *Using language*. Cambridge: Cambridge University Press.

Clark, H. H., & Brennan, S. E. (1991). Grounding in communication. In L. B. Resnick, J. M. Levine, & S. D. Teasley (Eds.), *Perspectives on socially shared cognition* (pp. 127–149). Washington, DC: American Psychological Association Books.

Cooley, M. J. E. (1987). *Architect or bee? The human price of technology*. London: Hogarth Press.

Coupland, J., Coupland, N., & Robinson, J. D. (1992). "How Are You?": Negotiating phatic communion. *Language in Society, 21*(2), 207–230.

Cross, I. (2011). Music and biocultural evolution. In M. Clayton, T. Herbert, & R. Middleton (Eds.), *The cultural study of music: A critical introduction* (2nd ed.). London: Routledge.

Cross, I. (2012). Music and communication in music psychology. *Psychology of Music, 42*(6), 809–819.

Di Paola, S. (2001). Gesture and narrative creation in avatar-based 3D virtual communities. Invited paper at Gesture and Dialogue Seminar, CSLI, Stanford University. http://www.dipaola.org/sig99/sld002.htm

Dourish, P. (2004). *Where the action is. The foundations of embodied interaction*. Cambridge, MA: MIT Press (First paperback edition).

Dreyfus, H. L. (1990). *Being-in-the-world: A commentary on Heidegger's being and time*. Cambridge, MA: MIT Press.

Ehn, P. (1988). *Work oriented design of computer artifacts*. Stockholm: Arbetslivscentrnm.

Ekman, P., & Friesen, W. V. (1969). The repertoire of nonverbal behaviour: Categories, origins, usage, and coding. *Semiotica, 1*, 49–98.

Ellis, W. D. (1938). *A source book of gestalt psychology*. London: Routledge & Kegan Paul (includes an introduction by K. Koffka).

Florin, M., Goranzon, B., & Sallstrom, P. (Eds.). (1991). *Dialogue and technology: Art and knowledge* (Artificial intelligence and society series). London: Springer.

Gadamer, H. G. (1960). Truth and method (German: Wahrheit und Methode). In: *Truth and method* (2nd edn.). London: Sheed and Ward, 1989, XXVIII.

Garfinkel, H. (1967). *Studies in ethnomethodology.* Cambridge: Polity Press. First published in 1967, USA: Prentice-Hall.

Gaver, W. (2001). *The presence project (RCA CRD projects series) paperback.* RCA Computer Related Design Research (2001 Mar).

Gill, K. S. (1996). The foundations of human-centred systems. In K. S. Gill (Ed.), *Human machine symbiosis: The foundations of human-centred systems design.* London: Springer.

Gill, J. H. (2000). *The tacit mode. Michael Polanyi's postmodern philosophy.* New York: SUNY Press.

Gill, S. P. (2002). *The parallel coordinated move: Case of a conceptual drawing task.* Published Working Paper: Helsinki: CKIR, ISBN.

Gill, S. P. (2007). Entrainment and musicality in the human system interface. *AI and Society, 21*(4), 567–560.

Gill, S. P., Kawamori, M., Katagiri, Y., & Shimojima, A. (2000). The role of body moves in dialogue. *RASK, 12,* 89–114.

Göranzon, B. (1988). The practice of the use of computers. A paradoxical encounter between different traditions of knowledge. In B. Göranzo & I. Josefson (Eds.), *Knowledge, skill and artificial intelligence* (pp. 9–18). London: Springer.

Goranzon, B. (1992). *The practical intellect. Computers and skill* (Series of artificial intelligence and society). London: Springer.

Hall, E. T. (1983). *Dance of life: The other dimension of time.* New York: Anchor Books.

Heidegger, M. (1927). *Being and time, a translation of Sein und Zeit.* Albany: SUNY Press. 1996.

Henle, M. (1961). *Documents of gestalt psychology.* London: University of California, University of Cambridge in Berkeley.

Heritage, J. (1984). *Garfinkel and ethnomethodology.* Cambridge: Polity Press.

Husserl. (1931). *Cartesian meditations.* A Translation of Meditations cartesiennes, D. Cairns. Dordrecht: Kluwer, 1988.

Kendon, A. (1990). *Conducting interaction: Patterns of behavior in focused encounters.* Cambridge: Cambridge University Press.

Kendon, A. (2004). *Gesture: Visible action as utterance.* UK: Cambridge University Press.

Magee, Bertolami, Kubicek, LaJoie, Martino, & Sankowski. (2011). *Within music therapy.*

Merleau-Ponty, M. (1945/1962). *Phenomenology of perception* (trans: Smith, C.). London: Routledge and Kegan Paul.

Morrison, J. C. (1970). Husserl and Brentano on intentionality. *Philosophy and Phenomenological Research, 31*(1), 27–46.

Müller, A., Fuchs, J., & Roepke, K. (2011). Skintimacy: Exploring Interpersonal Boundaries through Musical Interactions. In *Proceedings of the 12th international conference on new interfaces for musical expression.*

Nagargoje, A., Maybach, K., & Sokoler, T. (2012). Social yoga mats: Designing for exercising/socializing synergy. In *Proceedings of the Tangible and embedded interaction 2012* (pp. 87–90).

Negrotti, M. (2012). *The reality of the artificial: Nature, technology and naturoids (studies in applied philosophy, epistemology and rational ethics).* London: Springer.

Nevejan, C. (2007). *Presence and the design of trust.* PhD Dissertation. University of Amsterdam.

Nevejan, C. (2009). Witnessed presence and the YUTPA framework. *PsychNology Journal 'Ethics in Presence and Social Presence Technology', 7*(1), www.psychnology.org

Nevejan, C. (2012). *Witnessing you. On trust and truth in a networked world. Participatory systems initiative.* Delft: Delft University of Technology.

Norman, D. A., & Draper, S. W. (1986). *User-centered system design: New perspectives on human-computer interaction.* Hillsdale: Erlbaum.

Oleksik, G., Jones, R., & Milic-Frayling, N. (2010). *Use of gestures in a multi-device environment* (Technical. Report MSR-TR-2010). Redmond: Microsoft Research 2010.

Polanyi, M. (1962). *Personal knowledge: Towards a post critical philosophy.* London: Routledge and Kegan Paul (Reprint of 1958 version with corrections).

Polanyi, M. (1966). *The tacit dimension*. Doubleday. 1983 Reprint.

Polyani, M. (1969). *"The Logic of Tacit Inference"*. *Knowing and being*. London: Routledge & Kegan Paul.

Rabinowitch, T., Cross, I., & Burnard, P. (2012). Between consciousnesses: Embodied musical intersubjectivity. In D. Reynolds & M. Reason (Eds.), *Kinesthetic empathy in creative and cultural practices*. Bristol: Intellect Press.

Ratkic, A. (2009). Dialogue seminars as a tool in postgraduate education. *AI & Society, 32*(1), 99–102.

Rauner, F., Rasmussen, L. B., & Corbett, M. (1987). *The social shaping of technology and work*. Universitat Bremen, Institut Technik & Bildung.

Rauner, F., Rasmussen, L. B., & Corbett, M. (1988). The social shaping of technology. *AI & Society, 2*, 47–62. London: Springer.

Rogers, E. (1998). *The meaning of 'Relationship' in interpersonal communication*. Santa Barbara: Praeger.

Rosenbrock, H. (1996). Rosenbrock's account of causality and purpose: A compilation of Howard Rosenbrock's works by Satinder Gill. In K. S. Gill (Ed.), *Human machine symbiosis: The foundation of human-centred system design*. London: Springer.

Ryle, G. (1949). *The concept of mind*. Chicago: University of Chicago Press.

Sacks, H. (1984). Notes on methodology. In J. M. Atkinson & J. Heritage (Eds.), *Structures of social action: Studies in conversation analysis*. Cambridge: Cambridge University Press.

Sacks, H., Schegloff, E. A., & Jefferson, G. (1974). A simplest systematics of the organisation of turn-taking in conversation. *Language, 50*(4), 696–735.

Schmidt, K. (2011). 'The concept of work' in CSCW. *Computer Supported Cooperative Work, 20*(4), 341–401.

Schutz, A. (1962). The problem of social reality. In M. Natanson (Ed.), *Vol. 1 of collected papers*. The Hague: Martinus Nijhoff.

Sha, X. W. (2013). Connected knowledges and practices: An experiment in autonomous cultural production. *AI & Society, 28*(2), 133–146 (also see: http://topologicalmedialab.net/xinwei/).

Shannon, C., & Weaver, W. (1949). *The mathematical theory of communication*. Urbana: Illinois University Press.

Shutz, A. (1932). *The phenomenology of the social world*. Evanston: Northwestern University Press.

Turino, T. (2008). *Music as social life: The politics of participation*. Chicago: University of Chicago Press.

Turkle, S. (2011). *Alone together*. New York: Basic Books.

Vesna, V. (2012). Mind and body shifting: From networks to nanosystems. In J. Kastner (Ed.), *Nature*. London: Whitechapel Gallery; Cambridge, MA: MIT Press. http://www.victoriavesna.com/index.php?p=projects

Weiser, M. (1994). *Creating the invisible interface*. Keynote address at UIST'94 symposium on user interface software and technology, Marina del Rey, 2 Nov 1994.

Weizenbaum, J. (1966). ELIZA – a computer program for the study of natural language communication between man and machine. Communications of the ACM. *9*(1), 36–35.

Weizenbaum, J. (1976). *Computer power and human reason: From judgment to calculation*. San Francisco: W. H. Freeman.

Whitehead, A. N. (1978). *Process and reality*. New York: Free Press.

Winograd, T., & Flores, F. (1986). *Understanding computers and cognition. A new foundation for design*. Norwood: Ablex Corporation.

Wittgenstein, L. (1953). *Philosophical investigations*. (trans: Anscombe, G.E.M.) Oxford: Basil Blackwell (English Edition).

Wolf, K., Dicke, C., & Grassel, R. (2011). *Touching the void: Gestures for auditory interfaces*. Proceedings of TEI'11, ACM, New York, pp. 305–308.

Zemel, A., Koschmann, T., Lebaron, C., & Feltovich, P. (2008). What are we missing? Usability's indexical ground. *Computer Supported Cooperative Work, 17*(1), 63–85.

Chapter 2
Knowledge = Skill

Abstract This chapter provides a historical discussion for conceptions of data, knowledge, and skill, in order to understand how they came to underlie conceptions of machines, tools, and computer-human interfaces, and the tensions that arise from these conceptions. It investigates why there is a distinction between knowledge and skill, finding it to be rooted in a dualist concept of knowledge where mind is distinct from body and is given salience as the vehicle for knowing about the world. The mapping of mind to computation has given prominence to propositional knowledge, representation, and the rule, over how we conduct our everyday embodied lives with others and go about making judgements. This is questioned in discussions on embodied knowledge in performance arts, on engineering as an art, on calculating with data and judging with wisdom, on rule-following as practical knowledge, and the irreducibility of culture, all of which share the quality of a personal act of knowing.

2.1 Introduction

During the twentieth century, one particular model of communication stands out as a reference marker for the paradigm of the explicit. It is commonly referred to by the names of its authors as the Shannon and Weaver model (1949). This describes communication as being the transmission of information from a sender to a receiver. Since then, of course, many have challenged the simplicity of this model for accounting for the complexity of human communication. Yet the primacy it gives to the transactional continues to permeate conceptions of interaction in interface design. The sender-receiver model of communication, combined with the model of human cognition as computation, has facilitated the conception of the human as a computer. This has extended much older concepts of the human compotator (someone who does calculations) and has consolidated the idea of the human as machine that underlay the development of the automaton and was promoted by the Enlightenment (for example, the influence of materialist determinists, such as La Mettrie (1709–1751, "L'Homme, Machine")): "Automata figure in the sciences of the Enlightenment as machines in the form of humans and as humans who perform like machines. Some of these sciences proposed the organization of productive bodies in disciplined settings, then understood production in terms of the workings of automata" (Schaffer 1999). The automata of the eighteenth century include the famous life size chess player called The Turk, which was hugely popular, and housed a little person in its central chamber unbeknown to most. What is crucial about automata is that they make explicit the actions of the human body and specifically gesture, as the representation of knowledge and skill i.e. human thought processes. The Turk was believable and was successful due to the invisibility of the operator of its body. This contrasts with the success of later automata that lay in the visibility of the workings of the body, i.e. of the automata. These later automata were inspired by the drive of medical science to create cadaver automata for teaching purposes, that could function like a human cadaver. Schaffer proposes 'a connection between these medical debates and economic theory because the economy itself was figured as a perpetual moving automaton.' The explication of the human body and of gesture in the evolution of automata was believed to give information about the economic worth of all forms of work, as noted here by the chemist and economist Lavoisier, "how many pounds weight correspond to the efforts of a man who recites a speech, a musician who plays an instrument. Whatever is mechanical can similarly be evaluated in the work of the philosopher who reflects, the man of letters who writes, the musician who composes" (Schaffer op. cit. p. 134). Babbage, considered as the father of the modern computer, knew Lavoisier and experienced automata himself, and was influenced by this movement for the rationalisation and efficiency of man to improve productivity. By the twentieth century, the computer has become a potent model of the human mind and neural processes, whilst the robot and the virtual artificial agent have become the computational and biological automata of the human body and gesture and our interaction processes.

In this chapter, the discussion will revolve around one particular outcome of conceiving of the human as a computer, and that is the idea of the 'expert system'. This is a project of Artificial Intelligence (of the kind often termed Strong AI) and a field of cognitive science that sought to create autonomous systems that could operate like a human 'expert', such as a doctor. They are the automata of human cognition. Some of these systems were configured as tools or 'assistants' to human experts, or to human 'novices' (avoiding the need to train people to have the skills of an expert). A much lamented bottleneck to this expert system project was 'tacit knowledge', otherwise called 'know how'[1] (Ryle 1949). This lament may be seen to have its origins in an ancient "class distinction" in the West; the ancient Greeks made a qualitative distinction between 'techne' i.e. art or craft, and 'episteme' i.e. knowledge. 'Metics' (foreigners) did not aspire to episteme, and Philosophers did not (generally) stoop to techne. This class distinction remains in how they are perceived. Human experts were considered to be remarkably inept at being able to make their knowledge explicit in the form suitable for placing into a computer, hence various tools from 'cognitive psychology' were developed during the 1980s to extract this knowledge out of their heads, forming a new field termed 'knowledge engineering' (KE) which is still a strong field with its own Journal. The goal of KE was to represent someone's skill as explicit representations and explicit processes

---

[1] Gilbert Ryle, Knowing How and Knowing That.

for data and computation. This assumed that the tacit was merely the unformed explicit, and situated the concept of the tacit within a dualistic and divided framework of knowledge. This conception of the tacit contrasts markedly to Polanyi's original conception (The Tacit Dimension 1966) that collapses dualism, necessarily involves mediation (an *integrative process*), and is embodied and personal.

It is at the height of the debate about the Expert system and the bottleneck of tacit knowledge in the 1980s and early 1990s, that I encountered the debate about the nature of, and relationship between, explicit and tacit knowledge. During an apprenticeship with the Swedish Centre for Working Life in Stockholm (SCWL) I understood this debate as being about the limitations of representing human skill in propositional forms. The Scandinavian experience with these knowledge based technologies in spheres of working life spanned a decade, culminating in a major European conference on Language, Skill and Artificial Intelligence that took place in Stockholm in 1988. Being involved with this took me on a cultural journey to Germany, Italy, and Denmark to learn about humanistic approaches to technology and design. Each culture had its own conception of the relation between dialogue and knowledge, its own design and social/organisation cultures, and differed in philosophies and theoretical frameworks governing their conceptions of human and technology relations. It became clear that cultural practices shape the patterns of negotiation and organisational decision making, and also how people understand the meaning of words, such as 'participate', 'cooperate' and 'dialogue'. The Italian colleagues did not accept the use of the word 'dialogue' to denote any act lower than the communion with God; any other form of engagement is 'communication'. The British pragmatic culture was more comfortable with the idea of cooperation, whereas the Swedish democratic culture was more comfortable with the idea of participation. In the former, decisions can be altered relatively quickly if circumstances change, and in the latter, decisions undergo the rigour of the democratic process of participation involving all the levels concerned, for any alteration to be considered. Decision-making is a culturally rooted communication process, something the great anthropologist Edward T. Hall (1976 – Beyond Culture) understood well in his life's study of culture and communication.

The SCWL researchers undertook research on the concept of skill, the meaning of information, the role of imagination and reflection, and the use of language to express experiential knowledge, through conducting case studies of craft skills such as photography and boatbuilding, and the skills of nurses and mathematicians. In one of these studies, highly experienced mathematicians in the Swedish Forestry industry had worked with designers to build expert systems that would assist them in their daily calculations. Their experience of using these expert systems was tracked and analysed. Over a period of a few years, the researchers were finding that the mathematicians were sometimes doubting their own judgement (about their calculations) and passing it over to that of the computer. What had initially been intended as an assistive system to check calculations against, was now eroding their own confidence in their mathematical skills (Göranzon 1992a). If we know what information is being placed into a technology and we know the limitations of what that can achieve and we are ourselves highly skilled, why then, when we engage with this representation of our knowledge, do we lose our confidence to judge?

The research approach of the SCWL group to understand what constitutes human skill, was hermeneutic, drawing upon writings by Wittgenstein (1958) and Polanyi (1966), amongst other critical philosophers and writers such as Toulmin (1991), Searle (1990), and Dreyfus (1972), Dreyfus and Dreyfus (1986). In a similar vein to the Human Centred movement in the UK (Cooley 1987a, b; Gill KS 1986, 1996; Rosenbrock 1989, 1990), the German Social Shaping of technology approach (Rauner et al. 1987) and the Danish Participatory Design Movement (Ehn 1988) were critiquing the modernist Cartesian focus on data, propositions, and causality, and they did so by considering dialogue and reflection and the personality as the critical location of human skill and knowledge.

The expert system is considered in this chapter as an extreme exemplar of scientific or explicit knowledge, only surpassed by the concept of Big Data. It is based on a science of mind, wherein knowledge has become tangibly linked to technology. Orthodox cognitivism or computationalism[2] (Fodor 1976, 1981; Pylyshyn 1984; Simon 1985) holds that cognition can be defined as computations of symbolic representations. The focus is on representation and logic. Knowledge is non-contextual, in that it is time-independent and depersonalized, a conception with origins traceable to the ancient Greek thinkers, Socrates (469–399 BC) and Plato (429–347 BC). In the play Euthyphro, Plato relates how Socrates is complaining that experts are incompetent at being able to tell their knowledge, and they forget how they learnt it. This may have been a rhetorical ploy in Plato's literary restatement of Socrates' challenge to conventional political thought, however, it is a lament that is echoed over 2,000 years later by Knowledge Engineers trying to extract expertise out of the heads of experts. Socratic dialogue is commonly considered as the basis for our modern belief in objectivity and rationalism, as Socrates believed that we must question everything in our world with clear argument in order to find truth that is impersonal. He believed that thinking this way would liberate people from the societal and cultural conditions that bind them. However this was considered by some to undermine the social fabric and the collapse of moral behaviour. The playwright Aristophanes criticises the Socratic disembodiment from the reality of human existence, in his play the Clouds. Later, Plato gives further salience to the mind in asking people to free themselves of the noise of emotion and our senses in order to focus on pure thought to find truth.

The concepts of objective knowledge, of rational mind, and of causality, have historically been set in dualistic tension with the concepts of embodied knowledge, emotion as a source of understanding, moral values, and aesthetics. Whilst he was establishing the scientific methods of observation/empirical analysis and argument, and creating the disciplines that shape the university as we know it, Plato's student Aristotle, acknowledged the importance of human emotion for developing wisdom and being able to learn to make Just judgements. This concern with the role of the

---

[2] The terms 'orthodox cognitivism' or 'computationalism' is taken here in the sense of Fodor, JA (1981) *Representations: Philosophical Essays on the Foundations of Cognitive Science*. Brighton, Harvester Press.

personal is seen in post-modern philosophies, art, and literature from the end of the nineteenth century onwards. JGill, in The Tacit Mode (2000), describes it as reaching a pivotal moment in the 1960s where the dualism between mind and body is arguably collapsed within Polanyi's 'post-critical' conception of the tacit dimension (1966) that locates knowledge in both body and mind simultaneously. Polanyi explicitly calls this knowledge, a *'personal act of knowing'*. The Tacit Dimension comes 8 years after his publication of Personal Knowledge in 1958 where the personal and the objective are 'fused' into the personal, as "into every act of knowing there enters a passionate contribution of the person knowing what is being known".

From the person centred perspective, knowledge is context and praxis based and has an embodied, social, and experiential dimension. It is examined here for the interdependence of its various dimensions embedded in dialogue, and essential for the transfer and formation of knowledge between humans, for example, in making sustainable decisions, forming concepts and ideas, and innovating. The extreme cognitivist conception of knowledge in cognitive science will be termed the non-person centred perspective, which is disembodied and thereby unable to account for intersubjectivity. The essential disconnect in this conception, is between knowledge as a discrete property of the knowing individual (and therefore capable of elicitation) and as inherent in a complex way in a knowing social nexus. In systems terms, perhaps, this is the difference between an observable and an unobservable system.

In Chap. 1 reference was made to two design approaches that were questioning the dominant cognitivist approaches to technology, the Human Centred[3] and the Participatory. Both have their origins in the twentieth century's philosophies of dialogue, of Husserl (1931), Heidegger (1927), Buber (1923), Merleau Ponty (1962), Gadamer (1960), Wittgenstein (1958), and Polanyi (1966), amongst others, and a belief in technology having a societal or human purpose, other than economic efficiency.

2.2 Non-person Centred Tradition of Knowledge

The characteristics of the non-person centred approach to knowledge may be summarised as *propositional knowledge* and its *representation*, and *the rule* that governs it.

Propositional knowledge denotes formalised knowledge, wherein knowledge has to be explicitly defined or articulated. It has to be empirically supported or formally proven. It is knowledge which does not embody the personal and social dimension and can exist independent of time, and, therefore, context. For example, it cannot allow for social and personal values which exist in moral knowledge. Propositional

---

[3] This is a generic term for approaches to the study of issues pertinent to the design and application of computer-based technologies which differ from what is termed a machine centred approach. The human-centred approach is best explained in a comprehensive report by Dr. KS Gill, ref: *Summary of Human-Centred Systems Research in Europe*, SEAKE Centre, Brighton University, 1990. The idea of human-centredness has now become part of mainstream thinking but with a focus on 'technology' rather than 'system'.

knowledge has also been termed 'theoretical knowledge'[4] (Göranzon 1992a), 'scientific knowledge'[5] (Woolgar 1988; Winch 1958; Rosenbrock 1988; Collins 1974, 1975), 'rationalism'[6] (Dreyfus 1989; Gill 1988), 'positivistic knowledge'[7] (Johannessen 1988a), 'universal knowledge',[8] and explicit knowledge (Collins 2013), in the various contexts of its discussion.

Aspects of this notion of knowledge have been traced through the history of ideas to the 'dream of the exact language' of the seventeenth century in Europe (Toulmin 1991).[9] This 'dream' was an ambition to create a universal language that would allow one to express one's thoughts "as definitely and exactly as arithmetic expresses numbers or geometrical analysis expresses lines."[10]This language would embody shared understanding. It would not allow for misunderstanding as it "would embody and encode all valid modes of argument, so that different people reason together without fear of confusion or error".[11] This language would be an instrument of reason whereby knowledge is clear and unambiguous. The idea that knowledge must be well defined is central to traditional cognitive science, where the discipline

---

[4] 'Theoretical knowledge', in this context, is analogous to 'knowing that', as distinct from 'knowing how', cf. Ryle (1949). It has been described as mathematically structured knowledge (cf. Göranzon 1992a)

[5] NB. some of these authors, particularly those from the domain of the sociology of scientific knowledge (SSK) critique the descriptions/formal language of science, contrasting them to its practice. They do this by either undertaking apprenticeship in the specific scientific area, and/or by recording its everyday discourse. For further literature, in addition to Woolgar (1988) and Collins (1974, 1975), see for example, Gilbert and Mulkay (1984). Rosenbrock (1988) is critical of the application of the formalist notion of science (as in propositional knowledge) to the domain of engineering at the expense of sensibility and human purpose. This is discussed later, herein.

[6] Rationalism denotes the emphasis on objectivity in terms of the mind-body split., cf. Descartes (1639), Hume (1748), Kant (1929). Toulmin (1991) discusses the 'seventeenth century Cartesian ideal of intellectual exactitude, … it's idolization of geometrical proof', citing the 'rationalist procedures of Newtonian mathematics' (ibid. p. 41) and compares this ideal to that of the sixteenth century humanists, cf. Bacon, who believed in a 'humanly fruitful' science. The contrast lies between an emphasis on theory and on praxis.

[7] Johannessen (1988a) discusses the higher status in society placed upon analytical and empirical validity for one's having knowledge, versus the doing of knowledge, i.e. its practice. He traces this back to logical positivism, cf. the Vienna circle, Carnap (1956), Chaps. II and III.

[8] As in scientific law for nature, for example, Galileo: 'The book of nature is written in mathematical symbols'; Newtonian physics – 'a vote in favour of theoretical cosmology, not for practical human dividends', cf. Toulmin (1991). Toulmin describes Leibniz's characteristica universalis (universal system of characters), published in 1666, as the dream for a universal unambiguous, context independent, language, and thereby knowledge.

[9] For an outline of the development of the dream of exact language see Toulmin, op. cit. He discusses Leibniz's (op. cit.) project to develop a language based on mathematical symbolism. Johannessen also cites this period and the idea of an exact language in a discussion on the rule and the positivist conception of knowledge, in Johannessen, K (1988a) *Rule-Following and Tacit Knowledge*, in AI & Society Journal, Vol. 2.4. Springer-Verlag, London.

[10] Leibniz, see footnote 9.

[11] Toulmin, op. cit. p. 36.

of programming is regarded as scientifically useful for generating hypotheses about the mind. Underlying this idea of knowledge is the belief that the attempt to express vague concepts helps to clarify them.[12]

The philosophies of Descartes, Kant, Hume, and Hegel gave rise to modern cognitivism, from Descartes' analytical philosophy (rationalism), 'I think therefore I am', to Hume's evolution of empiricism and Kant's discovery of causality, i.e. that data in the mind is connected via causal links and this constitutes mental processing (thinking), and Hegel's equivalence of rationality and reality. Together they formed the powerhouse of ideas founding Western science and the modernist project of economic rationality as constituting social progress, materialised in the machine.

It is helpful to see how these ideas evolved. Hume's empiricism[13] embodies a foundationalist approach to questions of epistemology, beginning with a rock bottom analysis of human cognitive experience upon which to construct the structure of knowledge. Hence the basis of all human knowing is sensory experience, the data of empirical input to the mind. The mind is empty of any content when it comes to the world. What is needed is an analysis of the process by which sensory experience conveys information about the world to the mind. Sensory experience is also a test of whether a knowledge claim is reliable, hence if it can be traced to a sensory input then the idea or claim is reliable, and if not, then it is a figment of the imagination. Hume divides human perception into two classes, 'ideas' and 'impressions'. The latter are the data of thought and come into the mind directly via the senses. Ideas form memory and come into the mind via impressions and represent them. Impressions in turn have two sources, sensations and reflections: the former come directly through the senses, and the latter are derived from reflections on the processes of the mind as it organises these sensations. These organisational principles and activities of the mind enable the 'association of ideas'. By means of 'resemblance', 'contiguity in time and space', and 'cause and effect', the mind processes and organises sensory and reflective data provided by experience into memory, and imagination draws on this memory bank to produce fresh combinations. Hume did have his doubts, and was concerned about the principle of cause and effect, a principle that he considered to be central to the entire process of 'knowing', that is, being able to anticipate future experience on the basis of prior experience is dependant on establishing causal connections between events. His doubt was with finding a rational foundation for causation.

Within cognitive science the causal concept of inference is traceable to Descartes (1596–1650), and denotes that one can move from the premises and data to a conclusion and back again in a reversible process. This concept is in marked contrast to Polanyi's idea of tacit inference (1969), a *personal act of knowing*, which is a process of *integration* that is not reversible. For example, you cannot unlearn a skill once the integration of particulars has occurred, such as when learning to drive a car or when speaking a language. The idea of inference is essentially Cartesian; Descartes believed that knowledge is only acquired from within the mind. Hume assumed the

---

[12] Boden, op. cit. p. 32.

[13] See An Enquiry Concerning Human Understanding, first published in 1748.

mind to be devoid of all knowledge from the outset and that it must find a way to bridge the distance between self and the outside/external world. Kant also construed the relation between the knower and what it is to be known in the inside/outside structure. Twentieth century reactions to this Cartesian view include deconstructionism (Derrida 1967) and existentialism (Sartre 1943; Nietzsche 1961; Kierkegaard 1971), and Polanyi's placement of the body at the centre of cognitivity provided a connection between the knower and what is to be known, denying the dichotomy.

The concept of propositional knowledge draws a boundary between that which is knowledge and that which is not, in a somewhat hegemonic way, located within modernism. Modernism holds that reality is about ideas and knowledge is a function of rationality where human thought can comprehend the essential structure and meaning of human existence and reality itself; "what is real is rational and what is rational is real" (Hegel 1977) was tied to a belief in societal progress rooted in the evolutionary 'dialectical' struggle of ideas.

The origins of rationality are traceable to Socrates (469–399 BC) who lived in Athens during a period of political uncertainty and wars. Socrates believed that all men and women can question and reason about their condition in life rather than accepting it, and thereby come to see the world differently. He devoted his life to personally engaging people from all spheres of life in such thinking, and presented a radical departure from the art of rhetoric which is the art of persuasion by discourse (Nussbaum 1980). The origin of a dialectic between mind and reality has been attributed to Plato (429–347) who believed that the mind is the eyes of the soul and that to see reality clearly people must liberate themselves from the tyranny of the senses by relying on the mind to lead them out of the cave of ignorance to the light of pure ideas (The Republic, written around 380 BCE). The mind sees reality through pure reason, especially mathematics and logic. This idea is taken further by the mathematician Descartes, in the Meditations (written in 1639), with the idea that knowledge is based on complete or rational certainty; "whatever forces itself of the mind clearly and distinctly in the logical sense of these terms will serve as a reliable source of knowledge". This is his methodology of intuition. He drew on the works of Euclid and Newton arguing that the foundation for certain knowledge is self-evident axioms that are intuitively true, and he sought these axioms through systematic doubt. He believed the senses deceive us so we must doubt all knowledge claims based on sense perception, and that extended to a doubt of logic itself with the idea of an evil demon who could be deceiving us in what follows from what, rationally. The only thing he found he could not doubt was his own existence, and as doubting is thinking, thinking necessarily entails existence, hence Cogito ergo sum, I think therefore I am. This was his intuitive foundation of knowledge. From this he believed we could deduce propositions of knowledge (further theorems) with the same clarity as the original axiom. JGill argues that Descarte's method of deduction that is laid out in four rules, is the base for the modern articulation of ideas in philosophy and science and of the machine. These four rules are: *certainty* – to be absolutely certain of one's beginning point setting aside all previous and/or merely probable claims to knowledge; *division* – to carefully analyse every idea and proposition into its smallest components so as to discern clearly and distinctly what is claimed and what follows from what; *order* – to move carefully from one proposition to the next in logical order; *number* – to continually review each step for argument. These axioms will be considered further in the chapter in Cooley's critique of the core beliefs of the scientific method and the machine, as being *certainty*, *causality*, and *predictability*.

Just over a century after Descartes, Hegel's rationalistic idealism becomes pivotal in modernism's materialistic project of societal progress. This held that rationality is reality and vice versa.

Socrates is often referred to as the father of Western philosophy and laid the foundation of modern scientific thinking to see truth. His motivation was to liberate people but that aspect became lost in the Enlightenment with the modernist quest for mechanisation, efficiency, and order. This was not about liberating the human from their condition but creating the conditions of controlling human action, the human body, values, and having systems of surveillance (Schaffer op. cit.). Babbage's computer is part of this development of automata and the human machine.

By the time we reach the early twentieth century, logical positivism[14] (see, for example, Ayer 1971) argues that the areas of metaphysics, aesthetics, moral inspiration, ethics, lie outside the boundary of knowledge. This is because they are not in full measure linguistically articulable and are not scientifically relevant.[15]

The application of propositional knowledge and its representation will be discussed in the context of logical positivism and the idea of an exact language, and also in the context of the traditional, or conventional, model of computational psychology in Artificial Intelligence,[16] a science of mind.

The idea of *representation* that lies within the concept of propositional knowledge, requires that the world be defined in terms of components, each of which mirrors the reality. This leads to a tendency towards reductionism. Ideas about representation of knowledge are tied to ideas about language and thought. The 'dream of a mathematical language'[17] in the seventeenth and eighteenth centuries resulted in the concept of symbolic representation of ideas and the use of logical rules for defining the relations between symbols. Algebra was the model for the ideal language. There was a desire to eliminate all ambiguous or imprecise words and misleading metaphors (Goranzon op. cit. p. 43). In the automaton, the need to make the operation of the human body explicit was driven by an underlying need to access and represent the operations of the human mind, and to control these for economic

---

[14] AJ. Ayer, (1971) *Language truth and logic*. Pelican.

[15] Johannessen, op. cit. p. 290.

[16] See Boden (1991), p. 10. This is in contrast to developments in parallel processing and connectionism (see for example, Rumelhart and Norman 1986) which have been seen to be a challenge to the conventional model based on the von-Neumann machine (cf. Fodor and Pylyshyn 1988). However, all these various approaches of AI and computational psychology have originated from the same mid-century ideas about the brain's logical-computational potential. See also Boden (1988) for a comprehensive overview of differing perspectives in AI and cognitive science.

[17] cf. Liebnitz, op. cit., see Toulmin, op. cit.

progress. The concept of a *rule* is linked to the concept of knowledge and its representation. Within the context of propositional knowledge, as defined above, a rule
lays down the way in which the knowledge is to be interpreted or used. The concept
of the rule in rule-based computer systems embodies the belief in a science of logical thinking which is historically tied to the idea of a scientific law for nature.[18]

2.2.1 Rationality and Technology: On AI and Knowledge Engineering

The aspect of knowledge based technology that is of interest to the discussion here,
is that of 'knowledge engineering' (KE), the core determinant of which is knowledge 'representation', be it of behaviour or of mind, which in turn is determined by
the representational infrastructure of the computer machine.

The relationship between the representation of knowledge and language has
been discussed in philosophy in the field of logical positivism[19] where great significance is given to linguistic knowledge. Logical positivism asserted that "we can
only possess knowledge if it can be formulated linguistically and in principle tested
on the basis of experience or proved by formal methods"[20] (Johannessen 1988a).
Logical positivism represents knowledge as context independent.[21]

The characteristics of propositional knowledge, representation and the rule are all
essential to cognitive science and Artificial Intelligence (AI). AI and cognitive science
have been described as the last stage of the rationalist tradition in philosophy (Dreyfus
1989). Cognitive science, also called 'computational psychology' (Boden 1991) and
'cognitivism' (Varela 1988),[22] postulates that psychological questions in general,
whether they concern belief, problem solving, purpose, choice, language, perception,
memory, or even emotion, can be understood as computational questions about
mental rules and representations[23] (Johnson-Laird 1983, 1993).

---

[18] See footnotes 9 and 10. Of course, quantum mechanics challenges this idea, as it recognises
contingency in the world of physics. Building a quantum computer is the next big challenge.

[19] See Johannessen op. cit.; see Ayer op. cit.

[20] Johannesen, op. cit. p. 288.

[21] It is important to note that the logical positivistic view of knowledge has been traced as far back
as Plato's dialogues about expertise and skill and his conception of rationality. NB the historical
context for understanding this thinking: cf. H. L. Dreyfus (1989), Is Socrates to Blame for
Cognitivism? p. 219. Johannessen, op. cit; Plato (1975). The Republic. Penguin, 2nd ed.
Translation, D. Lee; Toulmin, op. cit.

[22] F.J. Varela (1988) Cognitive Science: A Cartography of Current Ideas. Editions du Seuil, Paris.
See also F.J. Varela et al. (1991). Fodor and Pylyshyn (1988) describe 'classical cognitive science'
as an extended attempt to apply the methods of proof theory to the modelling of thought; Pylyshyn
(1984) describes cognition as a type of computation.

[23] Boden, op. cit. p. 30.

Within the computer metaphor, the concept of knowledge has been based within the domain of cognitive science and artificial intelligence.[24] AI is the literal construal of cognitive science. AI involves the use of computer programming to study the structure of and function of knowledge.[25] Psychological concerns are with the structure and content of mental representations and the ways in which they can be generated, augmented and transformed. They focus on planning and problem solving (for example, Newell and Simon 1972, Newell 1980).[26] The construction of knowledge-based systems, and in particular expert systems, is the physical representation of AI and cognitive science.

The relationship between representation and language, which exists in cognitive science and artificial intelligence, is embodied in the idea of cognition. Cognitivists claim that we can only account for intelligence and intentionality if we hypothesize that cognition consists in acting on the basis of representations of concepts that are physically realised in the form of a symbolic code in the brain or a machine. This is a formal syntactic system.[27] In this model of knowledge, it is the form of words that is significant, where they are physically represented as symbols. These say nothing about why x means x, that is they do not embody meaning. This particular model may be termed the 'formalist'[28] approach of the Von Neumann machine. Here, information processing rules are explicitly coded within and accessed by the program. AI programs and computer models are purely formal-syntactic in nature.[29]

Knowledge engineering is an essential part of the process of designing knowledge-based systems (Kidd and Wellbank 1984; Hart 1986; Boose and Gaines 1988, 1990)

---

[24] See for example, the classical AI paradigm works of Fodor (1976), Newell (1980), Newell and Simon (1972), Pylyshyn (1984), Michie and Johnston (1984), Minsky (1963), Feigenbaum and McCorduck (1983). Also see The Handbook of AI, (eds.), Barr and Feigenbaum (1981).

[25] Classic AI programming languages such as Prolog (Kowalski 1974, 1982), and PopLog (Sloman 1989) are based upon systems of logic. Prolog is based on predicate logic, and PopLog explores computational linguistics.

[26] NB. Newell (1981) discusses the significance of Polya's (1945) idea of heuristics which greatly influenced the work on problem solving in AI. Polya, himself was a mathematician, not directly involved in AI or cognitive science. AI drew upon his heuristics but omitted those aspects of his theory which were 'ambiguous' or intangible, for example, his emphasis upon personal motivation or commitment which he considered to be essential for effective problem solving.

[27] Varela, op. cit. p. 18–21.

[28] Boden, op. cit. p. 20.

[29] It is noted that Boden has questioned whether this model is purely formal-syntactic when she criticises Searle's assumption of this in his argument about translation and the Chinese box. Searle (1980) argues that a computer cannot understand. Understanding entails intentionality. A computer cannot have intentionality because it is a formal syntactic system. He therefore argues that AI ideas or computational theories based on them cannot describe or explain mental processes. Boden argues, however, that any simple program has some semantic properties and that computational theories are not essentially incapable of explaining meaning. This is because explanation involves assimilation of something to something else which is analogous to it but not identical with it. Searle also argues that the physical nature of the brain produces intentionality and that on intuitive grounds, the metal and silicon cannot. Boden argues that the brain's ability to generate intentionality is intelligible only through its information processing capability. The computer has such a capability.

where relevant information is selected for a system and consideration is given to how that information is made available to the system as well as to the user. Traditional knowledge engineering [TKE][30] claims that all knowledge can be represented in a propositional form. This embodies the idea that knowledge is universal.

A knowledge based system is a computer-based system which is made up of three parts: (a) the knowledge-base; (b) the inference engine [the programme]; and (c) the interface. The combination of (a) and (b) simulates the internal processes of the human mind. Knowledge-based systems were sometimes called 'expert systems' [ES][31] as they simulated the behaviour of an expert in a particular domain, for example in the domains of medicine [32] and law (see Susskind 1989; Leith 1988), etc. The function of these systems is to provide solutions to problems. Back in the 1980s there were very few successful applications[33] (SPRU report 1988; Coats 1988) and those that did succeed were constrained to very clearly definable domains such as configuration where they still needed a human support system; for example, XCON, a Digital Computers' system, and later ES involved neural networks[34] in order to compensate for their inadequacies.[35] The label 'neural' is misleading as they were not "neural" or in any meaningful way "networks". This physiological metaphor distracts attention from its limitations. Other uses of knowledge based systems are as decision-making aids where the system presents useful information for the human decision maker. The idea is that the human and the system form an integrated system, whereby the machine is regarded as being more efficient in carrying out some functions of a task (e.g., calculation), and the human is seen to be more efficient at others (using intuition, etc). However, in many of today's organisations, such as banks and building societies, the machine is making the final decisions and human intuition and judgement by bank managers about their clients is no longer a factor. This is a consequence of the knowledge engineering project of representing expertise according to the representational infrastructure of the machine.

---

[30] This is distinct from current approaches to knowledge engineering which embody a humanistic/ interdisciplinary approach to design. TKE is based on the ideas of Feigenbaum and 'traditional expert systems design'; see Feigenbaum, EA and McCorduck, P (1983) The Fifth Generation. Addison-Wesley, MA.

[31] For example, see cf. Bramer (1988), Ostberg et al. (1988), Whitaker and Ostberg (1988), Hayes-Roth (1984, 1985)

[32] Lipscombe (1989) provides a critique of the development of expert systems in medicine and suggest that approaching the design/purpose of these systems to facilitate problem analysis rather than problem solving will provide for more effective tools. See also Alvey (1983).

[33] Partridge (1987) puts this down to the explanation problem in ES technology which is inherently limited to the relatively static and relatively context free domain of abstract technical expertise. In this article, he strongly recommended ES designers to concentrate on 'low road' applications and stay away form complex 'high-road' ones, otherwise there will be a software crisis.

[34] For a comprehensive introduction to neural networks/connectionism, see the Special Issue on Connectionism, AI & Society, 4:1.

[35] See for example, Sprague, RH and Watson, HJ (1986), Jones and Walsham (1992).

The 1980s and 1990s saw a debate on the inability of experts to express their knowledge and skills in procedures, which was seen as a human shortcoming (Berry 1987; Kidd and Wellbank 1984; Kidd 1987). Early methods were from cognitive science (Gammack 1987, Gammack et al. 1989; Olson and Rueter 1987), and by the late 1980s (Hart 1986; Rector 1989, 1990) there was a shift towards using methods of communication from other domains, such as counselling, social psychology, and anthropology. The objective was to access the practices of the expert, and their tacit knowledge. These would still, however, be transformed into appropriate representational/propositional form for the knowledge base. It is rather curious to think that back in the fourth century BC Plato narrates about Socrates's frustration with getting experts to tell their knowledge: In one of Plato's earliest dialogues, *Euthyphro*, Socrates tries to characterise devotion. Euthyphro, a religious prophet, gives examples from his work. In this dialogue, Socrates pushes Euthyphro to formulate the rules defining an act of devotion, while Euthyphro claims to be able to judge what an act of devotion is, but he cannot explain the rules his judgment obeys. In Socrates' view, experts (in this case a religious prophet) have consciously used rules, but have since forgotten them. The philosopher's task is to remember the principles that determine their actions. The discussion on the rule continues in Johannessen's argument about rule-following in the following section on a person centred tradition of knowledge.

2.3   Person Centred Tradition of Knowledge

The Socratic quest to make knowledge about the human condition transparent to people in society and dispel the mystery of skill and wisdom by making their secrets explicit, later evolved in Europe as a quest to maximise and mechanise human productivity, and continued in this vein with knowledge engineering that sought to mechanise human cognition. This quest for the explicit has been countered in history by a questioning of the mind-body split and the damage to human life and knowledge from the primacy given to data and the propositional. The characteristics of this questioning *person-centred* approach are that knowledge is context-based and has a personal and social dimension. There is an interdependence of different aspects of knowledge embedded in knowledge transfer, *none of which are reducible to any one aspect*. This person centred approach draws on philosophical works that arose in response to Cartesian rationalism, empiricism and utilitarianism (discussed in Chap. 1), and within technology it permeates various human-centred traditions of design and is visible in the design of interactive interfaces that seek to better enable human to human engagement. Much of the literature is primarily concerned with the development and constraints of the concept of scientific knowledge and its use as a driving force for social progress. Polanyi's post-critical philosophy "places the epistemic process in the context of the personal and social dimensions of human experience. This renders our understanding more responsible and accurate and more honest. Knowledge is a human enterprise, and we lie to ourselves when we distort the modernist concern to define it by pretending it can exist independently of humans. Polanyi's work is pivotal in contemporary philosophy" (JGill op. cit.).

2.3.1   Polanyi on Tacit Knowing

The concept 'tacit knowing' was formed by Polanyi in 1966 in his work on 'The Tacit Dimension'. In various discussions on tacit knowledge he is often cited for his expression that, 'we can know more than we can tell'.[36] Polanyi's postmodernism which he calls "post critical", reconstructs the intellectual achievements of modernism without its foundationalism of self-evident truths, primary sense data, intuition, and principles of commonsense. Note that intuition is here meant in its philosophical sense as what the mind can deduce, and the principle of commonsense denotes mental schema of reality. Polanyi maintains that there is a viable ground for human cognitive activity, and introduces the ideas of tacit and explicit knowing, where explicit knowing can be articulated and demonstrated and tacit knowing is where we always know more than we can say or prove. It has been argued, that Polanyi tries to avoid both skepticism and relativism in speaking about an axis of knowing, which avoids the need for an immovable foundation as an axis needs no support or justification other than itself. Knowledge can be and is reliable without being static and impersonal. Polanyi is concerned to show that the aim of exact science to establish a strictly detached, objective knowledge, is fundamentally misleading because tacit thought forms an indispensable part of all knowledge.

This idea of tacit knowing is based within a discussion which starts with questions about how we can recognise a face, or any object or phenomenon, and leads into questions about knowledge acquisition. He is interested in how we pass on to others knowledge that we ourselves cannot fully describe. He cites the use of practical classes, and the act of pointing to things to connect words to things, as methods of passing on such knowledge. This act of pointing leaves something out which we cannot tell, and for its meaning to be understood the other person must discover that which we have not been able to communicate. The discussion draws upon Gestalt psychology (Ellis 1938; Henle 1961) and the idea of shaping or integrating experience in the process of knowledge acquisition. Here we are introduced to two aspects of knowing: 'knowing how', and 'knowing that'[37] (Ryle 1949). The former denotes practical knowledge, and the latter theoretical knowledge. The concepts of integration, awareness, interiorization or indwelling form the core of his theory of tacit knowledge and explain the interdependence of the theoretical and practical aspects of knowing. For example, Polanyi argues that mathematical theory can only be learned by practicing its application. We can only understand that which is explicit if we can relate to it through practice.

Through the use of various examples, Polanyi identifies four aspects of tacit knowing: the functional, the phenomenal, the semantic, and the ontological. The functional aspect is his basic model of the structure of tacit knowing which he uses

---

[36] Cf. Polanyi (1966) *The Tacit Dimension. New York*: Doubleday, p. 4.

[37] G. Ryle (1949) *The Concept of Mind*.

throughout his argument. He explains it as follows. In recognising a face, we are aware of its features, yet we are unable to identify all those features. The ability to recognise the face occurs through a functional relationship between what he calls 'two terms of tacit knowing'. The first, proximal, term is the features, and the second, distal, term is the face. 'We know the first term only by relying on our awareness of it for attending to the second. It is the proximal term of which we have a knowledge that we may not be able to tell'.[38] He calls this the 'functional structure of tacit knowing'.[39]

Polanyi sees a direct relationship between our bodies and the external world, for example in the way we see things, in his discussion on perception as an instance of tacit knowing. He cites physiologists who maintained that the way we see an object is determined by our awareness of certain efforts inside our body which we ourselves cannot feel. In this context, Polanyi includes the activity of neural traces in the cortex of the nervous system. His focus on the relationship between our bodily processes and the external world has been of interest to discussions on the nature of craftsmanship skills, such as engineering. He talks of the transformation of the tool into a sentient extension of our body.

He identifies tacit knowing with indwelling. It is not by looking at things, but by dwelling in them, that we understand their joint meaning. This relates back to the point that we can only understand a mathematical theory if we can relate ourselves to it in practising it. We can only understand something if we are within it and understand its practice. We cannot look at the parts and have an understanding of the whole. If we try to focus on the particulars, we can destroy our conception of an entity. For example, if a pianist whilst playing starts focussing on the movements of her fingers, she will be paralysed. However, if she focuses again on her music, she will be able to play again. With this distance the particulars will come back to life and recover their meaning and their comprehensive relationship. Thinking of the parts, rather than of the whole, as the real entity, is a misconception. It can be explained by the fact that the parts seem more tangible. Polanyi does not think, however, that a knowledge of the parts is of no use in the understanding of the whole. For example, he contrasts someone who knows how to use a machine without fully knowing how it works, with an engineer who, he says, has a deeper understanding of its construction and operation. He states, however, that a knowledge of the parts cannot replace its tacit counterpart. For example, the skill of a driver cannot be replaced by the teaching of the theory of the motorcar.

Polanyi talks of the personal dimension of knowing.[40] He considers how a scientist can see a problem. He argues that all knowledge is of the same kind as the knowledge of seeing and working with a problem. To hold such knowledge is to be committed to a conviction that there is something there to be discovered. This experience cannot be represented by any exact theory. It is a personal act of knowing.

---

[38] Polanyi, op. cit. p. 10.

[39] Ibid. p. 10.

[40] Polanyi has developed his theory of personal knowing in his work, *Personal Knowledge: Towards a Post Critical Philosophy* (1962), first published in 1958.

To summarise, Polanyi's discussion on how we know something to be something is explained through his model of tacit knowing which has a particular structure of going from particulars to the entity which does not involve an explicit identification of these particulars. His theory of indwelling or interiorization claims that we can only understand that which is explicit if we can relate to it through practice. Knowing has a personal dimension.

2.3.2   Ikuta: Language and Performance

Ikuta (1990) and Polanyi speak of the hidden, and along with Merleau Ponty they give significance to the role of metaphor. JGill says of Merleau Ponty that his writing is metaphorical, and his whole philosophy requires a commitment to the notion that the world is best understood indirectly or 'mediationally'. The craft language of learning Waza is metaphorical.

The role of "craft language" is often used in the process of teaching and learning a skill of Japanese traditional performance. Ikuta explores two core ideas: "Waza" and "craft language". The term "Waza" refers to the skill of Japanese traditional artistic performances such as Japanese dancing, Noh play or Kabuki play ("Waza" may also refer to traditional martial arts such as Karate, Judo, or Kendo). Craft language means a special metaphorical language often used in the process of teaching a skill such as Japanese traditional performance, "Waza", as opposed to using a descriptive or a scientific language. The skill of Japanese traditional performance, "Waza", can be only mastered by a novice through the activity of imitating and repeating what a teacher does. The process of learning "Waza" is considered mysterious and is learned by "stealing in secret", *nusumu*, in Japanese. Kata and Katachi are two key stages in achieving waza. "Katachi" is a physical form of action expressed by a performer of a certain "Waza". This may be decomposed into parts and described as a sequence of procedures. Kata, however, is considered the crucial for attaining waza, and far from being a simple collection of parts of action, it is an artistic and personal expression that bears the meaning connected with a socio-historical factor of the world of a certain "Waza". Kata is reached through the activity of imitating and repeating superficial "Katachi" with great pains. Ikuta cites Zeami, concerning the mastery of Noh, saying there would come a state for the learner, who has been engaged in imitating and repeating "Katachi", such that the consciousness with which he tries to imitate "Katachi" disappears all of a sudden. He calls such a state "Ushu-fu". While the novice is imitating and repeating the form of action, the novice is in a state of "Mushu-fu". "Ushu-fu" comes through committing to and indwelling in the world of Noh. There are old Japanese sayings about mastering "Waza": "enter into katachi first, and then get out of it", and "get accustomed to it rather than be taught".

The special metaphorical language used in the process of teaching and learning "Waza" is important. For example, in Japanese traditional dancing there is a form where a performer holds his right hand up with a fan. To make the learner master this form, the teacher says, while showing him this form, "Hold your right hand up just as if you were trying to catch snow falling down from the sky". He would not say, "Keep your right hand up exactly at an angle of 45 degrees". Or to make the learner understand the tempo of a performance, he says "Store it, store it!" (*Tamete, tamete*) *rather* than saying "Keep the same form for five and a half seconds".

Craft language is effective in inducing or provoking sensation in the learner's body. Why can a metaphorical expression work more effectively than a descriptive one when the teacher wants to transmit "Kata" to the learner? Ikuta explores this by drawing on Hugh Petrie's work on metaphor as being "comparative" and "interactive". The interactive aspect of a metaphor provokes a certain physical sensation in the learner's body. The teacher who already knows the similarity between the metaphor and the form that is supposed to be mastered by the learner, seeks to help the learner imagine and discover the similarity between the metaphor and the form to be mastered by himself/herself.

Hence, if the teacher makes a metaphorical suggestion, "Act as if you are catching snowflakes falling down from the sky", this might confuse the learner at first, but he may begin to imagine the scene of snow falling on a cold day, and to compare the image of catching snow with his hand with the knowledge he has stored so far through committing himself to the world of Japanese traditional dancing. And in that process of comparison between the two through his imagination, he gradually discards inappropriate properties of snow such as "white", "cold", or "melting" which have nothing to do with the dancing form itself. And he would finally reach an appropriate property of snow, which is exactly similar to the form his teacher implies. He finally understands that "lightness" or "fragility" of snow must be the one he is supposed to express in the form of holding his right hand up. To catch snowflakes with his hand, he has to hold out his hand as gently as possible, otherwise they will surely fly away from his hand. He is convinced that although he needs to hold out his hand, it is not enough that he does so mechanically. What is important is how he holds out his hand. As soon as he can understand what the metaphorical expression means in practice, he can experience the same physical sensation as his teacher, in his own body, and can simultaneously grasp the meaning of "Katachi" as being real, and thereby master "Kata". Ikuta describes craft language as intermediating, i.e. having the effect of encouraging the learner to activate his creative imagination. This is an indispensable factor for mastering "Kata" and relates to John Dewey's (1975) (JGill op. cit. p. 43) description of how we learn by doing: "In attempting to practice an art or skill, we indwell it to the extent that it eventually comes to indwell us, even though we generally cannot say how this happens. In learning a new dance step, a new language, or how to think philosophically, there is no substitute for practice."

However, it is not necessarily the case that any learner, whether novice or expert, who is given metaphorical suggestions, can activate his or her imagination. To be able to do this, the learner needs to already have implicit and explicit knowledge not only of "Katachi", but also its socio-cultural background through committing himself to or indwelling in the world of a certain "Waza" by the time he receives such a metaphorical suggestion from his teacher. Without such knowledge, he can only imagine what the metaphorical statement means literally and will never be encouraged to activate his imaginative activity such as comparing the literal meaning with the form he is supposed to master, and he will stay in the state of "Mushu-fu". Craft language works only when the learner has already been engaged in the activity of imitating "Katachi", and indwelling inside the world of a certain "Waza". To those who are outside the world or have not stored enough knowledge yet, craft language is meaningless or is just an awkward expression at best.

This relates to Polanyi's reflection that the notion of 'part' only makes sense in relation to the whole of which it is a part. … "parts do not float around as independent units." This reminds me of an example from Taoist philosophy about appreciating the aesthetics of a view. A Monk asks a trainee Monk to describe the view in front of him, and the trainee monk replies that he sees trees, water, and the sky. The Monk then asks him to contemplate and reflect on the view, and leaves him to do so. After some hours, the elderly Monk returns, and asks the novice, what does he see?, and the novice answers, I see the trees, water, and the sky. His words are the same but his experience has been fundamentally altered, as the monk integrates his experience of seeing with his expression of what he sees.

2.3.3   Rosenbrock: Model of Symbiosis of Tacit and Explicit Knowledge

The concept of tacit knowledge has been discussed in the domain of engineering as being an essential dimension of expert knowledge. This discussion has taken place in response to an increasing emphasis upon scientific or explicit knowledge at the expense of tacit knowledge, particularly in relation to the development and application of computer based systems.

This emphasis has raised two fundamental concerns within engineering for the proponents of tacit knowledge such as Rosenbrock (1988, 1989, 1992) and Cooley (1987a, b). One is about the development of engineering theory and practice, and the other is about the construction of purposeful and beneficial systems. An overemphasis on theory or scientifically based knowledge does not adequately explain the nature of engineering skills[41] (cf. Rosenbrock 1977). It undervalues the interrelationsip between theory and practice. It also ignores the dimension of human purpose in the explanation of skills and in the design of systems. In the case of design, the most extreme representation of the scientific perspective of knowledge is the automated machine[42] (cf. Feigenbaum et al. op. cit.). This is illustrated in Fig. 2.1 where

---

[41] As in the case of control systems design.

[42] Rosenbrock is concerned that the notion of the automated machine allows for the idea of a workerless factory. It rejects the tacit dimension of worker's knowledge and skill, seeing them as automata, reducing their tasks to ever simpler and more closely definable fragments (cf. Fordism). He cites Needham's view in the 1920s (cf. 1927) that 'in science, man is a machine; or if he is not, then he is nothing at all'.

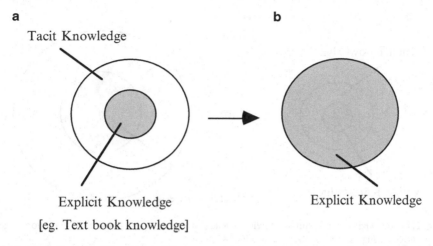

Fig. 2.1 Explication of expert knowledge: an analogy to the idea of the automated machine

explicit knowledge denotes theoretical knowledge or scientific knowledge, such as the kind of knowledge found in a text book. The idea of the automated machine embodies the belief that expert knowledge can be completely explicated (Fig. 2.1b, cf. Rosenbrock 1988, p. 318).

Figure 2.1 above illustrates the formulation of the tacit dimension in explicit form; the belief that the tacit can be completely explicated. However, the concept of autonomous entities, whether they are machines or humans, is fallacious. In the case of machines, some human intervention will always be needed in unexpected situations, such as machines malfunctioning.

The model of *symbiosis* between tacit and explicit knowledge proposed by Rosenbrock, who is himself an engineer, provides an alternative model of knowledge which meets both of the concerns about the development of engineering theory and practice and the development of systems. The model of symbiosis between the tacit and explicit aspects of knowledge [see Fig. 2.2, cf. Rosenbrock 1988, p. 318] challenges the emphasis on explicit knowledge and the concept of the automated machine [as in Fig. 2.1b above]. The symbiotic interdependence of tacit and explicit aspects of knowledge means that knowledge can never be made completely explicit as it is in Fig. 2.1b. Instead as knowledge is explicated it gives rise to new tacit knowledge which is required to use this explicit knowledge (Fig. 2.2). This formulation expands both the explicit and tacit dimensions of knowledge, which is the essence of the symbiosis.

It is in the context of seeing knowledge as a symbiosis of tacit and explicit aspects that Rosenbrock proposes that seeing engineering as an art rather than as a science will provide a better explanation of engineering skill. It is an art because of the tacit knowledge involved in being a skilled practitioner. Although a skilled engineer uses scientific knowledge and mathematical analysis, his/her skill also 'contains elements of experience and judgement, and regard for social considerations

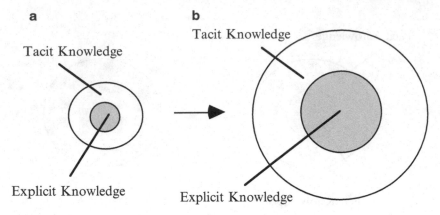

Fig. 2.2 The expansion of explicit knowledge leads to a reciprocal expansion of tacit knowledge required for using the new explicit knowledge

and the most effective way of using human labour. These elements partly embody knowledge, which has not yet been reduced to an exact mathematical form. They also embody value judgements which are not amenable to the scientific method' (Rosenbrock 1988).[43] These elements make up the tacit knowledge of the skilled engineer. Social studies of science show that science in practice also involves making value judgements using experience, reading in between the lines, and considering the social applications. However, when it comes to building machines, the praxis of science and engineering which makes it an art, is left out.

In further describing these elements of *experience* and *judgement*, Rosenbrock draws upon Polanyi's (1966) concept of tacit knowing wherein we have knowledge that we are unaware of having. That is, there are certain things we do correctly but which we cannot explain or make explicit in scientific terms. Rosenbrock gives an example of how an engineer performs a task to show the use of tacit knowledge in making judgements. The example focuses on the *ability to doubt*. An engineer may set up a problem according to an accepted theory and use a computer to process the problem, but he or she may doubt the answer. Further analysis may reveal a mathematical error or the misapplication of the theory thereby confirming the doubt. The doubt involves intuition, experiential knowledge and a personal commitment on the part of the engineer. There is commitment because it is a major responsibility of the engineer to decide when the discrepancy between theory and the real world will lead to error.

Rosenbrock thinks that it is important that engineers recognise the essential element of art and tacit knowledge of their profession. If it is difficult to convince them that this exists, it will be more difficult to persuade them that other professions have this element. This would leave little room for the essential human input when an engineer designs systems in which other people will work. The process of explicating knowledge for systems development will subsequently follow the

---

[43] Rosenbrock, H (1988) *Engineering as an Art*. AI & Society Journal, Vol. 2 No. 4.

direction illustrated in Fig. 2.1, and focus on explicit knowledge at the expense of tacit knowledge. This would also ignore the social and personal dimension of working life practice.

In the symbiotic model of knowledge, illustrated in Fig. 2.2 above, as aspects of tacit knowledge are made explicit through new theories about expertise or in the development of new technologies, there is a reciprocal expansion of art and tacit knowledge. This is required in order to make this new explicit knowledge meaningful and for it to be used. For example, with the development of new technologies, new skills are needed. These could be built upon previous skills. Future technological systems could be designed which accept existing skills. Such systems would enable existing skills to develop through experience with the new system into skills which the changing technology requires. Existing skills need to be seen as relevant and useful, but not static. Technological systems need to be designed so that they cooperate with human skill to make it more productive. This is as opposed to eliminating that skill.

The relationship between tacit and explicit knowledge expressed in Fig. 2.2 provides an explanation of the development of engineering theory and practice. As engineering builds its scientific basis, some of the tacit knowledge embodied in earlier practices becomes redundant. A new body of tacit knowledge emerges with the setting up and interpretation of new methods. The symbiotic model draws attention to human purpose in engineering practice. Rosenbrock's symbiotic model is driven by his wish to see the development of technology and skills as a positive beneficial process whereby purpose is essential (Rosenbrock 1988, 1990, 1992).[44]

2.3.4   Cooley: On Common-Sense

Cooley (1972, 1987a, b, 1991) deals with the nature of knowledge and skill of craftsworkers. He believes that knowledge consists in a *symbiosis* between its objective and subjective parts. These cannot be separated. Cooley attacks three presumptions of knowledge-based computer technology embodied in the description and attitude towards the nature of knowledge and skill. The first is the objectification of subjective knowledge. The second is the reduction of skill acquisition from being a process of *knowledge reproduction* to being a process of knowledge production. In both these cases, the designers of computer systems have assumed that the subjective can be separated from the objective. The third issue is the damaging effect of the subjective/objective split within human-computer interaction upon the common-sense and tacit knowledge of skilled workers.

---

[44] Rosenbrock was involved in a European venture upon Human-Centred CIM Systems. [CIM – Computer Integrated Manufacturing]. This project attempted to apply the symbiotic model in the construction of a human centred CIM system.

Fig. 2.3 The limits of
rule-based systems [p. 13]

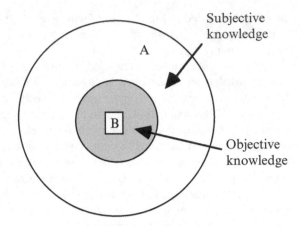

We will consider each of these issues in turn. Firstly, Cooley's symbiotic model
of knowledge is explained in Fig. 2.3 (cf. Cooley 1987a, p. 13) above.

In Fig. 2.3, A denotes the knowledge required to be an expert/skilled craftsworker. Within it there is a core of knowledge, B, which is the facts of the domain;
for example, text book knowledge. This can be reduced to a rule-based system, i.e.
objective knowledge. The annalus AB can be said to represent common-sense, tacit
knowledge and imagination, heuristics and fuzzy reasoning.

Common-sense for Cooley means "a sense of what is to be done and how it is to
be done, held in common by those who will have some form of apprenticeship and
practical experience in the area."[45] Common-sense is acquired through learning by
doing. Tacit knowledge, for Cooley, is that which is also acquired through learning
by doing and by attending to things. The relative levels of the subjective and objective aspects of knowledge which a person utilises vary as one gains expertise. An
expert uses more of the subjective aspects and less of the objective aspects of the
knowledge in, for example, the use of intuition. An expert has the ability to grasp
the situation in front of him/her and make judgements about it. A novice, on the
other hand, can only calculate by using explicit rules to make sense of what appears
to him/her to be a mass of data. Cooley describes this world of discrete and fragmented data as that of noise (Fig. 2.4). He presents the process of acquiring knowledge as a spectrum going from data to action: 'Data suitably organised and acted
upon may become information, and information that is absorbed, understood and
applied by people may become knowledge. Knowledge frequently applied in a
domain may become wisdom, and wisdom the basis for [normative] positive
action.'[46] Cooley calls this the cybernetic transformation[47] [Fig. 2.4, cf. Cooley
1987a, p. 12].

---

[45] Cf. Cooley 1987a, p. 12.

[46] Cooley, M. (1987a), Architect or Bee. Hogarth Press [new edition], p. 11. cf. cybernetics, see
Wiener (1949).

[47] Ibid. fig. 2.1. 'The tacit Area'. p. 12.

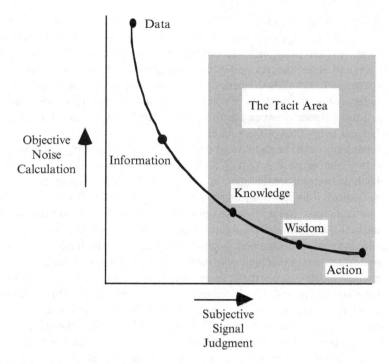

Fig. 2.4 Cybernetic transformation

Common-sense and tacit knowledge, which are essential requirements for skill, exist where there is wisdom. We can make calculations with data but we can only make judgements when we have wisdom. Being able to make judgements means that one has acquired expertise.

Cooley questions design philosophies which are based on the data/information end of the spectrum rather than on the wisdom/knowledge end (Fig. 2.4). For example, he rejects the traditional expert systems idea[48] where the ultimate aim is to objectify subjective knowledge (Fig. 2.2). This idea is based upon a belief that the subjective and the objective are separable. For Cooley, it is the interaction between the subjective and the objective that is important.

The second issue which Cooley is concerned with is information technology's focus on the production of knowledge. This focus is based on the notion that knowledge is objective. However, in order to understand the nature of skill, one needs to see knowledge as a reproductive process which is based on the continuous interaction between the subjective and the objective aspects of knowledge. The reproduction of knowledge is part of the process of knowledge and skill acquisition. Knowledge is acquired through learning by doing. Through this process human

---

[48] Feigenbaum and McCorduck, op. cit.

beings acquire 'intuition' and 'know-how'[49] (Dreyfus and Dreyfus 1986). Common-sense and tacit knowledge consist of intuition and know-how. Cooley draws upon Dreyfus and Dreyfus' assertion[50] that analytical thinking and intuition are complementary ways of understanding and making judgements. As one becomes increasingly experienced and skilled, there is a greater emphasis placed on intuition. Cooley believes that the analysis of working-life tasks and skills needs to account for the holistic balance between the use of analytical thinking and intuition, tacit knowledge and know-how of the worker.

The separation of the objective and the subjective in describing knowledge and skill, and in the subsequent design of computer technology leads to the third issue. This is that human-computer interaction does not allow for interaction at the subjective level. Instead, it imposes objectivity on working practice. This in turn, Cooley argues, damages the common-sense and tacit knowledge of skilled workers. Recognition of the symbiosis of objective and subjective knowledge would however require alternative design philosophies and practices which allow for the subjective aspects in human-machine symbiosis, termed 'human-centred'.

In summary, Cooley argues that it is essential that one recognises the relationship between the subjective and the objective aspects of knowledge. This relationship includes the dynamics of analytical methods and intuition, know-how and tacit knowledge of the skilled craftsworker. The relationship between the subjective and objective aspects of knowledge necessitates a rethinking about the relevance of computer technology and the development of symbiotic systems where the relation between the human and the machine places the human at the centre and not the machine.

---

[49] The terms, 'holistic similarity recognition', intuition', or 'know-how', have been adopted from Dreyfus and Dreyfus. They use them synonymously to denote, 'the understanding that effortlessly occurs upon seeing similarities with previous experiences ... intuition is the product of deep situational involvement and recognition of similarity'. They, in turn, have drawn upon Polanyi (1966).

[50] Dreyfus and Dreyfus (1986) present this balance between analytical thinking and intuition in their theory of skill acquisition. Here, there are five stages of development from being a novice to gaining expertise. These are (1) novice; (2) advanced beginner; (3) competent; (4) proficient; and (5) expert. A novice follows context-free rules. The relevant components of a situation are defined to enable the novice to recognise them. The novice lacks any coherent sense of the whole task and can judge his/her performance only in terms of how well the learnt rules have been followed. The advanced beginner, through practical experience in concrete situations, learns to recognise situational elements, which cannot be defined as objective context-free features. Recognition occurs through discerning similarities to prior examples. The competent learner can make plans and choices in order to achieve certain outcomes. Being proficient means that one has acquired an intuitive ability to use patterns without reducing them to features. The competent performer still relies on analytical thinking in combination with intuition. An expert, however can discern whole scenes without decomposing them into elements. Because of their experience they can use their intuition to make decisions and cope with uncertainties and critical situations. This framework has come under criticism from Harry Collins (2013) as not representative of other ways of learning that may involve more or less steps as in the case of touch typists.

2.4   Rules and Rule Following: A Hermeneutic Approach

During the 1980s the concept of tacit knowledge became the central theme in hermeneutic[51] discussions about professional skills and expertise in Sweden (Janik 1988; Johannessen 1988a; Nordenstam 1992, Göranzon 1991, 1992; Josefson 1988a, b, 1992; Janik 1988, 1991, 1992; Perby 1990). The implementation of knowledge based systems technology in many spheres of Swedish economic life since the 1970s raised concern both about the long-term effects of the technology upon skills and about the nature of design itself (Ehn 1988). A number of case studies were undertaken, which markedly showed that in the long-term, experts lose confidence in their ability to judge whether their methods and results are valid in comparison to those of the computer.

The case studies show that having confidence in one's own judgement and abilities is crucial to being skilled. The case studies and theoretical discussions concentrate on the concepts of praxis, craftsmanship, and skill acquisition. Within this context, the discussion on tacit knowledge focuses on the inter-relationship between tacit and propositional knowledge, that is, between practical and theoretical knowledge. This interdependence determines that propositional knowledge only has meaning when we know how to use it, or make sense of it. This entails its practice. This relationship extends from how we relate to the objects in our world, right up to the development of our skills and our language. There are two fundamental aspects of tacit knowledge expressed in the Swedish case studies.[52] These are practical knowledge, and knowledge by familiarity. Practical knowledge is the aspect of performing the knowledge in practice. Knowledge by familiarity covers the aspect of learning a practice through the use of examples of the practice. These may be examples of experiences given by those involved in the practice. Knowledge by familiarity makes for reflection upon one's own practice. It comes close to Polanyi's idea of indwelling (see pp. 48–49).

The Hermeneutic discussion draws upon Wittgenstein and Polanyi. Johannessen is a key philosopher in the development of this hermeneutic discussion.[53] Some of the central concepts he has been developing, rule-following and practice, are presented below.

---

[51] The hermeneutics of Goranzon and Josefson are based on interpretations of Wittgenstein, Polanyi, and Kuhn, whereas the hermeneutics of Ehn covers interpretations of Heidegger and Marx as well.

[52] Two additional aspects of tacit knowledge, based on an interpretation of the Scandinavian, (cf. Gill 1988, 1990, 1992) are 'experiential knowledge' and 'personal knowledge'. Personal knowledge is that which is specific to the individual personality, gained from our personal life experiences (like family culture, school, friends), and expressed in our social values, beliefs etc.; experiential knowledge is that of direct experience which can cover specific experiences, such as within the context of the workplace, e.g., knowledge gained from interaction with work colleagues, group culture, organisational culture etc.

[53] See Janik (1988) for an overview of the hermeneutic approach adopted in particular by the Scandinavian researchers based at the former Swedish Centre for Working Life.

2.4.1   Rule Following and Practice

A discussion on rule-following and practice has been undertaken at the Bergen
School of Philosophy (Johannessen 1988a, b, 1992; Nordenstam 1987, 1992). They
are challenging the emphasis generally placed upon linguistic knowledge or the
written word as being a superior form of knowing to that of practice.[54] This emphasis upon linguistic knowledge and the written word can be traced back to the
assumption that knowledge and language have a mathematical basis. Wittgenstein
(1958) challenges the concept of a rule as entailed in the concept of a mathematical
language, and undergoes a radical shift in his later philosophy in his development of
the concept of 'to follow a rule'. This is called his 'pragmatic turn'.[55] In the context
of the discussion on tacit knowledge the relationship between rule-following, practice, and language is a challenge to the idea of propositional knowledge.

Johannessen[56] (1988b) describes Wittgenstein's philosophy as a kind of practice
philosophy. To learn to master a language is a matter of mastering human reality in
all its complexity. It is a matter of learning to adopt an attitude towards it in established ways, to reflect over it, to investigate it, to gain a foothold in it, and become
familiar with it.[57] Wittgenstein includes physical communication such as gestures in
his extended concept of language. This is to show that we make use of a variety of
means to make ourselves understood. 'A sentence does not say of itself that it is to be
taken as, say, an assertion'.[58] Language and human action are intimately interwoven,
and so thereby is the relationship between language and reality. Wittgenstein became
very interested in the application of the rule and the situation of the user. One and the
same rule can be followed in many different ways. What guarantees that a rule is followed in the same way time after time cannot itself be a rule at all. It must depend on
our actions and different kinds of spontaneous reactions. Rule following is a practice.
If we do not know the closer details of the current use situation, we will not be able
to make up our minds about what is actually said. Therefore, our mastery of a natural
language must include a grasp or practical understanding of an enormously large
repertoire of situations involving the use of language. In order to understand and
respond, we must have situational understanding and judgemental power. The very
exercise of an activity might be a constitutive part of the formation of concepts. The
content of a concept can be regarded as a function of the established use of its expression. One has mastered a given concept when one is accepted as a competent performer of the series of established practices which incorporates the concept. It is our
application or practice which shows how we understand something. 'The practice

---

[54] They cover the fields of ethics, morality, and aesthetics, cf. Nordenstam (1968, 1987, 2013),
Johannessen and Nordenstam (1981), and Johannessen (1981).

[55] See Fann (1969) for a discussion of this shift.

[56] Johannessen (1988b) *The Concept of Practice in Wittgenstein's Later Philosophy*, in Inquiry.

[57] Johannessen, K (1992) Rule-Following, Intransitive Understanding and Tacit Knowledge.
pp. 41–63.

[58] Wittgenstein, L (1958) Philosophical Investigations. para 199, p. 81.

gives words their meaning'.[59] The identity of a rule over time is attained through the exercise of the established set of practices which guarantees that a rule is applied in the same way from one time to another and from one person to another. The rule itself cannot give this guarantee. 'The knowledge built into the mastery of concepts or rules has a partial and non-reducible expression in action. It is not possible to put into words this aspect of action in which the intellectually explicable part of the concept is necessarily embedded'.[60] There is an interdependence between the tacit and the explicit aspects of knowledge.

2.5 Explicit and Tacit Knowledge: Collins

The sociologist of science, Harry Collins, provides an alternative critique of tacit knowledge and the application of this concept to that made by, for example, the philosopher Hubert Dreyfus and the theorist of organizational knowledge Nonaka. It is the most recent critical evaluation of Polanyi's theory and it is helpful to lay it out in some detail, particularly as he dismisses the primacy that Polanyi gives to the body as the location of tacit knowledge, according to what he terms the social and minimal embodiment thesis p. 135). This is not the view taken in this book; in fact, Polanyi's famous expression that we know more than we can tell is referring to neuronal activity (body), which makes this claim by Collins redundant. The more interesting discussion is about what he considers to be irreducible to the explicit, and he lays the limit at human culture (in contrast to other animal behaviour) "that can only be accessed via experience".

He begins by describing the tacit as being 'parasitic' on the explicit, "If it were not for the idea of the explicit we would never have noticed that there was anything special about the tacit – it would just have been normal life. Having invented the explicit, however, we now have the tacit."

It is interesting that Collins' discussion of the explicit and the tacit revolves around interaction, and he takes the metaphor of a string as the basic unit of analysis of information about the interaction, to which he adds degrees of complexity, e.g. strings of different lengths. Hence in our interaction with physical objects, strings can have physical impact, or be patterns/inscriptions, or communicate either physically or afford interpretation. In the case of communication with other people, he refers to Wittgenstein's, 'ask for the use, not the meaning', where in order for the transfer of a string to count as communication, depends on the outcome: "A communication takes place when an entity P is made to do something or comes to be able to do something that it could not do before as a result of the transfer of a string", a case of cause and effect, e.g. if I can use the information to do something. He describes communication as jumping across a gap between two buildings, and presents *five enabling conditions of communication*.

---

[59] Wittgenstein, L (1977) Remarks on Colour. (ed) G.E.M. Anscombe. para 317.
[60] Johannessen, K (1988b).

Condition 1: The first is when everything is in place so that a gap can be easily jumped: trouble free.

Conditions 2–5: communication fails initially so something has to be changed to enable the gap to be jumped.

Condition 2: the string needs to be physically transformed to have a causal impact on an entity e.g. pressing on the keys of a keyboard to get the computer to do a sum that has been written on paper, i.e. transforming a paper string to a string of finger positions.

Condition 3: change the length of a string: a short string may fail where a long string succeeds, and here he gives two comparative different examples (which do not really have the same quality). An early computer fails to respond to 10×2.54 because it lacks a calculator program, it succeeds when supplemented with one; and the other example is regarding a joke about a joke: a man walks into a pub where the locals keep bursting out in laughter when one of them says a number. The man gives it a try and calls out numbers but not one of his gets a laugh. The landlord explains that it is not the joke that matters but how you say it. Collins explains the situation as follows. Over the years the locals frequenting this pub have become so familiar with each others jokes that they know them by their numbers, however, each number can only be understood by a 'local' to whom the number 'affords' the story. Each number could be communicated to the visitor with a longer string in which the joke was originally 'transmitted'. Collins point about this example is that, although it may be tempting to think that all tacit knowledge can be made explicit using longer strings, in this example that may sometimes work but it may not always do so.

Condition 4: In some cases where short or long strings will not do the job of communication, a fixed change in physical form of the entity will enable the strings to succeed in jumping the gap where they did not initially succeed e.g. additional memory in a computer, and a weight lifter building muscle to lift more weights. He also gives the example of new synapses being formed in the brain from learning something.

Condition 5: Fluency of language. For Collins, language is not the same as strings, and he makes a transformation-translation distinction: a string can be transformed and transformed back without loss of information (deduction, inference), and a language translated, involving irremediable loss of change of meaning.

Next, Collins presents three categories of tacit knowledge, weak, medium, and strong, which refer to their degree of resistance to being made explicit.

The strongest is *collective tacit knowledge* (*CTK*) which is defined as, "we do not know how to make it explicit. It is the domain of knowledge located in society. It has to do with the way society is constituted." For Collins this is unique to humans.

The medium level is *somatic tacit knowledge* (*STK*). This is to do with the properties of people's bodies and brains as physical things, something that is continuous with animals and other living things. In principle, human scientists could explicate it in their research, and it is possible that in the future we would be able to mimic animal behaviour with machines, and likewise for human animals.

The weakest level is what he calls *Relational tacit knowledge (RTK)*. He argues that this could be made explicit in the second sense of explicable (condition 2 above), but is not made explicit because of either the nature and location of knowledge or the way humans are made, as it is about how people relate to each other and the way societies are organised. It is about why the kind of knowledge transfer in condition 3 does not always work, and it includes cases "where the parties could tell each other what they need to know but either will not, or cannot, for reasons that are "not very profound", such as not knowing what the other party needs to know".

In summary, Collins describes the explicit as the transmission of something via strings; the tacit cannot be or is not transmitted, with strings. The explicit can be conveyed by middle persons or middle things with strings inscribed on them, whereas the tacit must involve direct contact. Thus if a middle person appears to transmit the tacit it cannot be in the form of a string inscribed, it must be in some other form. He explains that children and older students acquire tacit knowledge by socialising with parents, teachers, and peers, and in the workplace it is acquired by 'sitting by Nellie' or more organised apprenticeship. In science it is acquired by research degrees, talks at conferences, lab visits, and in the coffee bar.

He then goes on to talk about "asymmetry in intermediaries and knowledge", e.g. something passed on via others is explicit knowledge, but that passed on directly is not necessarily tacit, however not all knowledge passed on directly could be passed on via others. He makes an interesting point that it is a false inference to say that where a computer can read a string or produce a mechanical output where a human could not, that robots can replace us, and that with enough work, education can be transmitted via intermediaries such as the internet. "Education is more a matter of socialisation into tacit ways of thinking and doing than transferring explicit information or instructions."

It is useful to present in a bit more detail, what Collins means by Relational Tacit Knowledge, Somatic Tacit Knowledge, and Collective Tacit Knowledge. He gives examples as follows.

Relational

- *Concealed* – learning craft skills from a master craftsman e.g. the Japanese speak of 'stealing' the master craftsman's 'secrets'.
- *Ostensive* – knowledge learned by pointing to some object or practice because it is too complex to put into words. (According to Collins this is a condition 3 knowledge transfer i.e. it could be said to be explicit rather than tacit).
- *Logistically demanding* – someone who has been doing a job that could be done by a robot (a social prosthetic), if they are reliable then it is more efficient to keep him or her on.
- *Mismatched saliences* – people who are mismatched in their knowledge. It is difficult to see into the other person's head. This is a stronger case of relational

than the others as 'however hard the teller tries to tell all, he or she cannot do it'. He says the reasons this knowledge is not made explicit is because it is situated in an accident and these accidents cannot be avoided so no one can volunteer to tell the knowledge. In such circumstances, providers of knowledge welcome close proximity between themselves and learners so they can learn by every kind of interaction.

– *Unrecognized knowledge* – A carries out procedures in a certain way but cannot tell B about it as A does not know they are important things. A common problem for knowledge elicitation of expert knowledge is that the expert does not know what they know. The tradition or habit in which the knowledge is embedded may be picked up by imitation from close proximity with the other; how tacit knowledge is transferred.

In summary, Collins states that any piece of relational knowledge can be made explicit and all relational tacit knowledge cannot be made explicit at once.

For explaining somatic tacit knowledge, he gives the example of learning to ride a bicycle. This is learnt through a process of socialisation with other bicycle riders, and is a skill that once learned is never lost: the body's knowledge. Curiously, he presents a hypothetical setting that lies outside of human experience: he claims that if our brains and the physiology involved in balancing on a bike worked a million or so times faster or, what is the equivalent, if we rode our bikes on the surface of a small asteroid with zero gravity, we could adjust our balance by using Polanyi's rules, a manual. We are limited by our physiology. This claim is not clear.

He develops his argument with a criticism of Dreyfus's five stage model, stating that there are many other stages in learning a skill and different ways. He acknowledges that what remains important is that skills generally cannot be executed if we are self consciously attending to them e.g. the pianist watching their fingers, but he says this bears on nothing but on the way humans work and not on the way knowledge works. Collins appears to be disembodying knowledge as he criticises Dreyfus for a misplaced obsession with the body rather than an obsession with the nature of knowledge. There are fundamental problems with his criticism; one only needs to ask how do babies acquire knowledge from their mothers, to realise that Collin's separation between the psyche and soma is reductive.

His calls his third category of tacit knowledge, 'collective' and bases this in an idea of social Cartesianism. He gives examples of bike riding, copy typing, paint spraying, and chess, all of which could in principle be expressed in rules and executed by machines. However, if one takes the case of bike riding, riding in traffic involves negotiation with others. A mechanical bike cannot negotiate in traffic. Likewise, copy typists have to work with ambiguities and make judgements about how many mistakes to allow and how much time to spend on correcting them, and which correct putative mistakes to allow. In spraying paint, 'it's a matter of how thorough the job should be in different circumstances and will vary on what metals the paint contains', and in chess, it is about gamesmanship involving the setting up of challenges. Machines cannot manage trade offs and repairs that occur in human social context. Collective tacit knowledge is about negotiation and handling cultural differences in practices, and collective responsibility. People make social judgements about how individual and social responsibility are to be balanced, and the right way to do things can only be captured through experience, not through rules. He describes the explication of experience as the socialisation problem.

Collins considers improvisation as form of collective tacit knowledge, as it is a skill requiring the kind of tacit knowledge that can only be acquired through social embedding in society. Social sensibility is about knowing that an innovative dance step is improvisation whilst another step is foolish, dangerous, ugly. It is about absorbing social rules.

Now he talks about two stages of acquiring collective tacit knowledge. First condition: change must happen in an entity that is in touch with changing circumstances and somehow recognises the appropriate adjustments to what was initially transferred. This is what he calls "the mystery of social tacit knowledge", and asks, by what mechanism do humans stay in touch with society and how can one build a machine to do that? He argues that the Dreyfus model does not discuss the relation between bodily skills and social skills – i.e. the 'subdivision' between sensory motor skills and social skills. The division Dreyfus does make is between modalities of self-consciousness and unself-consciousness. This is an interesting point and one that I agree on, as I was unable to draw upon Dreyfus to develop an analysis of the tacit dimension in dialogue.

Collins' discussion on the irreducibility of the collective is based on culture. He does however base it within a social Cartesianism of human versus all other animals: humans can be social and animals cannot i.e. humans have the ability to absorb ways of going on from the surrounding society without being able to articulate rules in detail. Animals are taught to transform and respond to strings in desired ways by regimes of punishment and rewards. A personality of an animal, e.g. a dog, does not correspond to cultural differences between breeds. He dismisses all other animals as well that are arguably highly social, such as dolphins, elephants, macaques, etc. Collins' social Cartesianism is deeply rooted in a Judeo Christian concept of self. He describes social Cartesianism: "Humans can carry out polymorphic actions, whereby behaviour differs with context and interpretation of same behaviours (I would say, that 'appear' to be the same) in different contexts." He goes on to say that the distinction is between a species with fully developed language and culture, which no animal possesses other than humans, "all the many studies that purport to show that birds and chimps use language, tools, exhibit different behaviours in different groups, or learn different behaviours from each other, does not affect the distinction."

A more interesting discussion is on his metaphysics of the collectivity: "the collectivity rather than the individual is the location of the knowledge". He cites Emile Durkheim (1933) on collective consciousness, and how studies of children show how they acquire social collective knowledge, and how any individual who is isolated, will lose this over time. He gives the example of HG Wells story of 'The country of the blind', which is about an isolated social group where the language changes. Another example that many of us know is Golding's the 'Lord of the Flies' where children stranded on an island 'become animals'. Collins speaks about acquiring social knowledge through words and things, and immersion in talk and practices of society. He mentions the Sapir Whorf hypothesis, that words in a language depend on the physical environment, e.g. Inuits have 17 words for snow as snow comprises much of their business. People that speak a natural language possess a similar body type in three ways: (1) Physiology –this creates conditions for language, e.g. speech depends on the larynx, a certain kind of brain, lungs etc.; (2) The body determines the form of language in communication – alphabet structure and size, volume (amplitude) of voice; (3) The body shape affects the terms in the language and thereby conceptual structure of the world e.g. saying 'chair' – the fact that we walk on two legs, have knees that bend backwards enables us to take comfort from chairs.

To sum up, culture is about being able to negotiate with others, about making a social judgement about how individual responsibility and social responsibility are to be balanced and the right way to do things, all of which 'cannot be captured in any description on the page'. 'The right way to do things can only be captured through experience, and that experience and its application varies from country to country. The explication of the way such things are captured through experience is the socialization problem.'

2.6 Summary

The theory of human knowledge involves an ongoing dichotomy or dualism between knowledge as time and context independent, and knowledge that exists in praxis/experience and has a personal and social dimension. Attempts by philosophers, such as those by Heidegger, Polanyi, Buber, Merleau Ponty, and Wittgenstein, have sought to bypass this dualism that is inadequate for understanding the knowledge and skills of people.

And this inadequacy is explored through an analysis of knowledge transfer and knowledge formation with respect to the tacit dimension of knowledge in dialogue, discussed as the interrelationship between knowledge, language and action where knowledge is multidimensional.

The non-person centred view of knowledge is that it is propositional, and there is a distinction and a separation between that which is subjective and that which is objective. Emphasis is placed on objective knowledge, which is independent of time and context.

Within the context of designing technology, this is perceived as an objective entity whose application has universal pre-determined outcomes. Traditional knowledge engineering was rooted in the belief that knowledge lies in the heads of experts, and communication with the experts served the purpose of extracting data according to predetermined constraints. This is an extreme model of human cognition bounded by computation, and whilst the expert system project was flourishing, alternative design traditions were being developed that questioned the brittleness of such a perspective. Movements in design traditions have of course undergone a fundamental shift (Dourish 2004) where the emphasis is now on the user and their needs and knowledge, and their relations with others. This is evident in the growth in the fields of user experience design, interactive design, tangible computing, and responsive media interfaces.

The ultimate consequence of 'data' and 'knowledge' is Big data. Here disembodied analyses of data pulled out of situated contexts of culture, human relations, action and emotion, are made of online behaviour patterns such as search actions, preferences and consumption patterns. This creates a problem for the integration from particulars to the whole, such that we cannot see the wood for the trees, necessitating a knowledge engineering project on a mass scale even further disembodied than that of the expert system project. As a result of an increasingly technologically augmented existence, there is a growing demand to analyse the vast quantities of data of what are essentially human beings. Whereas the mathematicians in the Swedish Forestry industry had some key role in creating the data bases and processing rules of the systems they were to then use, the analyses of Big Data are being fed back to the people as being relevant to their needs and thereby directing their needs.

The person centred perspective is that knowledge is time and context dependent and has a social and personal dimension consisting of many aspects, which are interdependent. The subjective and objective aspects of knowledge are collapsed into each other or interdependent and cannot be separated. For example, intuition and analytical thinking are dimensions of knowledge.

Given that knowledge consists in interdependent aspects, how can one learn about these aspects of knowledge? For this purpose, knowledge is considered as analogous to skill and its performance (Gill 1995). The example of the computer has been used to illustrate the non-person centred perspective of knowledge. Humans have the ability to co-adapt and to innovate, i.e. improvise. This enables them to deal with uncertainty and breakdown. The computer, however, lacks the ability to adapt and to innovate. The key to these human abilities is praxis and experience, whereby knowledge has meaning in its performance. A computer performs according to predefined functions or rules. Human performance, however, is about rule-following which is a way of doing, whereby the application of a rule is dependent on the situation of the user. Our practice shows how we understand something. One and the same rule can be followed in many different ways. The computer, however, can only follow particular rules of causality that can be traced to Kant, and defined according to a universal logic. Combined with the utility concept of economic progress as expressed in the automation of humans and work, rules can only be followed in one 'best' way. However, unlike humans, in the event of breakdown, the computer cannot draw upon experience and the situational context to grasp the knowledge that the breakdown reveals (Winograd op. cit.) and to improvise with this understanding.

In order to consider how humans can adapt and innovate, the question posed is how do we acquire knowledge? In the non-person centred perspective, knowledge can be represented in terms of discrete entities. In contrast to this, the person-centred view of knowledge argues that knowledge is a continuous process embodied in dialogue. In embodied dialogue there is no finality about the meaning of a word (i.e. it cannot be represented as a discrete entity). Instead there are shared backgrounds which we tap into when we make an utterance or hear an utterance, and move with another person's body and voice, and touch, and have moments of stillness with them. It is through, or within, dialogue that we acquire knowledge and skill. The limits of reducing the tacit to the explicit lie in culture, in how we make social judgements, where the 'right way to do things can only be captured through experience (not through rules)' and is expressed in performance.

References

Alvey. (1983). *Annual report*. London.
Ayer, A. J. (1971). *Language truth and logic*. London: Pelican.
Barr, A., & Feigenbaum, E. A. (Eds.). (1981). *The handbook of artificial intelligence*. Reading: Addison-Wesley.
Berry, D. (1987). The problem of implicit knowledge. *Expert Systems, 4*(3), 144–151.
Boden, M. (1988). *Computer models of mind: Myths and mechanisms*. Cambridge: Cambridge University Press.
Boden, M. (1991). *Artificial intelligence in psychology: Introductory essays*. Cambridge, MA: MIT Press.
Boose, J. H., & Gaines, B. R. (Eds.). (1988). *Knowledge acquisition tools for expert systems*. London: Academic.
Boose, J. H., & Gaines, B. R. (Eds.). (1990). *The foundations of knowledge acquisition*. London: Academic.
Bramer, M. (1988). Expert systems in business: A British perspective. *Expert Systems, 5*, 2.
Buber, M. (1923). *I and Thou* (trans: Smith, R. G.). New York: Charles Scribner & Sons (English Edition).
Carnap, R. (1956). *Meaning and necessity*. London: Phoenix Books.
Coats, P. K. (1988). Why expert systems fail. *Financial Management, 17*(3), 77–86.
Collins, H. (1974). The TEA set: Tacit knowledge and scientific networks. *Science Studies, 4*, 165–186.
Collins, H. (1975). The seven sexes: A study in the sociology of a phenomenon or the replication of experiments in physics. *Sociology, 9*, 205–224.
Collins, H. (2013). *Tacit and explicit knowledge*. Chicago: University of Chicago Press.
Cooley, M. J. E. (1972). *Computer aided design, its nature and implications*. London: AUEW-TASS.
Cooley, M. J. E. (1987a). *Architect or bee*. London: Hogarth Press.
Cooley, M. J. E. (1987b). Human centred systems: An urgent problem for system's designers. *AI & Society, 1*, 37–46.
Cooley, M. J. E. (1991). *European competitiveness in the 21st century integration of work, culture and technology*. Brussels: Fast Commission of the European Communities.
Derrida. ([1967]/1978). *Writing and difference*. (trans: Bass, A.). Chicago: Chicago University Press (English Edition).
Descartes, R. (1639). In J. Cottingham (Ed.) (1996), *Meditations on first philosophy*. Cambridge: CUP.
Dewey, J. (1975). *Experience and education*. New York: Macmillan.
Dourish, P. (2004). *Where the action is. The foundations of embodied interaction*. Cambridge, MA: MIT Press (First paperback edition).

Dreyfus, H. L. (1972). *What computers can't do: A critique of artificial reason*. New York: Harper & Row.

Dreyfus, H. L. (1989). Is Socrates to Blaine for cognitivism? In B. Goranzon & M. Florin (Eds.), *Artificial intelligence, culture and language: On education and work* (pp. 219–228). London: Springer.

Dreyfus, H. L., & Dreyfus, E. (1986). *Mind over machine: The power of human intuition and expertise in the era of the computer*. New York: The Free Press.

Durkheim, É. (1933). *The division of labor in society* (trans: Simpson, G.). New York: Free Press.

Ehn, P. (1988). *Work oriented design of computer artifacts*. Stockholm: Arbetslivscentrum.

Ellis, W. D. (1938). *A source book of Gestalt psychology*. London: Routledge & Kegan Paul (includes an introduction by K. Koffka).

Fann, K. T. (1969). *Wittgenstein's conception of philosophy*. Oxford: Basil Blackwell.

Feigenbaum, E. A., & McCorduck, P. (1983). *The fifth generation*. Reading: Addison-Wesley.

Fodor, J. A. (1976). *The language of thought*. Sussex: The Harvester Press.

Fodor, J. A. (1981). *Representations: Philosophical essays on the foundations of cognitive science*. Brighton: Harvester Press.

Fodor, J. A., & Pylyshyn, Z. W. (1988). Connectionism and cognitive architecture: A critical analysis. *Cognition, 28*, 3–71.

Gadamer, H.-G. (1960). *Truth and method* (German: Wahrheit und Methode). *Truth and method* (2nd Ed.). London: Sheed and Ward, 1989, XXVIII.

Gammack, J. (1987). *Modelling expert knowledge structures using cognitively compatible structures*. Proceedings of the third international expert systems conference, London, pp. 191–200. Oxford: Learned Information (Europe) Ltd.

Gammack, J. G., Battle, S. A., & Stephens, R. A. (1989). A knowledge acquisition and representation scheme for constraint based and parallel systems. In *Proceedings of the IEEE conference on Systems Man and Cybernetics III,* Cambridge, MA, 1030–1035.

Gilbert, G. N., & Mulkay, M. (1984). *Opening Pandora's box: A sociological analysis of scientists' discourse*. Cambridge: Cambridge University Press.

Gill, K. S. (Ed.). (1986). *Artificial intelligence for society*. Chichester: Wiley.

Gill, S. P. (1988). On two AI traditions, *AI & Society, 2*(4), 321–340, London: Springer. NB. A version of this, S. P. Gill. (1988). '*Knowledge and skill transfer through expert systems: British and Scandinavian traditions*', is published in Research and Development in Expert Systems V: Proceedings of Expert Systems' 88. Cambridge: Cambridge University Press.

Gill, S. P. (1990, April). A dialogical framework for participatory KBS design. In *Proceedings Tenth European meeting on Cybernetics and Systems Research*, Vienna.

Gill, S. P. (1992). Dialogue and design of computer-based technology. In Y. Masuda (Ed.), *Human-centred systems in the global economy* (pp. 217–228). London: Springer. Gill SP, 1990.

Gill, S. P. (1995). Dialogue and tacit knowledge for knowledge transfer. PhD dissertation. University of Cambridge.

Gill, K. S. (Ed.). (1996). *Human machine symbiosis: The foundations of human-centred systems design*. London: Springer.

Gill, J. H. (2000). *The tacit mode. Michael Polanyi's postmodern philosophy*. New York: SUNY Press.

Göranzon, B. (1992a). *The practical intellect: Computers and skills*. London: Springer.

Göranzon, B. (1992b). The metaphor of Caliban in our technological culture. In B. Göranzon & F. Magnus (Eds.), *Skill and education: Reflection and experience* (Artificial Intelligence and Society series). London: Springer.

Göranzon, B., & Florin, M. (Eds.). (1991). *Dialogue and technology: Art and knowledge* (Artificial Intelligence and Society series). London: Springer.

Hall, E. T. (1976). *Beyond culture*. New York: Anchor Books.

Hart, A. (1986). *Knowledge acquisition for expert systems*. London: Kegan Page.

Hayes-Roth, F. (1984). The machine as a partner of the new professional. *IEEE Spectrum, 21*(6), 28–31.

Hayes-Roth, F. (1985). Knowledge-based expert systems: The state of the art in the US. *Knowledge Engineering Review, 1*, 18–27.

Hegel, F. G. (1977). *Phenomenology of spirit* (trans: Miller, A. V.). Oxford: Clarendon Press. (1807).

Heidegger, M. (1927). *Being and time*, a translation of Sein und Zeit. SUNY Press. 1996.

Henle, M. (1961). *Documents of Gestalt psychology*. Berkeley: University of California, University of Cambridge.

Hume, D. (1748). In T. L. Beauchamp (Ed.) (1999) *An enquiry concerning human understanding*. Oxford: Oxford University Press.

Husserl. (1931). *Cartesian meditations*, a translation of Meditations cartésiennes, D. Cairns. Dordrecht: Kluwer. 1988.

Ikuta, K. (1990). The role of "craft language" in learning "Waza". *AI & Society, 4*(2), 137–146.

Janik, A. (1988). Tacit knowledge, working life and scientific methods. In B. Goranzon & I. Josefson (Eds.), *Knowledge, skill and artificial intelligence*. Artificial Intelligence and Society Series. London: Springer.

Janik, A. (1991). Reflections on dialogue. In B. Goranzon & M. Florin (Eds.), *Dialogue and technology: Art and knowledge* (Artificial Intelligence and Society Series). London: Springer.

Janik, A. (1992). Why is Wittgenstein important. In B. Göranzon & M. Florin (Eds.), *Skill and education: Reflection and experience*. London: Springer.

Johannessen, K. (1981). Language, art and aesthetic practice. In K. Johannessen & T. Nordenstam (Eds.), *Wittgenstein – Aesthetics and transcendental philosophy*. Vienna: Holder-Pichler-Temsky.

Johannessen, K. (1988a). Rule following and tacit knowledge. *AI & Society, 2*(4), 287–301. Springer.

Johannessen, K. (1988b). The concept of practice in Wittgenstein's later philosophy. *Inquiry, 31*(3), 357–369.

Johannessen, K. (1992). Rule-following, intransitive understanding, and tacit knowledge. An investigation of the Wittgensteinian concept of practice as regards tacit knowing. In B. Göranzon & F. Magnus (Eds.), *Skill and education: Reflection and experience* (pp. 41–63). London: Springer.

Johannessen, K., & Nordenstam, T. (Eds.) (1981). *Wittgenstein – Aesthetics and transcendental philosophy*. Vienna: Holder-Pichler-Temksy.

Johnson-Laird, P. N. (1983). *Mental models: Towards a cognitive science of language, inference, and consciousness*. Cambridge: Cambridge University Press.

Johnson-Laird, P. N. (1993). *The computer and the mind: An introduction to cognitive science* (2nd ed.). London: Fontana.

Jones, M., & Walsham, G. (1992). The limits of the knowable: Organizational and knowledge in systems development. In K. E. Kendall, K. Lyytmenk, & J. De Gross (Eds.), *The impact of computer supported technologies on information systems development*. North Holland: Elsevier Science.

Josefson, I. (1988a). The nurse as engineer- the theory of knowledge in research in the care sector. In B. Göranzon & F. Magnus (Eds.), *Skill and education: Reflection and experience*. London: Springer.

Josefson, I. (1988b). The nurse as an engineer. *AI & Society, 1*(2), 115–126.

Josefson, I. (1992). Language and experience. In B. Göranzon & M. Florin (Eds.), *Skill and education: Reflection and experience*. London: Springer.

Kant, I. (1929). *Critique of pure reason*. New York: St. Martin's Press.

Kidd, A. L. (Ed.). (1987). *Knowledge acquisition for expert systems: A practical handbook*. New York: Plenum Press.

Kidd, A. L., & Wellbank, M. (1984). Knowledge acquisition. In Fox (Ed.), *InfoTech state of the art report on expert systems*. Pergamon: InfoTech.

Kierkegaard, S. (1971). *Either/or: A fragment of life*, tr. Howard A Johnson. New York: Doubleday. (1843).

Kowalski, R. (1974). Predicate logic as a programming language. In *Proceedings of IFIP '74*.

Kowalski, R. (1982). Logic as computer language. In Clark & Tarnland (Eds.), *Logic programming* (pp. 2–16). London: Academic.

Leibniz, G. W. (1666). Dissertatio de Arte Combinatoria, G. Phil. University of Leipzig.

Leith, P. (1988). The application of AI to law. *AI & Society, 2*(1), 31–46.

Lipscombe, B. (1989). Expert systems and computer controlled decision-making in medicine. *AI & Society, 3*, 184–197. London: Springer-Verlag.

Merleau-Ponty, M. (1945). *Phenomenology of perception* (trans: Smith, C.). London: Routledge and Kegan Paul. (1962).

Michie, D., & Johnston, R. (1984). *The creative computer*. Middlesex: Penguin.

Minsky, M. (1963). Steps towards AI. In E. A. Feigenbaum & J. Feldman (Eds.), *Computers and thought* (pp. 95–128). New York: McGraw-Hill.

Needham, J. (1927). *Man a machine*. London: Kegan Paul.

Newell, A. (1980). Physical symbol systems. *Cognitive Science, 4*, 135–183.

Newell, A. (1981). The heuristic of George Polya and its relation to artificial intelligence. In R. Groner, M. Groner, & W. F. Bischoof (Eds.), *Methods of heuristics*. Hillsdale: Lawrence Erlbaum Press.

Newell, A., & Simon, H. A. (1972). *Human problem solving*. Englewood Cliffs: Prentice Hall.

Nietzsche, F. (1961). *Thus spoke Zarathustra* (trans: Hollingdale, R. J.), Penguin.

Nordenstam, T. (1968). *Sudanese ethics*. Uppsala: Scandinavian Institute of African Studies.

Nordenstam, T. (1987). On moral rules and paradigms. In *Archivo Di Filosophia*.

Nordenstam, T. (1992). Language and action. In B. Goranzon & M. Florin (Eds.), *Artificial intelligence, culture and language: On education and work*. London: Springer-Verlag.

Nordenstam, T. (2013). Practical knowledge and ethics. *AI & Society, 28*(4), 377–382. London: Springer.

Nussbaum, M. (1980). On Aristophanes and Socrates on learning practical wisdom. *Yale Classical Studies, 26*, 43–97.

Olson, J. R., & Rueter, H. H. (1987). Extracting expertise from experts: Methods for knowledge acquisition. *Expert Systems, 4*(3), 152–168.

Ostberg, O., Whitaker, R., & Amick, B. (1988). *The automated expert: Technical, human and organisational considerations in expert systems applications*. Sweden: Teldok.

Partridge, D. (1987). Human decision making and the symbolic search space paradigm in AL. *AI & Society, 1*, 103–114.

Perby, M. L. (1990). The inner picture. In B. Goranzon & M. Florin (Eds.), *Artificial intelligence, culture and language: On education and work* (pp 77–82). Springer.

Plato. (1975). *The Republic* (trans: Desmond Lee), 2nd Edn. (revised). Middlesex, England: Penguin.

Polanyi, M. (1962). *Personal knowledge: Towards a post critical philosophy. (Reprint of 1958 version with corrections)*. London: Routledge and Kegan Paul.

Polanyi, M. (1966). *The tacit dimension*. Doubleday. 1983 Reprint.

Polanyi, M. (1969). *Knowing and being*. London: Routledge & Kegan Paul.

Polya, G. (1945). *How to solve it*. Princeton: Princeton University Press.

Pylyshyn, Z. W. (1984). *Computation and cognition. Towards a foundation for cognitive science*. Cambridge, MA: MIT Press.

Rauner, F., Rasmussen, L. B., & Corbett, M. (1987). *The social shaping of technology and work*. Bremen: Universitet Bremen, Institut Technik & Bildung.

Rector, A. L. (1989). Helping with a humanly impossible task: Integrating knowledge based systems into clinical care. SCAI 1989, 453–465, Tampere, Finland.

Rector, A. L. (1990). Integrating knowledge based systems into medical practice. ECAI 1990: 531–534, Stockholm, Sweden.

Rosenbrock, H. (1977). The future of control. *Automatica, 13*, 389–392.

Rosenbrock, H. (1988). Engineering as an art. *AI & Society, 2*, 315–320. Springer.

Rosenbrock, H. (Ed.). (1989). *Designing human-centred technology: A cross disciplinary project in computer-aided manufacturing*. London: Springer.

Rosenbrock, H. (Ed.). (1990). *Machines with a purpose*. Oxford: Oxford University Press.

Rosenbrock, H. (1992). Science, technology and purpose. *AI & Society, 6*, 3–17.

Rumelhart, D. E., & Norman, D. A. (Eds.). (1986). *Parallel distributed processing: Explorations in the microstructure of cognition, vol. 1: Foundations; vol. 2: Psychological and biological models.* Cambridge, MA: MIT Press.

Ryle, G. (1949). *The concept of mind.* London: Hutchinson.

Sartre, J. P. (1943). *Being and nothingness: An essay in phenomenological ontology* (trans: Barnes, H. E.). New York: Philosophical Library.

Schaffer, S. (1999). Enlightened automata. In W. Clark, J. Golinski, & S. Schaffer (Eds.), *The sciences in enlightened Europe.* Chicago: Chicago University Press.

Searle, J. R. (1980). Minds, brains, and programs. *Behavioural and Brain Sciences, 3*(3), 417–457.

Searle, J. R. (1990). Cognitive science and computer metaphor. In B. Göranzon & M. Florin (Eds.), *Artificial intelligence, culture and language: On education and work* (pp. 23–35). London: Springer.

Shannon, C., & Weaver, W. (1949). *The mathematical theory of communication.* Urbana: University of Illinois Press.

Simon, H. (1985). Human nature in politics: The dialogue of psychology with political science. *American Political Science Review, 79*, 293–304.

Sloman, A. (1989). The evolution of Pop-II at Sussex University. In J. A. D. W. Anderson (Ed.), *Pop-II comes of age: The advancement of an AI programming language* (pp. 30–54). Chichester: Ellis Horwood.

Sprague, R. H., & Watson, H. J. (Eds.). (1986). *Decision support systems.* Englewood Cliffs: Prentice-Hall, Simon & Schuster.

Susskind, R. E. (1989). *Expert systems in law: A jurisprudential inquiry.* Oxford: Clarendon Press.

Toulmin, S. (1991). The dream of an exact language. In B. Goranzon & M. Florin (Eds.), *Dialogue and technology* (pp. 33–43). London: Springer.

Varela, F. J. (1988). *Cognitive science: A cartography of current ideas.* Paris: Editions du Seuil.

Varela, F. J., Thompson, E. T., & Rosch, E. (1991). *The embodied mind.* Cambridge, MA: MIT Press.

Whitaker, R., & Ostberg, O. (1988). Channelling knowledge: Expert systems as communication media. *AI & Society, 2*, 197–208.

Wiener, N. (1949). *Cybernetics, or control and communication in the animal and the machine.* New York: Wiley.

Winch, P. (1958). *The idea of a social science and its relation to philosophy.* London: Routledge & Kegan Paul.

Wittgenstein, L. (1958). *Philosophical investigations* (trans: Anscombe, G. E. M.). Oxford: Basil Blackwell.

Wittgenstein, L. (1977). In G. E. M. Anscombe (Ed.), *Remarks on colour* (trans: McAlister, L. L. & Scattle, M.). Oxford: Blackwell.

Woolgar, S. (1988). *Science, the very idea.* Chichester: Ellis Horwood.

Chapter 3
Knowledge Is Skilled Performance

Abstract This chapter applies ideas from Chap. 2 about knowledge and practice, by investigating expertise and knowledge as embodied human expertise. It discusses various case studies and corporeality in human sense-making. It investigates how knowledge is embodied in how we perform when we communicate, exchange ideas, present information to each other, train and learn, and become skilled. How we relate with others is a skilled performance.

3.1 Introduction

In this chapter we consider four ideas in the investigation of tacit knowing as a personal act of knowing: (a) I know what I know and can talk about it because I have become skilled in performing it. (i.e. It's not in my head); (b) with my imagination, I build a picture of the knowledge; (c) the identification of a problem that needs to be solved is not necessarily done by the 'expert' but by a mediator of the problem, however, only the expert can recognise the mediator and solve the problem; (d) I realise my knowing in my co-performance with you: knowledge cannot live outside dialogue, and dialogue is skilled performance, and since knowledge is carried in dialogue, knowledge is skilled performance. The discussion critiques the dominant model of expertise that has as its premise the concept of the autonomous expert. We engage in the world as skilled performers within context and culture.

Some may argue that we have moved beyond the expert systems model, and many of the researchers who were involved in the knowledge engineering field have moved to other research areas, yet the concept and the researchers who created it, along with those who still do so, has left a legacy that underlies the large scale data bases in our organisations both in the private and public sector. Bank managers in the UK's major high street banks are now constrained by computerised decision making systems, and if they seek to override the system's decision for a client whom they have formed a judgement about that conflicts with the digital system, they need to find a human in the system to talk to. I have had discussions with senior bank managers who lament the loss of being able to enforce their own judgements, and have experienced junior managers who do not think to question the computerised

© Springer International Publishing Switzerland 2015
S.P. Gill, *Tacit Engagement*, DOI 10.1007/978-3-319-21620-1_3

system's decision but simply input the 'relevant' data and inform you of its outcome. A few years ago, one trainee bank manager told me he was so disillusioned by this computerisation of skill that he was leaving and going to do something that made more use of his intelligence.

'The collectivity rather than the individual is the location of the knowledge' (Collins 2013). Collins critique of how far tacit knowledge (Polanyi 1966) can be made into explicit knowledge and finds the limits to be in the irreducibility of what he calls the 'collective'. By this he means culture, that includes how we make *social judgements* about balancing individual and social responsibility; about how the *right way* to do things can only be captured through experience (and not through rules). The knowledge based systems project reduced the collective to the individual and the individual to the cognitive.

ET Hall (1976) describes the process of culture in his ground breaking research on cross-cultural communication, and in contrast to Collins he believes that culture (our own and thât which is not ours) must be made explicit if we are to avoid collisions and conflicts. However, when Hall speaks about making culture 'explicit', he does not mean this in the sense of the juxtaposition of the tacit and explicit posed by the computer, but rather in terms of human conscious awareness.

> What gives man his identity is his culture, the total communication framework; words, actions, postures, gestures, tones of voice, facial expressions, the way he handles time, space, and materials, and the way he works, plays, makes love and defends himself. All these things and more are complete communications systems with meanings that can be read correctly only if one is familiar with the behaviour in its historical, social, and cultural context,… once learned, these behaviour patterns, these habitual responses, these ways of interaction, gradually sink below the surface of the mind. … the hidden controls are usually experienced as though they were innate simply because they are not only ubiquitous but habitual as well. …… What makes it hard to differentiate the innate from the acquired is the fact that, as people grow up everyone around them shares the same patterns. (Hall 1976, p. 42)

In an increasingly globalised world, for many of us who have grown up in a bicultural or tricultural situation, speaking more than one language accustoms us to the fact that people are really very different in the ways they behave, as Hall observes in his example of watching people shifting "from a Spanish to a German way of interacting without their knowing that the shift occurred." Those of us who speak more than one language experience how our gestures, our vocal intonations and accents change when we switch languages. The practice of language carries the trace of cultural behaviours, and as societies become more multicultural there is a behavioural adaptation with the mainstream culture. Efron's study (1941) of the minority communities in New York in the 1940s, particularly Italian and Jewish, showed that there is a differentiation between the groups of the later generations, but not between these groups and the evolving mainstream New York culture. Efron was concerned to show that the environment shapes cultural behaviour, that culture is not innate. In his research, he finds features of gestural communication that are motivated by processes in other behavioural patterns of the community to which the gestures belong. For example, he identifies a number of gestural acts that he calls hybrid gestures. This is the combination of elements peculiar to the gestures of traditional individuals of

Jewish or Italian communities with elements found in the gestures of Americans of Anglo-Saxon descent. From these findings, Efron concludes that,

> the same individual may, if simultaneously exposed over a period of time to two or more gesturally different groups, adopt and combine certain gestural traits of both groups.

Efron compares a hybrid gesturer to a bilingual person who *retains the characteristics of their first language in their performance in the second language.* He found that the assimilated Eastern Jews and Southern Italians in New York City differed from their respective traditional groups and resembled each other. The gestural characteristics of the first generation of Jews and Italians gradually disappeared with the social assimilation of individual Jews and Italians into the Americanised community which was also evolving with their assimilation. Efron concludes that 'gestural behaviour, or the absence of it, is to some extent at least, conditioned by factors of a socio-psychological nature'. One could say that the hybrid gesturer, the person with multi-cultural identity, inhabits a cultural space of betweenness.

Efron's work is the first major study of the hidden rules of gesture and culture, and remains a landmark study of the hybrid identity of multicultural persons. It touches on a starting point of my own research life, to understand how my culturally hybrid self affects how I can know that I have understood you, and how I can know that you have understood me.

Hall refers to Power's work on perception and feedback (1973), that addresses how 'man's nervous system is structured in such a way that the patterns that govern behavior and perception come into consciousness only when there is a deviation from plan." (Hall 1976, p. 43) In our everyday lives, we only become aware of 'hidden' rules when someone does not follow them, for example if I reach out my hand to shake yours and you move forwards to kiss my cheek, our greeting will be amusingly awkward. The examples that Hall unfolds for us have more serious consequences. Such hidden rules of culture may be described as *rule-following* (Johannessen 1988),[1] which is a way of doing, whereby the application of a rule is dependent on the situation of the person(s). Our practice shows how we understand something.

Collins (op. cit.) uses the examples of riding a bike, driving a car and dancing, amongst other activities, to explain how culture involves the kind of understanding needed to negotiate one's way through traffic (e.g. on a bike or in a car) and knowing how to improvise on a dance step: "Negotiating traffic ... includes understanding social conventions of traffic management and personal interaction such as knowing how to make eye contact with drivers in heavy traffic in just the way necessary to assure a safe passage and not to invite an unwanted response. And it involves understanding how differently these conventions will be executed in different locations." Riding a bike in London will be quite a different experience to riding a bike

---

[1] See Chap. 2 for a summary of Johannessen's discussion of Wittgenstein's philosophy on rule and rule-following. It can simply be understood as: a rule is abstracted from the situation, whilst rule-following is how one behaves in the situation.

in Delhi, and within the UK, riding a bicycle in Cambridge is different from a small country village, and further still, the specific context of riding a bicycle will shape the riding style ('display of skill') e.g. going to work through traffic or out across country on a cycling race. And he extends this analogy of culture and the conventions of riding a bike, to that of driving a car. In Italy drivers pass the responsibility for safety to other drivers, they expect the unexpected and cope with it well. This makes it much easier for you to drive as an individual since you do not have to do everything "according to the book" and Collins calls this 'diver collectivism'. In contrast, British and American drivers in Britain or America must take much more responsibility for smooth traffic flow, and tend to meet violations from the rules of this flow with expressions of rage. Collins makes an interesting point that relates to what Hall says about making the hidden rules explicit. He does not consider these descriptions to comprise a set of rules for driving in the countries he describes.

In all the countries there is a form of 'collective responsibility', for example in Britain and America if drivers resolutely ran over anyone who stepped into the road or crashed into any car that broke a rule, there would be chaos. What is required in every case is a social judgement about how individual responsibility and social responsibility are to be balanced and the right way to do things cannot be captured in any description on the page. The *right way to do things* can only be captured through experience, and that experience and its application vary from country to country. The explication of the way such things are captured through experience is the socialization problem.

At some level both Hall and Collins share the need to describe our behaviour in order to understand how we are social beings; the difference is that Collins places the limit to description at the level of experiencing, whilst for Hall the details of experiencing need to be made visible in order to handle these cultural differences in a way that facilitates the experiencing within the life world of the cultures one is engaging in.

3.2   Somatics and Skill

"Negotiating traffic is a different problem to balancing on a bike" (Collins op. cit.). Why, and is this the case? The distinction that Collins is making is between what he categorises as 'collective tacit knowledge' and 'somatic tacit knowledge'. He claims that the 'somatic body' can be made into explicit knowledge, whereas collective tacit knowledge cannot. He presents the example of the android named 'Data' in the American Science Fiction series called Star Trek: The Next Generation. Data is being taught dance steps by a Dr. Crusher which he is able to immediately repeat without making any mistakes. Collins argues that us humans would need to practice such dance steps in order to be able to repeat them without making mistakes, and he calls this acquiring somatic tacit knowledge. Data 'has the kind of quick brain' that could learn how to balance on a bike just as easily as he could learn dance steps. A quick brain is aligned with a 'somatic limit'.

As Data is so good at repeating the dance steps, Dr. Crusher suggests he improvises with the ones he has learnt in order to be able to 'dance with verve' i.e. some style. And he does. For Collins, this is where 'Star Trek' goes wrong as improvisation is a skill requiring the kind of tacit knowledge than can only be acquired through social embedding in society. Social sensibility is needed to know that one innovative dance step counts as an improvisation while another counts as foolish, dangerous, or ugly, and the difference may be a matter of changing fashions, your dancing partner, and location. Social sensibility does not come from having a quickly calculating brain, it comes through having the kind of brain that can absorb social rules.

Whilst agreeing with Collins that Star Trek has got it wrong about the android's ability to improvise, I would also suggest that he has got it wrong in assuming that the somatic dance step can be considered apart from the improvisatory dance step. Putting the example of the android aside, when we learn a dance step, that step improves as we perform it, and each rehearsal of the step improves it. The first part of the process of becoming skilled in practice is to learn the techniques (techne), and then with practice in rehearsal and performance the step becomes a skilled step, as the dancer embodies the step and it becomes part of their person. Collins is assuming that a dance step is something that can be abstracted from its purposive evolution into skilled performance, which is necessarily in relation to other people, whether these people are one's teacher, one's fellow dancers, and one's audience.

In traditional dance such as ballet where there is a clear repertoire of dance steps, would a ballet dancer be considered as only having somatic tacit knowledge but not collective tacit knowledge as they do not improvise on these steps? The more experience they have of performing their steps, the more skillfully will they execute each step. The mastery of a movement has been beautifully illustrated by Ikuta (1990; see Chap. 2) where she describes how a Noh actress acquires the skill of performing the act of reaching out her hand to catch a snow flake, firstly by learning the precise movement as instructed, then over time using her imagination and placing her person into the act so that it becomes her movement. In their skilled performance of a dance step and the movement of catching a snow flake, the ballet dancer and the Noh performer share the quality of skill essential for improvisation, that of embodying the action with their person, i.e. a personal act of knowing.

Dancing is highly cultural and about communication. In some parts of the world, there is no distinction between the word for dance and for music, and it is part of the rituals that socialise you into the culture. Collins' claim that the somatic body is something that could be made explicit is problematic as it fragments the body from the person and the culture of the practice, and this has implications for the consequences of its mechanisation.

A more interesting and useful question that he poses is to ask, by what mechanism do humans stay in touch with society and how can one build a machine to do that?

3.3 Social Beings

Understanding what makes us social beings is studied extensively across anthropology, social sciences, and music. Our social behaviour is dominated by 'complex hierarchies of interlocking rhythms' and in studies undertaken by Hall and his students (op. cit.), such interlocking rhythms have been likened to a symphonic score (Hall 1983). These rhythms, he suggests, hold the key to the interpersonal processes between 'mates, co-workers, and organizations of all types on the interpersonal level and across cultural boundaries'. Rhythms express the truth of interpersonal encounters.

Even how close we stand with each other is expressed in rhythm, notable when adjusting to cultural difference. Hall called this the proxemic dance (Hall op. cit.). A study of conversing 'Americans and Mediterranean peoples', discovered that distances were maintained with accuracy to 'a fraction of an inch', and the process was rhythmic. People adjusted their distances approximately every 30 s.

In studies on group synchrony, one of Hall's students found that children in a playground were all playing in synchrony with each other. On close scrutiny, it emerged that one active girl was skipping and dancing all around the playground, and whenever she came near a cluster of children they would synchronise to her. This girl was 'orchestrating' the movements of the playground.

These examples give us a glimpse into how much rhythm is part of our co-existence and survival as growing children and as adults. If we do not have this survival skill we become isolated. Hall proposed that depression may have its roots in the person who is out of sync in deep and basic ways.

Hall (1976, 1990) found that each culture he investigated had its own beat, tempo, and rhythm. Furthermore, that the behaviours of people embodied the culturally based intervals for corrective action that affect how we connect at the emotional level. For example, the Spanish of New Mexico keep close tabs on each other's emotions so that even slight variations are immediately detected and commented on. This short interval or short cycle on feedback, can create volatility. Anglo Saxons have a long time interval, long feedback cycle, taking mood shifts for granted and avoiding interfering or intervening in others lives. People frequently feel they are alone and that it is right and proper they should be able to solve their own problems. When things go wrong it only becomes obvious when it is out of hand.

Rhythm is a powerful dimension of identity and culture. The proxemics example of people adjusting a fraction of an inch at a time to cultural differences in proximity whilst moving every 30 s around a room as they are standing and talking, illustrates the power of interpersonal synchrony but also shows what happens when this lacks mutual adaptation of the cultural embodiment of space. Hall found that few people can function unless it is within the limits of their own rhythm system (culture). He addressed the need for differing rhythm cycles of cultural identity to calibrate especially in cross-cultural communication, and that if different systems are not calibrated, unless a deliberate and successful effort is made to bring them into phase, the interaction could be problematic.

The everyday act of a human greeting is incredibly complex and rooted in the rhythms of culture. We shake hands, hug each other, kiss on cheeks, etc. Greetings are highly culturally variable (Duranti 1997; Garrick Mallery 1891): Maori rub noses, Russians kiss on the mouth, and Japanese bow. But universally, irrespective of culture, these bodily acts are about gauging one person's sense of another. Greetings are essential to giving us a chance to trust in the communication that will unfold and affords us time to achieve the possibility of mutual synchrony later in that unfolding (Condon 1970). The greeting is a parallel coordinated act, and the mutual synchrony of body and voice in greetings expresses "a commitment to communicate" that may be likened to a form of phatic communion (Malinowski 1923) for social bonding.

In the field of music psychology, Cross's works on music and sociality (Cross and Woodruff 2009; Cross 2006), music and evolution (Cross 2011), and music perception proposes that music is fundamentally social and bodily, and that the relation between music and movement in time is evolutionary and cognitive. This relation shapes our capacity to both perceive and anticipate when an event, be this a gesture or vocalisation, is going to occur, and to mutually respond to it in coordinated time. Cross has developed the concept of 'floating intentionality', which brings together the idea of shared intentionality from pragmatics in language (Sperber and Wilson 1986) and intentionality from a musical context, that is intrinsic to both these domains. He makes the distinction that language is primarily transactional and music relational (Cross 2011).

Linguistic models focus primarily on turn-taking structures that can be considered outside the dynamics of experiencing in time. Recently, Levinson (2006), director of the Max Planck Institute for Psycholinguistics, has begun to build a bridge between music and language that considers the temporal dynamics of the turn-taking structure as possibly facilitating the rhythmicity in speech and also orienting us towards a positive convergent outcome.

If knowledge is skilled performance, and dialogue is skilled performance, and skilled performance is rhythmic, and knowledge is formed and shared in dialogue, then knowledge is carried in rhythm.

3.4   Data and Dialogue

In the last chapter, the expert system provided an extreme example of the cognitivist paradigm of human knowledge and skill against which to explore the limits of this paradigm for capturing tacit knowledge (cf. Polanyi 1966).

The discussion below will collapse the distinctions made between *knowledge* and *skill* that consider these as distinct ways of knowing, by considering knowledge as skilled performance where *skilled performance is dialogue*. The meaning of data and information, the role of imagination and reflection, and the use of language to express oneself, will be explored through various case studies.

Following my apprenticeship with the Swedish Centre for Working Life (SCWL) in the late 1980s I undertook some case studies of skilled performance in different areas of 'expertise'. The first study was about creating a knowledge base for consultancy practice. As a result of presenting a paper about tacit knowledge at a British AI conference (Expert Systems, Gill 1988), the chairman of the conference session invited me to join a workshop on consultancy organised by his consultancy company. The workshop formed part of a comprehensive process that sought to transform the company's corporate identity. This was a large multinational, and at that time its members did not have a corporate concept of 'consultant'. They performed in their jobs as 'experts' in specific areas of work, e.g. financial, engineering, etc. However, to keep up with the times and be competitive, the company decided to develop the concept of consultancy and reconstruct its identity. This necessitated asking its highly skilled 'experts' to articulate and think of themselves as 'consultants', something they were unfamiliar with seeing themselves as. My role was to 'elicit' the tacit dimension of their knowledge formation as they underwent this process in the workshop. The ultimate goal was to develop an interactive and intelligent multi-modal knowledge based system for training experts to become consultants. Unfortunately, it was not possible to video or audio tape any of the interactions due to sensitivity and confidentiality. During my week with these experts (sales, engineering, marketing, top management, computing, etc.), I experienced many forms of expression of practice and experience being used to build the identity of 'consultancy', such as role play, cartoons, metaphors and video film. The following is an example of 'consultancy' performance that took place during the week long consultancy workshop.

3.5   What Does It Mean to Be a Consultant?

A group of four upper-middle and senior management practitioners (experts in their fields) are giving a presentation of about 20 min each. They are seated around a table and are provided with an overhead projector to use. Each is given the task to present themselves to the others as a consultant and talk about what a consultant is, and sell the idea of consultancy to them. I was invited to observe the proceedings of the workshop.

The first 'consultant' dressed in a suit and tie, stands facing the group and presents a 'tool kit' of consultancy using the overhead slides. This toolkit essentially consists of a list of propositional statements – descriptors, definitions and rules. After a few minutes this consultant has to stop giving his presentation, saying he has lost the thread of information, i.e. the connection between himself and the information he has been presenting.

The second 'consultant' dressed more casually but smart, also stands and speaks of how consultants 'pull rabbits out of hats' whilst presenting hand drawn overheads of a rabbit being pulled out of a hat and one with the word 'magic' in large letters. His forms of expression disturb his 'clients' who accuse him of mocking their profession and expertise in what they see as his portrayal of them as insincere or dishonest. His expressions make them unreceptive to his 'content'.

The third consultant also dressed casually but smart, stands and speaks about rules or conduct and emphasises the good things a consultant does. His handwritten overheads are measured and consistently paced. He is perceived as sincere and the others feel he understands them and supports them.

All these three 'consultants' had stood and presented overheads. The fourth consultant remains seated but places himself on the other side of the table to the other three, facing them. He begins to tell them a confidential story of some political rumblings at the top of their corporation. This consultant is very high up in the organisational structure hence he has an authentic voice on these matters. The others become troubled and deeply involved in unravelling the story trying to find out as much as they can and work out the nature of the problem. After 20 min, this fourth consultant breaks the illusion of reality and tells them it was all a story. This is a disorienting experience for the others and they are very impressed by what he had done with them. It was of great interest to me, for this fourth consultant had fully engaged his 'clients' in the performance of *practical knowledge* where their *experiential knowing* immersed with his and with each other's. It was powerful acting with *audience co-performance*.

The second consultant who is seen to offend the others' moral well-being has in fact given a sound presentation at the level of content. The chairman of the workshop session later showed me the copy of the overheads by this consultant pointing out that there was actually nothing offensive or wrong in what he was saying. The problem had lain in how he had presented the content and how he was perceived as a person. The third consultant provided the feeling of safety and comfort in his use of moral and ethical forms of expression and a calm, paced voice. He was described as genuine.

In all these performances, the posture, position and clothing of the performers in relation to their 'clients' set the stage. If the forms of expression were not embodied (e.g. first consultant), the performance failed, and if the forms of expression did not meet the perceptions of self (e.g. of the moral position of the client as in the case of the second consultant), there was breakdown in the communication process.

This study (Gill 1995) made it clear to me that what someone knows is expressed in their performance of knowing, hence the study of the tacit dimension of knowledge needs to be considered as a process within dialogue itself, and not outside of it.

3.6 Knowledge as Skilled Performance in Dialogue: Underwriters Making Judgements

This was reinforced by the second case study which took the form of an informal interview with an expert and a novice underwriter, where I applied ideas about how to engage with 'eliciting' the tacit through and within dialogue, where dialogue is the method and the observation. This second study (Gill 1995) is of a dialogue with underwriters as they are evaluating insurance applications, and it is taking place at their company.

In the Spring of 1989 I was invited to Bristol by researchers (with Bristol University) who were developing a data base for underwriters that could process applications for life insurance policies. The work on the data base was becoming cumbersome and the processing of all the possible data input categories was creating bottlenecks. The relationship between the knowledge engineers and the underwriters had followed a one way flow, of the knowledge engineers eliciting knowledge from the underwriters using methods from cognitive psychology. The communication was largely functional. I requested to be alone with the 'experts', in order to avoid them making associations between myself and what I may be wanting from them, and what the knowledge engineers had been seeking from them. I had the opportunity to talk with a senior underwriter and a junior underwriter for a couple of hours. We sat at a table, with myself seated on one side and they on the other, facing me. They had brought along a set of application forms with them that they laid on the table, and were curious about my presence. I told them that I was not there to extract any information out of them but that I wanted to learn about what they do and spoke a bit about my interest in the tacit and experiential dimension of human knowledge and skill. They were interested and began to talk about their skill, explaining to me what they do by going through each of the forms and thinking aloud as they analysed them. The dialogue was that of a senior expert teaching and imparting his skill to his junior colleague, and to me. As they worked through the information on the forms they built up a clear *picture* of each person represented there and *imagined* their past and future lives, their habits, lifestyles, personalities, values, etc. On the basis of these imaginings they formed judgements as to whether this was someone who could or could not qualify for a certain type of life insurance policy. The experiential knowledge and imagination of the senior underwriter was made available to the imagination and knowledge of his junior colleague who could then follow and work with him to understand the personality and life-style of their applicants.

It was clear from this 2 h session that there was no one salient procedure of data processing that could be applied to each form, as each person (each applicant or rather each completed application form) presented a different picture of salient information for the underwriters. It would be problematic to predefine rules for connecting the categories of data on the forms (processing the data) that are rooted outside 'relevance', i.e. outside how the information on the form is meaningful to the underwriter in building a picture of a person.

There are two problems here and they relate to the idea of not being able to see the wood for the trees. If one functions at the level of data and procedures, then one builds composites, but these composites may not form a wholeness, instead they may simply remain a collection of parts. It is the human who can make the wholeness by applying experiential knowing and imagination, but the skill of achieving this may become lost if the system automates the expert's creation of the applicant as the composition of parts. There are undoubtedly corporate factors (around risk and profit) which shape the imaginative construction of the client, but these are not the foci of the analysis. This experience took me back to my early conversation with my Scandinavian mentors about what role imagination, experience, and culture plays in human knowledge. One study by the SCWL group that bears directly on the work with the underwriters is Maja Lisa-Perby's study (1990) of how weather forecasters form an inner weather picture when they make weather forecasts.

3.7 Inner Weather Picture: Weather Forecasters

Perby studied the skill of meteorologists and investigated the reliability of forecasting by computers compared to forecasting by meteorologists. This study was undertaken in the early stages of the use of computers for numerical forecasting and for automating map plotting. They were being used as it was assumed by management that the computer would help to make forecasting more efficient, due to a belief that the weather forecasting is a process of calculating data.

Perby investigated how the use of these numerical forecasts was affecting the tacit knowledge of the meteorologists, and why given the huge increase in the availability of data, there was too much and not enough relevant data at the same time. Her study focuses on a group of meteorologists at an airport, where they are providing the local weather forecasts for pilots. The computers were making numerical forecasts based on mathematical models that could predict large scale weather for up to 10 days ahead. They provided on average, forecasts for up to 12–24 h ahead. For the meteorologists, this was not sufficient for making local weather forecasts which need to be made within 9 h ahead. They found their traditional methods of analysing the weather more effective for this purpose, and this is what Perby's study is about. Her argument is that computer solutions tend to be general and standardised whilst skilled work is formed by concrete and specific circumstances. The interest I have in her study is the role of imagination in making the weather forecasts.

Meteorologists look for patterns in weather. Through an integration of information and experiences (for example from colleagues and pilots) presented to them, they build an inner weather picture. This involves assimilating the information, and that gained from personal contact, e.g. with pilots, facilitates them in assimilating other information, even though it is a small percentage of the overall information used. Traditionally the meteorologists have used historical information/observations in their analysis and prediction of the weather. This includes being briefed by their colleagues when they take over the work shift. This briefing provides a 'sign-post'. Their colleague(s) also draws up synoptical maps during his/her own working shift. 'Synoptical' means that the observations are made at the same point of time at all places. The meteorologist also interprets the information against a theoretical model of the strata of the atmosphere. In contrast to the meteorologist, the computerised numerical forecasts contain future oriented information which does not enable the building of an inner weather picture. Hence, even though the availability of information increased with technology, much of it was of no use to the meteorologist.

Traditionally the meteorologist draws up synoptical maps every 3 h to form a sequence of maps in order to gain an insight into weather movement. The numerical forecasts produced every 12–24 h did not provide the detailed and precise information that was obtained from the synoptical maps. This caused the meteorologist problems in interpreting the numerical forecast as each model could be suitable for depicting some weather conditions and not other weather conditions. The meteorologist therefore has to gain experience over a period of, on average, a year in order to be able to use a particular model effectively for predicting the weather. Furthermore, they have to cope with an additional problem: the numerical meteorologists keep developing new models. This does not allow the meteorologist to get experience of the models and poses problems for interpreting the information and producing reliable forecasts.

The meteorologists in Perby's study resisted changes that undermined their ability to come up with an inner weather picture. They resisted a division of labour between making and communicating the weather, because this would require the meteorologist who is responsible for briefing to take over a ready made analysis and render him/her unable to form an inner weather picture. Meteorologists also resisted the idea that the synoptical map they produce is a product rather than a working material; they defended the active assimilation of information about various weather elements as opposed to passive reception of a lot of information. An active analysis guarantees a certain depth in the interpretation of the information.

The study was a project between Lund University and the local weather forecasting service at Stirrup. Perby's study showed that increased information through computerisation did not mean greater reliability in decision making. In weather forecasting, skill lies in the ability to select and interpret information, and using historical material to build an inner weather picture. In order to build such a picture, the meteorologists spent time reflecting and digesting the information. Computerisation and cost 'efficient' methods placed less importance on reflection and therefore on the processes of understanding which is facilitated through a variety of sources of knowledge such as talking to colleagues over tea and communicating with pilots. Perby's expectation was that the systematisation of the practice of weather forecasters that places an emphasis on formal knowledge would lead to a loss of skill and deterioration of their inner weather picture, their tacit knowledge.

3.8   The Expert and the Mediator

The above examples of consultancy, underwriting, and weather forecasting, present an understanding of knowledge as it is expressed in the performance of expertise. Expertise is not reducible to a matter of representation, but lies in dialogue, communication and conversation, reflection, and imagination. Thereby 'data' or 'information' taken from its living context loses its meaning; it becomes redefined if we seek to reconstruct it within a system of rules. The project of the knowledge based system assumes that an expert has all the knowledge needed to perform their expertise in practice and that he/she is an autonomous decision-making entity. The examples above along with studies in the field of the sociology of scientific knowledge, show that this is a limited and misplaced picture of expertise. The next example is from my doctoral work (Gill 1995) and is a critique of the basic unit of knowledge that might be represented in a data base, i.e. that of data itself, by analysing its life within dialogue, its living context. The critique is situated within a quest to understand what is the relationship between the tacit and the explicit dimensions of knowing as they unfold in dialogue, i.e. how knowledge is acquired and transferred in dialogue, and it questions the concept of the autonomy of an expert.

The study of is of the meetings of a design team in a company, who are creating an audio–visual communications infrastructure in their building, which is architecturally not conducive to unplanned interaction as it separates the space into two pod areas per floor, where each pod is a square with offices. People find it very difficult to know what is happening with others at any time unless they send an email or phone them or go to the top floor where seminars are held and where people can eat their lunch. The aim of the audio-visual infrastructure is to increase awareness of what is happening at any time. I had an opportunity to track the design team's discussions, primarily their team meetings. This involved participatory observation, which included making video and audio recordings, as well as conducting informal interviews, and partially inhabiting the space as an affiliated researcher.

To begin a critique of the life of a piece of data in dialogue, I considered what might count as salient information in the design meeting, such as 'topics' discussed. For this inspiration I have to thank Judy Olson (from the field of human-computer interaction, HCI) who was researching the processes in collaborative design, and in her analyses of salient events during a design discussion she had the category of topics. I selected 'topic' as a data entity, bearing in mind that the etymology of topic, topos, is 'place'. I identified topics that were raised in the conversations of the audio-visual design team and treated these as 'information'.

In analysing the nature of this 'information', I traced the path(s) of each topic and found that where a topic began there was a discrepancy in knowledge amongst the team. A discrepancy could be that someone does not have the information that another person assumes they have; it could be that a person's status makes their contributions less credible and they are ignored; it could be differences in experiences and opinion about an event; or it could be that the ways in which a person expresses some information is not being perceived in the intended way, etc. There are many factors that give rise to a discrepancy in knowledge. What I found is that the end of each discrepancy coincided with new salient information being raised, i.e. a new topic, indicated by a move for a topic shift. At that moment the discrepancy is resolved, or at least a consensus reached such that the conversation could move forward, or alternatively the person with the [corporate] authority in the team decided that there was no more time to spend on the topic and closed it and initiated a new one. The last scenario of closing a topic by force is unstable as there has been no mutual agreement even to disagree.

Quite unexpectedly, the quest to understand the relationship between the tacit and the explicit dimensions of knowledge in dialogue had become an analysis of the nature of discrepancies in communication and the means by which we can become aware of these discrepancies and resolve them. And the critical factor in becoming aware is the *mediator* of the discrepancy, and I shall explain what I mean by this below.

The design team that I was following was composed of five persons (four men and one woman) of whom one was the Director of the Company. Each had a particular skill in a specific knowledge domain (hardware engineer, software engineer, user-designer relations, free thinker, Director). The Director of the Company (also the chairperson of the team) chose four people to represent the salient elements necessary for the successful design of this technology in a complementary way.

The topics that I identified within the conversations held discrepancies that unfolded different patterns of dialogue. For example, one of the topics revolved around a gap in knowledge between two people where one is talking from within his expertise and the other is trying to engage with him outside of his own expertise. This necessitates some third party person who can bridge the gap. This scenario of mediation comes most readily to our minds when we think of the word mediation in the context of communication. However, we would typically assign the person who lacks the 'expert' knowledge to be the problem of the gap in communication, whereby a mediator will bridge the gap by helping the expert to provide the necessary information to the other person who lacks it. This picture is probably rooted in what Hall called the identity extension transference (see above) where we assume that the problem in communication lies with the other. In the context of the design discussion, the mediator was able to make the 'expert' understand that in fact he (the expert) had not understood the nature of the design problem that he was supposed to be responsible for and that this is the gap between him and the non-expert, not the lack of knowledge of the non-expert. The problem in communication lay with the expert, i.e. as Hall says we need to come to realise that the problem with the other is me.

Another scenario, which does not come as readily to mind when we think about the meaning of mediation or mediator, is where many people are recalling something such as an event or a past conversation, and they remember different things about their experience of it. This happens to us in every day life, and a popular example shown in movies is of a couple who recall the day they first met, such as the clothes they wore and what they said, and each corrects the other's memory. Sometimes when we are relating a shared experience, say at a dinner party, we can be swayed by a friend's conviction that what they saw happening was what happened and not what you remember, and you find yourself aligning your story with theirs. In the design team, there is some confusion around the problem of lighting in one part of the building that can be seen by everyone in the group, as all the offices and all the spaces in the building (except for one space in the eating area on the top floor) are connected by the audio-visual system. Each member of the team remembers something different about the view, and some change their mind based on what another one says: 'I cannot see a very clear view through that camera lens', 'that area looks very dark', 'maybe the light is on too low', etc.… As the designers in the team share their experiences, one of them says something pertinent, the name of a particular camera lens. At that moment the 'expert' amongst this chattering of recalled autobiographies hears this pertinent utterance and suddenly realises what the problem is, and solves the matter that he now understands is with the camera lens. The person who said something pertinent is the *mediator* of the problem, and made the person who can solve the problem aware that they are in fact the 'expert' for this problem.

In both scenarios, the 'expert' in the life of the topics that I analysed did not see what the design problem was. It is someone else, whom I term the 'mediator', who provides the key to solving the source of the differences of opinion and perception about an issue. The mediator does so with the precision of the appropriateness of their utterance at the right time and in the right style and in the right role. The only person who can recognise the mediator of the problem is the 'expert' for the problem, i.e. only the expert for the problem can recognise the key as being the key and know how to use it.

There are three points to be considered:

- The first is that the concept of an autonomous expert is artificial and not grounded in human praxis;
- The second is that expertise is distributed in mediation;
- The third is that there is a relation between mediation and tacit knowing in human relations.

3.8.1   Mediation Process

Next it is helpful to look into the structure of the mediation process in light of the examples given above. It is proposed that the mediator enables resolution in discrepancy and consensus in knowledge by being empathic with the critical discrepancies (Gill 1995). By empathic I do not mean sympathic, but rather I mean an aesthetic quality that is akin to aesthetic emotion, for example, of our personal resonance with the structures, textures, forms and colours of a painting, as well as the theme presented (e.g. depicting a landscape, people walking in the country side, etc.). Imagine you are viewing a work of art, you experience the work as a whole yet you have an awareness that it is composed of the brush strokes, dots of paint, textures of paint, and colours. Together, these particulars enable you to see the picture and experience any aesthetic pleasure it may give. These particulars, marks on the page, form patterns of recognizable human forms, forms of nature, artifacts, and a narrative, i.e. they give us a mediated quality of meaning and affect. Polanyi (1966) said that we attend from the particulars of a work of art to attend to the aesthetics of the artist who created it. Within human interaction, such particulars may include the forms of expression (the gesture stroke, the intonation of the voice, the rhythm of the body and voice), a person's style, a person's role in relation to others, and the kind of knowledge they are expressing (e.g. narrative form – are they talking about an experience they had the other day whilst walking into town; or descriptive form – are they describing the dress they saw in the shop; or propositional form- are they giving you instructions on how to say run a particular software you need to use). Our perception of these particulars, that is evident in how we engage with them or not, affects how we understand what someone says. I call such particulars in human relations, compatibilities, *whereby particulars become relational*; empathy is the compatibility and ability to generate shared understanding with respect to a particular combination of compatibilities where compatibilities include levels of knowledge, forms of expression, personality, role, etc.

Hence, when a mediator in the design group utters the key to the problem of the poor view, there is a resonance between the mediator and the problem, and between the mediator and the expert, hence the mediator mediates the key to the problem to the expert, enabling the expert to resonate with and solve the problem. Neither are attending to the particulars but attending from them to see the problem. The mediator's personal act of knowing is distinct from that of the expert's in that the mediator cannot solve the problem. Furthermore, once the expert recognises the problem, all the participants in the group become aware that the problem has been identified.

Mediation is needed to provide the bridge for the particular discrepant aspects of the tacit and explicit dimensions of the knowledge in the communication to meet, and enables the participants to share awareness of the tacit dimension of the discrepancy.

Hence, the success or failure of knowledge transfer in dialogue is dependent on how knowledge (content) is carried and shaped in dialogue, and this includes discourse processes and group dynamics. Dimensions of knowledge (content) considered in this study are propositional, experiential and personal, knowledge by familiarity, and practical. These modes or categories were arrived at after reflecting on how to apply ideas about tacit knowledge that have been developed in discussions on skill, to analyse the relationship between the tacit and explicit dimensions of knowing within the processes of dialogue. Hence, these are not categories in a strict taxonomic sense.

- *Propositional knowledge* is domain specific knowledge, or knowledge, which can be expressed in the form of rules, made explicit, and is non-personal and non-experiential. In this case study the term propositional knowledge covers technical knowledge, rules about the use of the technology, descriptions of the functionality of the technology, knowledge which has the status of fact ('The menu, it says glance'), design issues (privacy), and design topics (background, glance and sweep connections). The range and variety of expressions just listed are specific to this design context. For example, if the context were that of a conflict between parents and children, between lovers, between a teacher and children in a classroom, within a courtroom, etc., the variety of possible expressions are expected to differ.
- *Experiential knowledge* is that which comes from one's own direct experience, or it is cultural/social knowledge,[2] or it is knowledge of another's experience (that one can relate ones own experience to, or imagine with). Experiential knowledge includes autobiographical information, which is personal knowledge. This may be either direct experience which is indicated by the use of personal pronouns such as 'I', 'we', etc. (I had a delicious lunch); or generic knowledge[3]

---

[2] This may be general knowledge e.g. of a specific culture, or specific experience e.g. work based, gained from interaction with work colleagues, group culture.

[3] This is based on the idea of generic structures in memory, which summarise similar events, cf. Barsalou (1988) i.e. refer to memory descriptions which refer to repeated actions over extended periods of time, e.g. 'we also went to the movies while we were there; everyday we would leave our house' cf. Table 8.1, p. 200.

(a frequent experience: 'whenever I do…'), or episodic knowledge[4] (a specific experience: 'the other day I was…'). Experiential knowledge encompasses how people use their knowledge and how they can relate their knowledge appropriately to specific problems. It encompasses practical knowledge.

- *Personal knowledge* is that of the individual personality, expressed as values, beliefs, and emotions. It is influenced by society, culture, family, education, friends and work colleagues.
- *Knowledge by familiarity* is the use of examples by a speaker to help the transfer of knowledge by opening the dialogue to engage the other(s) from their own experiences, and thereby help bridge discrepancies. Examples illustrate a person's knowledge and invite others to connect at that person's level or kind of knowledge.
- *Practical knowledge* is the skilled performance itself. It can be inferred but not made explicit: decisions, judgements, analyses, indicate (point to) practical knowledge but do not represent it.

Through dialogue, participants may acquire knowledge or fail to do so, and the dialogue may alter their group (collective) knowledge, and achieve dynamically stable knowledge[5] and build trust. Knowledge acquisition is successful when the communication between participants is consensual and compatible. Knowledge acquisition fails where no compatibility in communication can be established around the source of the problem and for it to be solved. If one were to perform a knowledge engineering exercise on these dialogues, one would face a problem that is reminiscent of, but of far greater complexity, to that of the example of the underwriters when they are making sense of the information contained within an application form to imagine a person's life – the relation between content and processes in communication is orthogonal and cannot be predefined. Knowledge is a process embodied in the dynamics of dialogue and the persons involved.

Hence propositional knowledge can be expressed in a variety of ways. It can be effective if both speaker and listener share the same knowledge base. If they do not, then it is not effective and you have breakdowns and misunderstandings. I was communicating with David Smith about this recently. David has been working in the area of knowledge transfer and tacit knowledge for many years, and he brought my attention to how we may also *know differently*, depending on our *cultural frame*:

---

[4] This is as in episodic memory, cf. Tulving (1972). Episodic memory refers 'to situations in which a person remembers an experienced event which contains spatio-temporal knowledge (i.e. details of time and place)' cf Conway (1990) p. 3.

[5] The term 'stable' refers to a person's relation with their knowledge and is used in a colloquial sense, as opposed to a scientific sense, i.e. it does not mean that knowledge is in a state of stable equilibrium. It denotes an individual's ability to have acquired the knowledge such that they can use it in a sustainable manner; a kind of psychological state whereby someone can maintain their performance of the knowledge over time. This may be behavioural, involving automaticity. In this case one is not necessarily consciously aware of one's knowledge. Stability of knowledge may also exist where someone has confidence in using their acquired knowledge. It requires the person to be true to themselves.

If I grow up in a society which explains certain phenomena and events in terms of (say) sympathetic magic, I will 'know', understand and use those phenomena differently from someone whose cultural frames include "science". I've come across this in Africa many years ago.

People will use the culturally located conceptual frameworks they have to draw robust and (internally) valid conclusions, especially where more "correct" alternatives appear both counter-intuitive and less robust.

3.8.1.1   Background to the Knowledge Categories

I have mentioned above that I had drawn upon a range of discussions and research on tacit knowledge and human skill to arrive at the various modes of knowing in order to have a way of analyzing the relationship between tacit and explicit dimensions in human dialogue and they include the works of[6] Cooley (1987a, 1987b), Goranzon and Josefson (1988), Rosenbrock (1990, 1992), Gill (1996a, b), Rauner et al. (1988). Cooley and Rosenbrock's fundamental work on human-centredness laid the ground for a movement that questioned the depersonalised automation of human skill that assumes the personal is not significant for skilled practice. Although a skilled engineer uses scientific knowledge and mathematical analysis, his/her skill also "contains elements of experience and judgement, and regard for social considerations and the most effective way of using human labour. These elements partly embody knowledge which has not yet been reduced to an exact mathematical form. They also embody value judgements which are not amenable to the scientific method" (Rosenbrock 1988).[7] In the seminal book *Architect or Bee*, Cooley, describes how the relative levels of the subjective and objective aspects of knowledge which a person utilises vary as one gains expertise. An expert uses more of the subjective aspects and less of the objective aspects of the knowledge in, for example, the use of intuition. An expert has the ability to grasp the situation in front of him/her and make judgements about it. A novice, on the other hand, can only calculate by using explicit rules to make sense of what appears to him/her to be a mass of data (Cooley 1987a).

I also drew upon work in autobiographical memory research for the category of experiential and personal knowledge (Conway and Bekerian 1987; Bekerian and Dritschel 1992), in particular the role of personal history in the organisation of specific autobiographical memories. Bekerian (at the former Applied Psychology Unit, Cambridge) and her colleagues showed how personal history cues access autobiographical memories, whereas cues that the person cannot relate their self to are less likely to do so. They found that autobiographical memory may be organized in a hierarchy of kinds of personal information that ranges from abstract to specific knowledge, where more abstract levels of the hierarchy are the thematic aspects of a person's life that include such things as location, activities and time period. These

---

[6] See Chap. 2 for details.

[7] Rosenbrock (1988) *Engineering as an Art*. AI & Society Journal, Vol. 2 No. 4.

abstract levels can index more specific levels,[8] for example, 'I remember a time when I was in my teens and dreamt a lot', or 'a mother was remembering a time when her children were growing up during which she was doing a lot of house-work'. Life period themes ('I remember a time') are fairly common across people, therefore individuals may represent these periods in terms of 'culturally specified norms' (op. cit. p. 130). Autobiographical memories may also be accessed through 'contextual cues' such as odors, sounds, etc. At the time that I met her (as her PhD student), Bekerian was consulting for the police. She had found that the police were selective in their judgements about what counted as 'evidence', limiting it to what could be proven either by witnesses or by some other empirical evidence, and in both the questioning during an interview and analysis of the case, what was per-ceived as being a personal matter, including a personal memory, was left out of the case records. Yet asking questions that trigger personal memory can be important for accessing memories that provide 'evidence'; research in autobiographical mem-ory shows that semantic, situational and personal knowledge are connected in mem-ory. Furthermore, asking questions that connect to personal memory can access other information more effectively and in a shorter time than impersonal questions (Conway et al. op. cit.).

The category of practical knowledge was drawn from Goranzon and his group's work at the Swedish Centre for Working life (1977–1989) on dialogue and tacit knowledge. This work, that developed and applied a hermeneutic approach to understanding knowledge and skill, sought to understand why there was a loss in the ability to make judgements on the part of the professional, during the mass applica-tion of information technology in organisations in Sweden in the 1970s and 1980s. Goranzon (1992) argued that in traditional approaches to knowledge and skills, importance is given to propositional knowledge at the expense of practical knowl-edge and this includes not recognising the importance of communication amongst professionals in their practice. What his group called 'knowledge by familiarity' is completely left out. Knowledge by familiarity is acquired from learning within a practice by seeing or examining examples of the tradition in the work. One member of this SCWL group, Josefson (1988, 1992) focused on knowledge by familiarity in

---

[8] Conway and Bekerian (1987) conducted three experiments to investigate timed autobiographical memory retrieval to cue words and phrases. In the first experiment, subjects retrieved memories to cues that named semantic category members and were primed with the superordinate category name or with a neutral word. No prime effects were observed. In the second experiment, subjects retrieved memories to primed and unprimed semantic category cues and to personal primes and personal history cues. Personal primes named lifetime periods (e.g., "school days") and personal history cues named general events occurring in those lifetime periods for each subject (e.g., "holi-day in Italy"). Only personal primes were found to significantly facilitate memory retrieval. A third experiment replicated this finding and also failed to find any prime effects to primes and cues nam-ing activities not directly related to an individual's personal history. In this experiment, character-istics of recalled events (e.g., personal importance, frequency of rehearsal, pleasantness, and specificity of the memory) were found to be strongly associated with memories retrieved to per-sonal cues and only mildly associated with memories retrieved to other types of cues. These find-ings suggest that one way in which autobiographical memories may be organized is in terms of a hierarchically structured abstracted personal history.

her work with nurses where she engaged them in philosophical work that they could relate their practical life to (e.g. Wittgenstein's Philosophical Investigations 1958) and narrative works (Ancient Greek and other fiction) to enable them to articulate their practical knowledge and thereby evolve a language of nursing practice. She held that propositional forms are an important feature of practical knowledge, tested and validated through the experience of unique events (each patient case), and assessed by similarities and disparities with previous examples. Any practice consists in rules and examples.

These discussions from human-centred systems, dialogue, and autobiographical memory in some way question the separation of the explicit from the tacit, the objective from the subjective, and the semantic from the situational and personal. A traditional cognitive approach (e.g. as in Anderson 1983) would say that practical knowledge is procedural knowledge, and can be represented as an algorithm of some kind. That is, it can be represented as a set of rules about how you use your knowledge which are based upon a summary of the content of experiences. The approaches I have drawn upon argue that one cannot represent all of experiential knowledge as a set of propositions or as an algorithm. One can relate some content of autobiographical information to propositional knowledge, e.g. 'my car is red'. But one cannot easily represent reactions of self, i.e. emotions, attitudes, values, beliefs, as propositional knowledge.

I adapted the various concepts in the discussions on skilled practice (see Chap. 2) in order to apply them to the analysis of dialogue. The work on autobiographical memory was based on the analysis of discourse and hence the concepts were transposable for the design team discussions.

3.8.1.2 Mediation Process Continued

To return to mediation, the conventional model that most of us are familiar with is that this is something that a person does in resolving dispute situations or in facilitating a meeting (e.g. a chairperson). This person serves as a conduit of information between the parties concerned, and is a go-between. In this study, mediation is considered as the mediation of discrepant knowledge within a knowledge environment, where a mediator serves to clear the noise, so to speak. The conventional model is one form of this.

Within any conversation (knowledge environment), we sometimes meander around a topic talking about things that may not seem to be necessarily relevant to it. In the case of a dispute or a difference of opinion, or in a group meeting where people are trying to brainstorm over a problem, such meandering may appear irrelevant (e.g. rhetorical) to the particular problem by the various negotiators or participants involved. Yet such 'irrelevant' information may be functioning to sustain the dialogue and open opportunities to discover the source of problems and clear up the noise. The belief of 'the one best way' (cf Cooley 1987a) to do things in order to achieve a goal and produce an outcome, permeates perceptions of what constitutes relevant information and the analysis of salient paths for problem solving and decision making. However this can miss the relevance of verbal and non-verbal contributions that serve to move the discussion and support the emergence of ideas, solutions, and decisions, just as in my conversations with the underwriters. Likewise, in the perception of what counts as evidence in police interviews Bekerian (see above) found they left out personal memories, deeming them irrelevant to the case. In fact, in any dialogue, take for example a dinner party or a business meeting, 'topic irrelevant' interventions can create the possibility for someone to emerge out of the 'noise' and perform a mediating role that causes people to rethink the nature of the gossip or the source of a design problem.

In one of the design team meetings, during a period of 5 min there were three topics identified in the discussion, and each topic carried different kinds of discrepancies in the knowledge of the participants. In each one, a different person emerged as a mediator.

The study drew three basic requirements for a person to be a successful negotiator or mediator:

1. Understanding the other; or understanding the situation of discrepancy in the knowledge environment (i.e. amongst two (or more) participants).
2. Knowledge of the gap between oneself and the other; knowledge of the gap in the knowledge environment (e.g. amongst the participants).
3. Ability to express this understanding and knowledge to other or others, i.e. produce the bridge.
4. Only the person who can solve the discrepancy recognises the mediator.

It is not sufficient to understand the nature of the discrepancy nor to have the key knowledge; one needs to be able to convey this in a form that others can perceive and that thereby makes sense to them. Personality also played a role as this influences the perceptions people have of each other, and affects how they understand the information being expressed, as shown in the consultancy study above.

The analysis of the tacit and explicit dimensions of communication for knowledge transfer and formation, supports the finding from the consultancy study that embodiment of forms of expression sustains one's own performance and engagement with others (dynamically stable knowledge). Various kinds of knowing form the tacit dimension in communication. The explicit, e.g. in this case a topic, or something that could be constituted as being a piece of data, is a process within dialogue, and a critical factor in the formation of knowledge in human communication that is necessarily a personal act of knowing, is mediation. Polanyi's concept of tacit knowing has a mediational structure (Gill 2000) of integrating our attention to something from our awareness of its particulars. It is this quality and in this sense that I assign the expression mediator to a person in human dialogues. The mediator is a mediator because the 'expert' or the person who needs to grasp the source of the problem in order to understand how to resolve it, does understand that whatever the mediator has expressed shows them this possibility. The expert recognises the mediator. *Mediation is not an individual's action (be this a gesture or/and an utterance), but a collective moment between the mediator and the expert (i.e. two or more persons), and once the expert recognizes the mediator in his/her response, the whole group also understands that the source of the problem has been identified.* This in part supports Collins' (op. cit.) category of collective tacit knowing as being irreducible to the explicit, which in this case would be of 'expertise' being reduced to an 'autonomous expert'.

3.9　Conclusion

Dialogue is skilled performance, and since knowledge is carried in dialogue, knowledge is skilled performance. Dialogue is improvised, and at its best it flows and feels good and we feel connected. I was asked recently that if a person speaking were speaking in Chinese to someone who speaks in Japanese where neither can understand the words (speech content) of the other, would they be transferring knowledge? I would say they would be, and of the kind that underlies our everyday contact with others we encounter in our lives. It is of the kind that was crucial for my Japanese colleague (Chap. 1) to make sense of my utterances where neither I spoke fluent Japanese nor he spoke fluent English, but which was inaccessible to him in the video conference setting to the extent that he could not understand what was said and know how to engage. Someone whom I met briefly at Stanford spoke of her experience of ordering food in a restaurant in France whilst visiting with her husband. She is deaf, her husband is not and neither spoke French well. He had tried without much success to make himself understood to the waiter using his poor French, so she gave it a try, and using gestures and sounds, she was able to convey their needs with success. Her husband had attended to words, she had attended to movements and sounds that would engage the waiter. Such improvisation is not about the one best way, nor is it possible to abstract it outside the person(s) involved in it; it is a personal act of knowing. It is not about certainty but about moving with uncertainty. Certainty blocks it. Yet we build technologies of information of certainty for certainty. Such technology caused the skilled mathematicians in the Swedish Forestry Commission (Goranzon 1992) to lose their ability to trust their own judgements when using the knowledge based system that they had been involved in creating.[9] Certainty gradually caused them to doubt their uncertainty and to pass over judgements to the computer. The senior bank managers whom I spoke with are from an era when they were expected to make judgements about a client, and they lament this wall of certainty of the data base which they have to feed information into and that computes decisions which are sometimes contrary to what they think. They try to find humans in the system in attempts to override this computation if they can, whilst there is a generation being trained to accept these abstract decisions and do not know how to judge or are not encouraged to judge.

The dominant model of expertise with its premise that an expert is an autonomous cognitive entity has shaped the concept of the knowledge based system and its zenith, the expert system. However, expertise is about being able to improvise which

---

[9] See Chap. 2.

necessarily is about handling uncertainty and working with doubt. Handling uncertainty involves mediated awareness. For example, for the weather forecasters, this occurs in their tea break discussions with colleagues and in reflection. The skilled 'consultant' created an imaginary world to engage his colleagues in thinking through a problem that they believed to be real, and the underwriter and weather forecaster formed an inner picture to understand the problem. In the examples from the design team meetings, it was not the 'expert' for the problem who grasped its nature, but a 'mediator' who made the expert aware that he/she is the expert for it. In all these, expertise is not conducted autonomously. It is about engaging in the world as skilled performers within context and culture and this involves, *knowing that, knowing how, and also knowing when*. The personal act of knowing, of being committed to know, is necessarily embodied.

A visceral example of this is Chesley Sullenberger's landing of US Airways flight 1549 on the Hudson River in 2009 where all the passengers survived. Within minutes of leaving New York's la Guardia airport, and at a height of just 2,818 ft, the plane struck a flock of geese flying in perfect formation towards them and lost thrust in both its engines. Sullenberger took over from his co-pilot and decided not to fly back to La Guardia or over dense population but to head for the Hudson River. After gliding the plane over the George Washington Bridge, he picked a stretch of water near Manhattan's commuter ferry terminals to land, where rescuers were able to reach in minutes. All this analysis, communication, and decisions took place in the 3 min from the engines cutting out to landing the plane. Sullenberger's 40 years of experience of flying, combined with his experience in handling and understanding risk and safety, and also his personality, helped him to skillfully navigate the plane and in trust with his co-pilot. It is interesting that those who knew him were not surprised that he was able to do this, commenting, 'he is an unbelievable professional', 'he was the right person to help passengers survive a crisis'.

Skill, be it Sullenberger's flying of the plan or a dancer's beautiful step, has an aesthetic quality. Aesthetics, along with ethics, has been considered to lie outside the realm of explicit or propositional knowledge (Ayer 1971) because they are not in full measure linguistically articulable and are not scientifically relevant. Flying a plane like Sullenberger or dancing a beautiful step requires a great deal of skill, and it is acquired in an apprenticeship, and it is in this way of learning that people develop both an ethic and an aesthetic quality of performance (Smith 1992). Within dialogue itself, mediated awareness may be said to be aesthetic. The study of the design team meeting showed that mediation involves empathy, which in turn embodies aesthetic emotion arising with the resonance in the confluence of compatibilities between the expert and the mediator.

This conceptualisation of empathy is to be explored further in the next chapter on our bodies and the mediation of knowledge in human interaction. There we continue the discussion on how co-presence in physical space facilitates the transfer and acquisition of experiential knowledge. The methodology for understanding the tacit has so far drawn on dialogue, discourse analysis, ethnomethodology and participatory observation, and now extends to include ethnography.

References

Anderson, J. R. (1983). *The architecture of cognition*. Cambridge, MA: Harvard University Press.

Ayer, A. J. (1971). *Language truth and logic*. London: Pelican.

Barsalou, L. W. (1988) The content and organisation of autobiographical memories. In U. Neisser & E. Winograd (Eds.), *Remembering reconsidered: Ecological and traditional approaches to the study of memory* (pp. 192–243). New York: Cambridge University Press.

Bekerian, D., & Dritschel, B. H. (1992). Autobiographical remembering: An integrative approach. In M. Conway, D. C. Rubin, H. Spinnler, & W. Wagenaar (Eds.), *Theoretical perspectives on autobiographical memory* (pp. 135–150). Dordrecht: Kluwer Press.

Collins, H. H. (2013). *Tacit and explicit knowledge*. Chicago: University of Chicago Press.

Condon, W. S. (1970). Radio interview, Boston University Radio. http://www.edu-cyberpg.com/Literacy/WhatresearchCondon.asp

Conway, M. A. (1990). *Autobiographical memory: An introduction*. Milton Keynes: Oxford University Press.

Conway, M. A., & Bekerian, D. (1987). Organisation in autobiographical memory. *Memory and Cognition, 15*(2), 119–132.

Cooley, M. J. E. (1987a). *Architect or bee*. Hogarth Press [new edition], p. 11. cf. cybernetics, see Wiener (1949).

Cooley, M. J. E. (1987b). Human centred systems: An urgent problem for system's designers. *AI & Society, 1*, 37–46.

Cross, I. (2006). Music and social being. *Musicology Australia, 28*, 114–126.

Cross, I. (2011). Music and biocultural evolution. In M. Clayton, T. Herbert, R. Middleton (Eds.), *The cultural study of music: A critical introduction* (2nd edn.). London: Routledge.

Cross, I., & Woodruff, G. E. (2009). Music as a communicative medium. In R. Botha & C. Knight (Eds.), *The prehistory of language* (pp. 1–113). Oxford: Oxford University Press.

Duranti, A. (1997). Universal and culture specific properties of greetings. *Journal of Linguistic Anthropology, 7*(1), 63–97. American Anthropological Association.

Efron, D. (1941). *Gesture and environment*. Kings Crown Press. Republished as Gesture, Race and Culture, Mouton, 1972.

Garrick, M. (1891). Greeting by gesture. Part 1, Popular science, Vol 38. Reprinted by D. Appleton, NY.

Gill, S. P. (1988). Knowledge and skill transfer through expert systems: British and Scandinavian traditions. In B. Kelly & A. Rector (Eds.), *Research and development in expert systems V: Proceedings of expert systems '88*. Cambridge: Cambridge University Press.

Gill, S. P. (1995). Dialogue and tacit knowledge for knowledge transfer. PhD dissertation. University of Cambridge.

Gill, K. S. (Ed.). (1996a). *Human machine symbiosis: The foundations of human-centred systems design*. London: Springer.

Gill, S. P. (1996b). Rosenbrock's account of causality and purpose. A compilation of Howard Rosenbrock's works by Satinder Gill. In K. S. Gill (Ed.), *Human machine symbiosis*. London: Springer.

Gill, J. H. (2000). *The tacit mode. Michael Polanyi's postmodern philosophy*. New York: SUNY Press.

Göranzon, B. (1992). *The practical intellect: Computers and skills* (AI & Society series). London: Springer.

Goranzon, B., & Josefson, I. (1988). *Knowledge, skill and artificial intelligence*. London: Springer.

Hall, E. T. (1976). *Beyond culture*. New York: Anchor Books.

Hall, E. T. (1983). *Dance of life: The other dimension of time*. New York: Anchor Books.

Hall, E. T. (1990). *The silent language*. New York: Anchor Books. First published, 1959 by Doubleday.

Ikuta. (1990). The role of "Craft Language" in learning "Waza". *AI & Society, 4*, 137–146.

Johannessen, K. (1988). Rule following and tacit knowledge. *AI & Society, 2*(4), 287–301. Springer.

Josefson, I. (1988). The nurse as an engineer. *AI & Society, 1*(2), 115–126.

Josefson, I. (1992). Language and experience. In B. Göranzon & Magnus Florin (Eds.), *Skill and education: Reflection and experience*. London: Springer.

Levinson, S. C. (2006). On the human "interaction engine". In N. J. Enfield & S. C. Levinson (Eds.), *Roots of human sociality: Culture, cognition and interaction* (pp. 39–69). Oxford: Berg.

Malinowski, B. (1923). The problem of meaning in primitive languages. In C. K. Ogden & I. A. Richards (Eds.), *The meaning of meaning* (pp. 451–510). London: Kegan Paul, Trench, Trubner and Company.

Perby, M. L. (1990). The inner picture. In *Artificial intelligence, culture and language: On education and work* (pp. 77–82). London: Springer.

Polanyi, M. (1966). The tacit dimension. Doubleday. 1983 Reprint.

Rauner, F., Rasmussen, L. B., & Corbett, M. (1988). The social shaping of technology and work: Human-centred systems. *AI & Society, 2*, 47–62.

Rosenbrock, H. (1988). Engineering as an art. *AI & Society, 2*, 315–320. Springer.

Rosenbrock, H. H. (Ed.). (1990). *Machines with a purpose*. Oxford: Oxford University Press.

Rosenbrock, H. (1992). Science, technology and purpose. *AI & Society, 6*, 3–17.

Smith, D. (1992). The psychology of apprenticeship. In B. Göranzon & M. Florin (Eds.), *Skill and education: Reflection and experience* (pp. 83–100). London: Springer.

Sperber, D., & Wilson, D. (1986). *Relevance*. Oxford: Blackwell.

Tulving, E. (1972). Episodic and semantic memory. In S. Tulving & W. Donaldson (Eds.), *Organisation of memory*. New York: Academic.

Wittgenstein, L. (1958). Philosophical investigations.

Chapter 4
The Body: Knowing How, Knowing That, Knowing When

Abstract The discussion in this chapter continues an investigation of tacit knowing as a personal act of knowing by considering: *I can only see how you see if we share the experience in the same physical space.* In doing so, it takes the discussion on mediated expertise further by considering mediation as an embodied process involving a collective act. This is a personal act of knowing where the body mediates experience of knowing how, knowing that, and knowing when simultaneously.

4.1 Introduction

The discussion in this chapter continues an investigation of tacit knowing as a personal act of knowing by proposing that, *I can only see how you see if we share the experience in the same physical space.*[1] Being present is a bodily experience, and involves all the human senses. Consider the various forms of the human greeting in our cultures: The Maori rub noses in greeting each other, Russians kiss on the mouth, and in some Arab cultures, they bring their faces close enough to smell the breath of the other. All these acts are part of gauging one person's sense of another, essential to building trust that is required for committed engagement. Placing a glass plane between two people in any of these situations would block their tacit ability to interpret their relation to each other, and thereby comprehend each other's meaning, through the impacts between their bodies; it requires them to focus on the visual and speech channels that have a narrower bandwidth for tacit knowing.

When my Japanese colleague tried to communicate in English with American clients via a video conference with his broken English, he was rendered unable to understand what they were 'saying'. His Japanese colleagues who spoke English well had an easier time. Yet he was known and valued for his skills in engaging with others and building trust, such that the company sent him to the US for a few years. In the cross cultural situation the richness of sensory embodied engagement that my colleague drew upon to make sense of someone else by connecting with them, seems to have been reduced to the act of looking and having grammatical competence.

---

[1] This has emerged from the studies presented herein about seeing colours, sharing an aesthetic view, and collaborative sketching.

© Springer International Publishing Switzerland 2015
S.P. Gill, *Tacit Engagement*, DOI 10.1007/978-3-319-21620-1_4

It might be just a matter of time before we can become as skilled in using computer based communication tools, such as the video conference and skype, as we have become in using the telephone and writing letters, and learn to understand when to use them and when not to, and how to interpret what someone is saying.

It has been proposed (Hood 2012, 2014) that children growing up using new media to regularly engage with others may be evolving a different form of self out of their technology mediated relations with others, than that of say my generation. Our brain has evolved for pro-social behaviour, and our capacities for mentalizing, coordinating movement, emotional connection, are encultured from when we are born, and this includes our development of self, i.e. identity. If a child's social development is affected in early life that can have an effect on their social development throughout life. We may need to think carefully about the effects on children who are increasingly using new media technologies at a very young age, compared to the technologies of the past of writing letters and talking on a telephone.

Although this is not the focus of this book, we can reflect on how we engage with others in the same physical space and come to share, for example, a sense of what is a beautiful shade of colour. Communicating well with someone else, be it to shake hands, to kiss, or dance, draw together, or have a wonderful conversation with food, has an aesthetic and ethical quality.

4.2   The Body as Mediator of Experiential Knowing

In the winter of 1996/1997, Gordon, an apprentice landscape architect with company 'BETA', sent a set of completed coloured maps that he had made at the company's Welsh office, to John, a senior architect based at its headquarters located in North England. The company was going to make a bid for project work to reshape a major road in North Wales where the frequency of traffic accidents was high, and these coloured maps were part of the depiction of the changes to the road design and effects upon the landscape. For example, colours depicted old woodland and new woodland. To Gordon's surprise, John judged the colours that he had used to be 'wrong' and that the maps needed to be correctly recoloured. Company BETA had barely 2 weeks left to submit their bid and re-colouring all these maps was no small task. John brought in other experienced landscape architects at his branch to help, and asked Gordon to travel up from Wales and re-colour the maps with them. It was felt that Gordon lacked experience and the only way he was going to get it was by experiencing the doing of colouring in a shared practice.

The problem of 'seeing' the colours was partly due to the company's economic condition. BETA was downsizing, as a result of which Gordon was the sole landscape architect left at the Welsh branch. Architects, however, do not interpret the material in isolation when they first handle it. In talking aloud and moving pens over paper, they engage the other person(s) in their conceiving. This, it is suggested enables one person to adapt upon another person's view, producing the conditions for a coherent development of the design (Gill 1997), and a process for 'seeing-as' (interpretation) until they come to 'see' (unmediated understanding) (Tilghman 1988).[2] This is likewise with colouring activity: as the apprentice colours with the team and more experienced architects, he/she learns how they select, for example, a specific shade of blue to set against a particular shade of green (seeing-as) to create a 'pleasing effect' that 'looks professional' (Gill SP, op. cit).

Because of the distance between the two branches and because of their commitments, John had been unable to visit Gordon and work with him. Instead, he had sent him a set of previously coloured maps (examples of experience), colour coded keys, and a set of instructions. These are *descriptive* and *propositional forms of expression*, all located in the experience of the architects at the North England Branch. For Gordon, they are outside his experience, and as he has no other landscape architects in the Welsh branch to consult, he brings his own experience to bear in interpreting these fragmented representations of his colleagues' practice.

In his study of how a team of geophysicists judge when material fibres in a reaction vat are jet black, Goodwin (1997) shows how simply saying 'jet black' is not sufficient for helping an apprentice measure and make this judgement competently. Rather, the 'blackness of black' is learnt through physically working with the fibre, and in talking about the experience, "transforming private sensations and hypotheses into public events that can be evaluated and confirmed by a more competent practitioner". Geochemists use their bodies as 'media that experience the material' being worked with through a variety of modalities. In the case of the apprentice, Gina, in Goodwin's study, her interlocutor's ability to recognize and evaluate the sensation she is talking about requires 'co-participation' in the same activity.

The example of Gordon's 'failure' to correctly interpret the forms of expression sent to him, is an example of how breakdown can take place when 'co-participation' is missing from the interpretation process, and how essential it is for repair within a distributed apprenticeship setting. Knowledge becomes clearly more than a matter of applying learnt rules, but of learning 'rule-following' (Johannessen 1988) within the practices that constitute it. The need for Gordon to colour with the other architects in order to be able to correctly interpret any such future fragments that might be sent to him, shows that *experiencing in co-presence motivates the personal act of knowing* and enables Gordon to acquire tacit understanding of his peers' aesthetic view. Gordon's acquired knowledge will become evident in his skillful performance of these forms of expression in the future.

The equivalence in meaning of 'forms of expression' (Chap. 3; see Gill 1995) and 'representations of practice' denotes a range of human action, artefacts, objects, and tools. Human action includes cues, which may be verbal, bodily, of interaction with a physical material world (tools, e.g. pens, light tables, etc.,), and construction of the physical boundary objects (e.g. colour, maps, sketches, masterplan sketches, masterplans, plans, functional descriptive sketches, photographs, written documents, etc.).

---

[2] Tilghman's use of the term 'mediated' is in the sense of a conduit.

The dilemma of this distributed setting is that in the future, any interpreting or understanding that Gordon as an apprentice makes of different fragments of knowledge, will still take place in isolation from his landscape architecture colleagues.

I spoke about this problem, of the apprentice trying to learn to share his and his team's sense of what looks good from a distance, with John, and posed him a question: suppose it were possible for his team and the apprentice to colour maps together in a distributed setting with the help of some hypothetical and perfectly seamless computer interface,[3] would he be interested in exploring this possibility? John declared that this was not a matter for technology, but quite simply that when the apprentice 'lacks experience' the only way he will acquire it is by colouring with them in the same physical space. John was not an anti-technology person, in fact the firm was steadily replacing its traditional methods with computer based systems in order to improve 'efficiency' and compete with the 'professional' aesthetic look produced by new technology; hand coloured maps and writing looked 'amateurish' compared to the clean lines and smooth even colourings produced by computer software. However, and paradoxically, on the matter of developing the skill to share a group's aesthetic view, John was adamant that the apprentice would only come to see with them if he was physically in the same space and doing activities of seeing with them. He said that no technology, however seamless, would enable the apprentice to acquire this. Given what happens when we place a glass pane in between us, this makes perfect sense.

His conviction, made me reflect on what it means to share a space and be present as a *precondition to acquiring experience*; experience that would have helped Gordon to interpret the examples of the company's previous coloured maps produced for similar bids, and interpret the colour keys and instructions, that had all been sent to aid him.

John was certain that once Gordon had this experience of colouring with him in the same physical space, he would have no trouble in the future in aligning his aesthetic 'seeing-as' with theirs when given such materials or representations (exemplars) to interpret and 'see', wherever he might be. *Seeing-as* requires interpretation, and Tilghman terms this, 'mediated understanding'. Once you have the skill to see, you can understand without interpretation, and just perform. The tacit knowing that Gordon had acquired would be 'retrieved and made active by sensing' (Reiner 2009) in his act of seeing. *The role of mind and imagination is important for such retrieval in sensing that brings together the past (memory), the present, and anticipates the future.* In such sensing, our minds draw upon our bodies: 'wherever some process in our body gives rise to consciousness in us, our tacit knowing of the process will make sense of it in terms of an experience to which we are attending' (Polanyi, op. cit. p. 15). So how do we embodied beings acquire experiential knowing in shared physical space, and what are the constraints of disembodied communication upon distributed knowledge acquisition?

---

[3] Whilst I was speaking with him I was thinking of the ClearBoard by Hiroshi Ishii.

4.3   The Body and Tacit Knowing

It may help here to consider Polanyi's discussion of the body and tacit knowing (Polanyi 1966), particularly in learning tasks that involve the body, such as playing chess, dance, etc. He describes a skilled human performance as a comprehensive entity, and when two people share the knowledge of the same comprehensive entity, two kinds of 'indwelling' meet. "The performer co-ordinates his moves by dwelling in them as parts of his body, while the watcher tries to correlate these moves by seeking to dwell in them from outside. He dwells in these moves by interiorising them. By such exploratory indwelling the pupil gets the feel of a master's skill and may learn to rival him." Gordon and Gina are undertaking such exploratory indwelling in discerning colours through movement and their sense, in order to share the knowledge (experiential) of the same comprehensive entity (e.g. colour black, or aesthetic judgment).

For Polanyi, the body is the 'ultimate instrument of all external knowledge', and 'wherever some process in our body gives rise to consciousness in us, our tacit knowing of the process will make sense of it in terms of an experience to which we are attending'. In performing Body Moves, we grasp and sense someone's motions, and respond to them appropriately (skillfully) in spontaneous co-action.

Further, tacit knowing has two terms, *proximal*, that includes the particulars, and *distal*, their comprehensive meaning. A simple example is a wood full of trees: a wood is the distal term, and the trees, the proximal term consisting of particulars (trees). When we look at a wood, we are aware of its trees but do not look at each specific tree in order to understand that this is a wood in front of us. How do we achieve this understanding of the entity, the wood? Polanyi develops a theory about the processes of such understanding or comprehensive meaning, called tacit knowing. We draw upon this to consider how we resonate with structures in communication. Polanyi has a specific meaning in using the word 'comprehension'. A comprehensive entity has a number of levels that form a hierarchy. These levels are structures of sets of particulars that constitute the entity. Each level (set of particulars) has its own principles that operate under the control of the next level up. For example, in performing a speech, the voice you produce is shaped into words by a vocabulary. However, the operation of higher levels cannot be accounted for by the laws governing its particulars that form the lower levels. For example, you cannot derive a vocabulary from phonetics. The two terms of tacit knowing, proximal and distal, are described as being two levels of reality, and between them, 'there is a logical relation which corresponds to the fact that the two levels are the two acts of tacit knowing which jointly comprehends them'.

There are two important points to be made here. Firstly, that in resonating with the particulars of each level in the communication structure, we do so by being 'aware' of the particulars of the entity such as a gesture, for attending to it. This is distinct from saying we resonate with the particulars, such as the elements of the gesture, by attending to them. If we did so, this function of the particulars, i.e. enabling us to attend to the entity, is cancelled and we would lose sight of the gesture itself because all we would see is fragmented elements. A popular example of this in discussions about skill, is of playing the piano. If in the middle of performing a piece of music we suddenly began to focus on the movements of each of our fingers we would have difficulty in being able to play. Tacit knowing is about achieving the performance of playing the piano such that the finger movements and the piano keys are *'invisible' to us, as an extension of our selves*.[4] This is an important aspect of riding a bike, driving a car or flying a plane: the skilful cyclist, driver or pilot acquires the machine as part of the body.

In a similar sense, and the second important point, is that our ability to grasp communication cues and the content that they frame is invisible to us until we feel awkward in the communication situation, at which point we become aware of its particulars. For example, a handshake not quite working makes us aware of the particulars of our and the other person's hands and awkward movements, and we perceive the other as distinct and make judgements about him/her and our relation with them. A simple handshake becomes a conscious event.

Experiencing the performance of representations of practice (e.g. gestures, vocalisations) by moving with these representations in a joint activity (activity such as colouring together or sketching together), may be seen as alignments in our behaviour (selves) called *Body Moves* (Gill et al. 2000, Gill 2004). The idea of the Body Move emerged from a need to understand how the body mediates knowledge. It does so when we perform collective acts, and these behavioural alignments have a rhythmic quality. The reason for John's (the landscape architect) insistence that co-presence, colouring together in the same physical space, is a precondition to gaining experience and sharing an aesthetic sense of what looks good, may lie here. Being present may be described as a precondition for committed communication, and the nature of this precondition has a bearing upon how we coordinate with each other.

4.4   Body Moves in Dialogue

The identification and conceptualisation of Body Moves emerged during my research stay (1997) at ATR (Advanced Telecommunications Research) Media Lab, located between Kyoto and Nara, with a group of computational and psycholinguists. This group were designing various multi-modal conversational agents, one of which was simply a cartoon eye and another a cartoon face composed of few lines of eyebrows, eyes, and mouth. I sat in on their audio analyses of feedback and fillers, for example 'hai, ne, so ne', which would be the equivalent of 'uhuh, ok, mmm' in English. These analyses would be fed back into the design of the conversational agents. Although I was not fluent in Japanese, I had experienced enough of the sound of the language and contexts of use to feel the meanings that were intended in the prosody of these utterances. Prosody is the way in which we say something, for example the rise and fall in the pitch of our voice, the loudness with which we

---

[4] The idea of invisibility and extension of self is drawn from Polanyi's work on Personal Knowledge (1962).

speak, the softness of a tone, the pace of our voice, etc. They were analysing these features which provide information about the psychology of the linguistic interaction (psycholinguistics) at the level of how we are moving the information within the communication situation (metacommunication), rather than being about the content of the information (Shimojima et al. 1997; Kawamori et al. 1998). In this way they are analysing the pragmatics of the communication.

Bearing this in mind and thinking about how the body mediates knowledge, I viewed the videos I had made of the landscape architects and noticed how their bodies operated differently in different design stages. For example the architects position themselves around a table and engage with their bodies very differently when discussing what happened at a recent meeting with a client than they do when they are sketching out a conceptual idea together on a sheet of paper, or when they are looking at photos of an aerial scene to discuss the layout of the landscape and its features. The scenario of sketching together revealed a great deal of bodily activity and one could observe the expression of the architects' ideas as they used their hands, pens and bodies. Hence I selected this design stage in their practice for analysis.

To begin with, I reflected on Wittgenstein's language games in the Philosophical Investigations (1958), of learning a language game through action and reaction. My Japanese colleagues were looking into feedback in order to design their multi-modal interactive agents, so a good place to start seemed to be to explore how the body performs feedback by firstly identifying moments of action and reaction. This would be of interest to both our purposes. My colleagues gave me Sotaro Kita's PhD thesis on gesture and cognition (1993), Traum's PhD thesis on grounding (1994), a paper on conversation moves (Carletta et a
````1. 1997) and Allwood et al.'s (1991) work on 'Linguistic (interindividual) Feedback'. Kita's thesis informed me about the category of 'beats', or batons, first classified by Efron (1941) in his seminal study of ethnic groups in New York. Efron was concerned to find out and demonstrate that gestures are not genetic and racially determined but are formed within the social and cultural environments that we grow up in. The category of a 'beat' was very useful. Traum's work was on joint acts that *ground* our understanding, a concept developed by Herb Clark (Clark and Brennan 1991). From Carletta et al.'s work, a 'move' denoted the movement of the conversation forwards and was adopted in coining 'Body Moves'. Unlike the speech 'move', these body moves may be considered as synchronised 'beats' that help ground our understanding of each other.

The communicative act theories considered above by Traum, Carletta and Allwood, provided a description of an empirical framework for considering this phenomena of bodily interactions, that we called Dialogue Act Theory. The body moves show that such acts exist for interactive body movements. We proposed that body moves work in harmony with the intention of the speech act and assumed the categories of the body moves we identified (in Gill et al. 2000) to be co-related to communicative acts. The idea of 'Body moves' expanded into the area called 'pragmatic acts' (Mey 2000) seeking to widen the 'narrow conception of strict natural language pragmatics'. Body moves create '*contact*', i.e. a space of engagement between persons, and they can move in a rhythm of bodily take-turn. At the time the
````

work was being undertaken, natural language pragmatics was too limited to capture this aspect of communication, and thus of understanding, but Body Moves were soon incorporated into pragmatic theory in Mey's work where the body move is a pragmeme (Mey 2000, pp. 223–227).

Work on gestures (Streeck 1993; McNeill 1992; McNeill et al. 1994; Furuyama 2000) shows that gesture and speech are co-ordinated activities, suggesting a dialectic in cognition, and that this relationship is essential for effective communication. The analysis of body moves indicates the construction/establishment of mutual ground within a space of action as they facilitate the flow of information in dialogue. 'Body move' does not refer to the physical movement itself but rather the act that the movement performs. They form part of the knowledge environment of our physical co-presence. As *body language* they are considered both as a *form of expression* and as *communication dynamics* (see Chap. 3). Such moves are distinguished from representational or iconic gestures of the verbal utterance, which serve primarily to illustrate it. Where in conversation, a 'move' is described as a verbal action that causes the conversation to move forward (Carletta et al. 1997), the body move is a collective bodily action, a 'dialogue act'.

It may be helpful to look further at the linguistic theories that we drew upon for characterising the body moves. Allwood's theory (Allwood et al. 1991) of 'Linguistic (interindividual) Feedback' describes four basic communicative functions that are essential for human, direct face-to-face communication. Special attention is paid to the type of reaction conveyed by feedback utterances, the communicative status of the information conveyed (i.e. the level of awareness and intentionality of the speaker), and the context sensitivity of feedback utterances. 'Context sensitivity' means the type of speech act (mood of the person), the factual polarity (positive or negative), and the information status of the earlier utterance influencing the interpretation of feedback utterances. The four basic communicative functions are:

Contact – whether the interlocutor is willing and able to continue the interaction
Perception – whether the interlocutor is willing and able to perceive the message
Understanding – whether the interlocutor is willing and able to understand the message
Attitudinal reactions – whether the interlocutor is willing and able to react and (adequately) respond to the message, specifically whether he/she accepts or rejects it.

According to Allwood et al., these four basic functions arise from four basic requirements of human communication:

(a) The willingness and ability to communicate;
(b) The fact that the receiver (listener) is willing and able to perceive the behavioural or other means whereby the sender (speaker) is displaying or signalling information;
(c) Whether the receiver is willing and able to understand the content that the sender is displaying or signalling. It is also helpful if the receiver can perceive and understand various types of indicated information;
(d) The receiver's willingness and ability to react attitudinally and behaviourally to various aspects of the content that the sender is displaying or signalling. It also helps if the receiver can react to indicated information.

Within this theory, the importance of linguistic feedback lies in the need to elicit and give information about the basic communicative functions, i.e. providing continued contact, perception, understanding, and emotional/attitudinal reaction, and doing this in a sufficiently unobtrusive way to allow communication to serve as an instrument for pursuing various human activities. Linguistic feedback is therefore an essential instrument for successful communication and for the incrementality of communication, i.e. the step-by-step build up of consensual, joint understanding, which in its turn is a means for pursuing a variety of other human activities.

In his theory of 'Grounding' (1994), Traum identifies categories of speech acts, grounding acts and turn taking. Grounding is about the act of building common ground. Conversants need to bring a certain amount of common ground to a conversation. The process of bringing in and adding to this common ground has been called grounding (Clark and Schaefer 1989). With regard to communicative acts and their application to interactive body movements (gestures), key features of communicative acts can be described as *core speech acts* and *turn-taking acts*, whilst the key features of body moves are *grounding acts* and *turn-taking acts*. To account for the mutual understanding of core speech acts, Traum proposes the idea of a discourse unit (DU). This consists of an initial presentation and as many subsequent utterances as are needed to make the act mutually understood, or grounded. The initial presentation is a core speech act termed 'attempt'; it is fully realised when the DU is grounded. A minimal DU contains an initial presentation and an acknowledgement, and may also include any repairs or continuations needed to realise the act. Some of these speech acts are: inform, check, request, accept and suggest. In short, a DU represents a unit of conversation at which grounding takes place; at the same time, it is composed of individual utterance-level actions. The opening utterance of a DU is called an initiate act; subsequent utterances are called continue acts. An example of a grounding act is turn-taking:

- A '*keep-turn*' may be any instance of continuing to talk. An extreme case of a 'keep-turn' is a 'floor battle', where one person tries to keep the turn while another tries to take it.
- A '*release-turn*' is usually signalled by intonation.
- A '*take-turn*' succeeds when no-one else speaks; however if someone is speaking, the attempt has been successful if they stop. Within each turn, a take-turn action occurs at the beginning of the first utterance.

Carletta et al.'s (1997) theory of 'Conversational Moves', presents different kinds of initiations and responses classified according to their purposes. The two categories we drew upon were *check* and *acknowledge*.

'*Check*' requests a partner to confirm information that the speaker has some reason to believe is true, but is not entirely sure about. Typically, the information to be confirmed is something the partner has tried to convey explicitly, or something the speaker believes was meant to be inferred from what the partner has said. Check moves are invariably about some information that the speaker has been given.

   e.g.

- G: Ehm, curve slightly to your right.
- F: To my right?

- G: Yes
- F: As I look at it?

'*Acknowledge*' is a verbal response that minimally shows that the speaker has heard the move to which he/she responds; often it also demonstrates that the move was understood and accepted. Carletta et al. refer to Clark and Schaefer's (1989) five kinds of evidence that an utterance has been accepted: 'continued attention', 'initiating a relevant utterance', 'verbally acknowledging the utterance', 'demonstrating an understanding of the utterance by paraphrasing it', and 'repeating part or all of the utterance verbatim'. Carletta et al. count only the last three as acknowledge moves, as the first response leaves no trace in a dialogue transcript to be coded, and the second involves further dialogue moves.

- Example:
- G: Ehm, if you …. You're heading southwards.
- F: Mmhmm
- Example:
- G: Do you have a stone circle at the bottom?
- F: No.
- G: No, you don't.

The first of Clark and Schaefer's evidence for acceptance, 'continued attention', is useful for the case of body moves.

Body moves are rather like moves in a game; however, unlike moves in a game, which are of a strategic nature, body moves do not embody specific intentions. While in speech, the communicative acts we have cited above are strategic in that they embody some intention, and this intention is expected to be understood by the listener in the context of the communication situation, we cannot say there is an intention in the body move itself. We could, though, say that they embody an intention of communication as such.

The body moves were defined and identified through a cyclical process, which began with the identification of various acts in bodily action and reaction, and which seemed to mimic acts which occur in speech. We found that in the process of defining and clarifying the nature of these moves, we could not apply the same definitions as for speech. In addition, we identified a number of acts which do not exist in speech, or were not yet considered as relevant to the speech situation. In order to provide a definition for such a body move, we drew upon aspects of the communicative act theories cited above. Hence it is not possible to say that the body moves were developed either by a derivative or an inductive method; rather the process involved both.

4.5   Engagement Space

Body moves take place within shifting spaces of engagement. An *engagement space* may be defined as the aggregate of the participants' body fields of engagement. An engagement field is based on a certain commitment in being bodily together. Hence we can call the engagement space, the *body field of engagement*. *In defining this space*, we found it most useful to draw upon Allwood's theory of communicative acts, as laid out above, particularly the communicative function, 'contact'.

The body field of engagement is set as the communication opens and the bodies indicate and signal a willingness to cooperate. The body field is a variable field and changes, depending on participants being comfortable or uncomfortable with each other. For instance, in the case where one person moves their hand over into the other's space, and that person withdraws their hand, this indicates that the 'contact' between these persons is disrupted. There are also examples where the participants hold their bodies back from entering the other's field of engagement, an indication of disagreement or discrepancy in the communication, signaling distance rather than contact. The degree of contact and the nature of the distance are expressed in terms of commitment and attitude. Hence an *immediate* space of engagement involves a high degree of contact and commitment to the communication situation; a *passive distance* is less involved and committed, whereas *disagreement* is very distanced and commitment is withheld. Disagreement or discrepancy can necessitate a *reconfiguration* of the body field of engagement.

Reconfiguration occurs when there is a disturbance in the relationship between the speakers; this discrepancy between them is expressed by their need to bodily re-arrange their relation to each other, so that a feeling of sharing an engagement space is re-established. After a momentary detachment or distance, the response move is akin to a motor reaction. It is a rhythmic reconfiguration of the body space between the participants creating a new engagement situation by reshaping the field of engagement.

The action category of reconfiguration occurs because there is a problem in the overlap in one person's body's field of engagement with another person's when one person moves into the other person's body field, at any particular moment. But if the overlap of their respective fields poses no problem the participants can undertake parallel coordinated moves.

Within the space of engagement, bodies can move in a coordinated manner to shift the focus within the communication situation to a specific point. Focus involves a movement of the body towards the area the speaker is attending to, i.e. his/her space of bodily attention; in response, the listener or other party moves their body towards the same focus. In as much as body moves control the management of focus, they become significant as a dimension of embodied interaction.

4.5.1 Body Moves

Body moves occur within the arena of the engagement space. In developing the category of BMs below, we have found it helpful to draw upon communicative acts and features of these acts that are parallel to the phenomena observed. Some features of communicative acts are specific to speech and are not embodied in body moves, such as intonation, or asking questions and giving commands. Some body moves have required the development of new terms, either in order to distinguish between them and their conversation analytic counterpart, such as in the case of 'check' (here, a body move is called a *b check*); or because there appears to be no clear counterpart in the theory of communicative acts (CA), for instance *dem-ref, attempt contact* and *focus*. (All these categories are explained below).

A body move is a Composite Dialogue Act (CDA) (see Engle 1998, on 'composite signal'), i.e. a collective act involving the movement of bodies and voices of two or more persons. Where bodies and voice form a collective act, we describe the body move as involving a related communicative act (CA) and the nature of this relation is dependent upon the context of the body move. Examples of associated communicative acts are suggest, confirm, acknowledgement and information-reference. *Suggest* (Traum 1994) happens when the initiator propose a new item as part of a plan; *confirm* is when either the initiator elicits confirmation and/or the responder confirms they understand; *acknowledgement* (*ack*) (Carletta et al. 1997) shows that the speaker has heard the move to which he/she responds, and often demonstrates understanding and acceptance; the newly constructed communicative act of *information-reference* (*info-ref*) denotes the content of the speech for which the body move provides the evidence. Below are some examples of Body Moves.

4.5.1.1 Attempt Contact

This body moves draws the other person's attention to the situation. It can be used to involve other persons in the dialogue, increasing their participation in, or commitment to, the dialogue situation, without explicitly asking them. *Attempt-Contact* increases the degree of contact in the engagement space by getting the other to move into the speaker's bodily field of engagement. It can be enabled by an eye movement, such as a looking gesture, or a hand and arm gesture. The associated communicative act is a *confirm* or a *suggest* action.

This body moves increases the participants involvement and commitment in the dialogue situation. In the example below, the person to the left of the picture, B, uses his hands and arm to get the person on the right, A's, attention.

Example 1 B is getting A's bodily attention (Fig. 4.1). The gesture, in content terms is iconic. However, it is also a *move*. Prior to this, B had been drawing in the same space as A, but moves back when he learns, to his disappointment, that he has missed a meeting when someone had presented some information about a part of the site that he had wanted to 'follow up'. A is still talking to B and giving him information, but B is not physically attending to him. B has just heard that a big pit is being excavated beneath this spot and he is asking about whether the water is able to get through. The discussion is about planting trees and making sure they have sufficient aeration. It *is* in this context that B makes this body move.

Here, the request act performed by the Body Move is different in level and nature from that performed by the Communicative Act *info-request*, (though related to it). The verbal act *is* a request for confirmation of information content. Although in this case, *Attempt-Contact* involves a representational gesture, or convention, the Body Move is also a request for attention. In fact, it is almost a

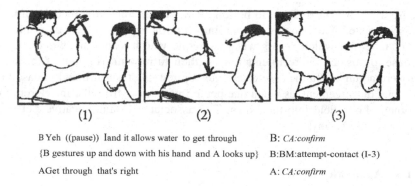

(1)	(2)	(3)

B Yeh ((pause)) Iand it allows water to get through	B: *CA:confirm*
{B gestures up and down with his hand and A looks up}	B:BM:attempt-contact (I-3)
AGet through that's right	A: *CA:confirm*

Fig. 4.1 Attempt-Contact

demand for attention in its exaggerated sweep. It is very hard for A to ignore it physically. Prior to this move, B had withdrawn from the immediate space of engagement and was participating from a physically passive distance; however his subsequent Body Move causes A to move into his field of engagement, making A turn his head around and answer his need. Hence the Body Move increases the degree of contact between the two.

The other Body Moves will be briefly described.[5]

4.5.1.2   Body Check: B-Check

This body move is identifiable as a 'check' in a manner that is parallel to the communication act 'check', but in a physical way, hence it needed another expression. To retain the idea of a checking action, we chose to call it the Body-Check or B-Check. In addition to confirming information, this body move signals understanding. Whilst the Body Move's associated Communicative Act is a request for confirming the information which is about the content of the communication, Body Moves are not questions or requests or commands which are about the content level of communication. The B-Check is much wider in its scope that the Communicative Act check. A B-Check in the study involved the architects mimicking each other, but that may have been coincidental.

4.5.1.3   Take-Turn

The Body Move *take-turn* occurs when the body moves prior to the speech turn. (cf. Traum's theory of turn taking acts). Whether bodily actions can be considered as turn-taking is a grey area. Some researchers suggest it is possible, thus Bavelas (1994) considers taking the turn to be an interactive gesture. According to Traum, the start of an utterance may be a take-turn act, whereas ending it might involve a

---

[5] Cit. Gill et al. (2000).

Release-Turn or a Keep-Turn, to be followed with another utterance when take-turn is attempted. We term this case an 'interruption movement'. Release-turn is a type of take-turn which occurs when someone who has the turn withdraws. In response to this act, the recipients release their turn by moving out of the space they were acting in. In the case of an interruption, the take-turn and release-turn can signal disagreement, as when one person withdraws from the interference of the other's body field into their own. The associated Communicative Act for a take-turn could be any.

4.5.1.4 Acknowledge: Ack

The Acknowledge move gives an idea of the respondent's attitude of response, i.e. how the person hears, and understands and perceives what is being discussed. It shows continued attention. This aspect of Acknowledge was identified by Clark and Schaefer (1989); it was not included by Carletta et al. (1997) because it leaves no trace in a dialogue transcript to be coded. However, it is part of the Body Move. The hearer and listener demonstrate, e.g. with their gesture, how they are acknowledging the other's proposal or request for agreement. The Body Move occurs in response to the other's Communicative Act of information reference or suggestion, and may be accompanied by a body release-turn or bodily place-holder. Its associated Communicative Act is the speech act 'acknowledge' or 'accept'. In one of the examples, the magnitude of a gesture and the physical proximity of a person's hands moving in close to the other's indicates the degree of engagement in that situation. The movement creates a change in the degree of contact, which may indicate the nature of the acknowledgement or acceptance.

4.5.1.5 Focus

Focus is a meta-discursive function of the type: 'I'm going to focus on this spot'. It is a signal for a change of level, causing a shift in the discussion towards the meta-level, and involving a movement of the body towards the area the speaker is attending to (the focus); in response, it causes the listener or other party to move their body forward towards the same focus. The category becomes significant as a dimension of body interaction as it shows how focus is managed. The response move may not involve understanding, but it does involve a willingness to perceive the message (Allwood et al. 1991). Maybe it is possible to describe Focus as mediating recognition on the part of the recipient, as the body move involving Focus causes the other persons to give their attention to what the focusing person is going to do next, by making them move into that person's space of bodily attention. It is distinct from the Dem-Ref body move, as the latter refers back to the noun-phrase and is ostensive, whereas Focus is about what the mover is going to shift towards, and thus creates increased Contact for engagement in this shift. The associated Communicative Act to the Body Move is a suggest act.

4.5.1.6   Demonstrative Reference (Dem-Ref)

This is a collective gesture that physically demonstrated the matter being referred to in the communication. It points to a specific location. It is possible to directly demonstrate, or ostensively assign referent to, a noun phrase by a pointing action. This body move facilitates the communication of the speech content that the speech alone could not achieve, and thereby adds a communicative dimension to that of speech. In comparison to the body moves, Attempt-Contact and Focus, Dem-Ref lies within the content of the communication. The associated CA is a suggest act.

4.5.1.7   Summary

Body Moves affect the way in which people are present to each other; they influence people's degree of closeness and their commitment to engage in action, and physically demonstrate this. This dimension of the way participants in a conversation relate to each other is not carried in the speech, but affects its import. In drawing on Allwood's theory of linguistic feedback (particularly the concept of 'contact') we developed the concept of 'the engagement space' between bodies interacting with each other. Traum's theory of grounding allows body moves to be seen as part of the process of achieving mutual understanding through turn-taking and grounding acts. In drawing upon these theories, *the dimension of contact becomes part of the grounding process.* Body Moves provide us with a dimension to the grounding process that is additional to the one covered by communicative act theory, and as such, can broaden the linguistic focus to encompass a wider concept of communicative or pragmatic acts. The Composite Dialogue Act was our bid towards this.

The idea of an engagement space or composite body field of engagement allows the spatial dimension of coordinated activity to become part of a dialogue act. It is a variable space as bodies are constantly negotiating and reforming their fields and their degrees of commitment to the situation. Moves such as Attempt-Contact and Focus enable the physical management of any possible loss of contact and lack of engagement or attention. In this way, these composite dialogue acts maintain the coordination process.

4.6   Rhythm and the Body Move

There is, however, one Body Move that was not possible to explain using a feedback, action and reaction, model of communication, and this was called the Parallel Coordinated Move (PCM). It would turn out to be critical in highlighting a common feature of the Body Moves, that of rhythm; their occurrence over the period of the video clip suggests a relationship between them which leads up to the moment of the Parallel Coordinated Move and makes it possible. This will be explored further below.

Here is a description of the activity in the video clip of the landscape architects sketching together. Two landscape architects are working on a design task that is typical of the daily practice in this firm. The senior architect is fully qualified and director of the company, whilst the other is an apprentice with the firm and due to qualify in a year's time. They are both familiar with each other and share a mutual respect, despite the difference in their status and experience (empathic relationship). Their task is to produce a plan for the car park of a site, and how to sign ways for people to move from the car park through the main site itself. Some time earlier, they had produced a sketch plan for the client. The site is to be transformed from being an old derelict brewery to a headquarters for this client. The client has produced a version of their sketch plan, largely following their own ideas and wants the landscape architects to take this further. Part of the discussion between the senior and junior architect is whether to go for something radical or generally remain within the bounds of what they have in front of them. They, or rather, the senior architect, decide that changing it would not greatly improve on what they have. Hence they decide to work with what they have.

4.6.1   Mediation

There is a great deal of body interactions in this design activity and their mutual respect means that B is able to express disagreements and produce his own suggestions however, they are communicating at different levels of design. The discrepancy in their status is evident in the take-turns and keep-turns that A performs. The senior architect is focusing on the 'conceptual structure' of the entire landscape, whereas the junior architect is focusing on 'one position' within that 'conceptual structure'. Their gestures and body movement correspond to the level of the design they are addressing. The senior architect makes large sweeping hand and arm gestures across the table. The junior architect makes small finger and hand pointing gestures and at one point leans down into the space. They never 'meet' – as one of them enters the space the other one moves out of it or shifts their position creating distance, except for the punctuations of Body Moves. This continues until the senior architect 'mimics' the junior architect's previous gesture and posture, moving his body down onto the drawing and proposing an alternative 'position' within the 'conceptual structure' to that which was the focus of the junior architect. The moment the senior architect's finger points at the position to indicate this intention, the junior architect also moves down into the space. The moment he touches the drawing paper with his finger and moves it in one stroke across the area of his proposal, the senior architect moves his finger as well – back and forth – across his alternative proposal. During this parallel coordinated action, they are finally synchronised in their proposals and entrained within each others' body motion and vocalisation. As the junior architect completes his drawing stroke and moves up out of the design space the senior architect's hand motion continues to move smoothly across into the junior architect's space, and in one pen stroke he acknowledges his proposal. As he does so, the junior architect's body relaxes; his tensed and hunched up shoulders relax downwards. The moment the Junior architect touches the paper to the moment the senior architect's hand motion acknowledges his proposal, lasts just 1.5 s.[6] We know that knowledge has been *mediated* (see Chap. 3) during the parallel coordinated action, enabling the senior architect to acknowledge his junior colleague. The acknowledgement is evident in the release of tension from the junior architect's body and his attempt at a topic shift.

4.6.2   Tacit

Between the junior architect's attempts to make his proposal and having it acknowledged, the moments where there is contact and a shared space between him and the senior architect are during Body Moves. Between his first and second proposal attempt, there are no Body Moves between them. Between his second and third proposal attempt, there are three Body Moves, two *attempt-contact* and one *b-check* (body check), that serve to pull attention and increase contact between the architects. Between the third proposal attempt and the parallel coordinated move there are two Body Moves which reconfigure (*body take-turn*) and *focus* attention. There is no gap between the last Body Move (*focus*) and the Parallel Coordinated Move. The specific occurrence of these Body Moves is not accidental and there is no resolution to the difference in the respective projects of these two architects until the Parallel Coordinated Move takes place.

As described above, Body Moves are composites of gesture, speech, and silence *of the participants together, not of the individuals* (as in the idea of a 'composite signal' (Clark 1996; Engle 1998)). This is an important distinction. Our skill in communication, as an individual, is impingent on our skill in performing with another self. In other words, *the understanding of the representations of the tacit dimension of another's action, is expressed in the skilled performance with the other, be this to agree, disagree, negotiate, acknowledge, or simply, to act at the same moment with the other (simultaneously).* In the 'Tacit Dimension' (1966) Polanyi described a relation between emergence and comprehension as existing when 'an action creates *new comprehensive entities*'. It is proposed that Body moves necessarily involve at least two people sharing the knowledge of the same comprehensive entity, namely, of their *joint skilled human performance. 'These comprehensive entities include, apart from our own performance, both the performance of other persons and these persons themselves'* (Polanyi, *op. cit. p. 49*). It is proposed that this sense of a person was important for my Japanese colleague to make sense of what a person says, and he was unable to gauge the person(s) in the video conference.

Another related and significant feature of the Parallel Coordinated Move is that it allows us to share our differences in co-existence. The architects are expressing

---

[6] In an earlier description of this move in Gill (2007) there is an error stating this period lasts 3 s. The timing is significant: we know from research into music perception that we have a 1.5 s limit for anticipating a beat (London 2004), and this parallel coordinated action and each of the other identified Body Moves, occurs within this window of time.

different but related projects at the same time. They are not producing the same particular movement, but by moving together at the same time (i.e. in synchrony), they are able to be aware of and perceive the other's point of view in a visceral way.

4.6.3 Rhythm and Body Field of Engagement

If two people are listening to a third person speaking, they are likely to synchronise their movements to that person, and by aligning themselves in this way they align themselves to each other (Kendon 1970, 1990). Observations of two people communicating show that they move different parts of the body at the same time (Condon and Ogston 1966; in the case of neonate synchrony with adult speech, see Condon and Sander 1974). In the parallel coordinated move example, the senior architect (A) and the junior architect (B) are moving with different forms expressing distinct projects. Their synchronisation may be enabled by their simultaneous alignment with A's speech rhythm. We know from studies of non face-to-face communication over a telephone (Bavelas et al. 2008) and via a microphone (Gill and Kawamori 2002) that gestural coordination on the part of the person speaking may be a self-maintenance motion, and this is one explanation for A's movement with his own speech.

To 'move with another is to show that one is "with" [that person] in one's attentions and expectancies' (Kendon 1990, p. 166). We described A's drawing action, which begins when B begins to draw, as a way of directly engaging with B's motion with his own body's motion. When bodies move together, it is a way of being 'open' to the other that is not possible in speech. If one situates this in the engagement space, *B stretches A's body field of attention with his own, by moving into it or touching its boundary*. When he touches down onto the drawing, he places his pencil physically very close to A's pen position; B's movement pulls A to move with him. The location that A has chosen on the drawing is close to the location of B's previous attempts (he made three attempts to get A's attention for his suggestion about signing a passage way from the car park). B's action is made possible by A's shift in gesture and in speech to his level of focus. In describing B's action as stretching A's bodily space of attention and into his own space of bodily attention, it is proposed that their personal spaces of action become expanded in their bodily connection, and that this creates a new open space for possible dialogue. This idea of moving inside or touching and stretching the space of bodily attention might be related to Kendon's thought of how 'the boundaries of [participants'] components coincide' (op. cit. 163); he spoke of the participants in his example as 'dancing to the same beat', and this is what the architects are doing during the Parallel Coordinated Move.

In the field of conversation analysis there is a concept called 'floor', which has conventionally assigned whoever is speaking at any time, to be holding the floor i.e. the attention of others. Some conversation analysts question this. Hayashi (1991) makes a distinction between the idea of taking the 'turn' to speak and holding a 'floor', arguing that a floor is a collaborative activity that can only be achieved by a person as an agreement obtained by feedback by the other person in the conversation, e.g. through backchannels. Most notably, Edelsky (1981) suggests that floor can lie outside of any specific person and arises out of the collaboration e.g. it can be referential to the topic of the conversation. In her work on group activities where there are simultaneous discussions, she argues that not only is it hard to talk about who has the floor, but there may even be multiple floors operating at the same time. And she extends the concept of the turn in speech to be the duration of the issue or point of view of any specific person, an on-record 'speaking'. Meierkord (2000) goes further and redefines a turn as a jointly completed unit of conversation that includes backchannels.

The idea of a collaborative floor is helpful for understanding how the idea of a floor might be applied to the parallel coordinated move and other body moves, a collaborative activity around a 'topic'. As both A and B are touching their spaces of bodily attention (body fields) as they move together, their bodies may be said to be *sharing the floor space, an* expanded personal space of action. Just as the Body Move and the Parallel Coordinated Move are a composite Dialogue Act across the participants, so is their floor a composite floor. It is proposed that this enables the quality of the 'open' space, allowing for common ground to be achieved via bodily experience.

4.7   Rhythm and Awareness of the Other

What would happen to our relations with each other if our possibility to move at the same time as each other is blocked?

This was investigated with the Interactive Workspaces Project at Stanford University (Guimbretiere et al. 2001) thanks to Terry Winograd and Jan Borchers, as an investigation of the role of non-verbal behaviour in cooperative interaction. By good fortune, the iRoom (the laboratory of the Interactive Workspaces project) contained a number of touch sensitive and large scale computer based graphical interfaces (Smart Boards), i.e. electronic whiteboards. At that time these only allowed one touch action at any time. This design constraint offered me the perfect drawing surface to explore with. By default, you could never act together on its surface, and thereby never achieve the parallel coordinated move whilst sketching. This would be useful for testing the quality and function of the Parallel Coordinated Move (Gill and Borchers 2004) and other Body Moves found in the study of the landscape architects sketching together. I involved undergraduates from the Faculties of Communication and Computer Science to work on the study with me. We decided that it would be engaging to ask pairs of students to create a shared dorm living space together on the Smart Board. Each pair was given some time to familiarise themselves with the Smart board, and quickly got to realize that they could not touch at the same time; if they did, there would be a disastrous zigzag of lines between the two points, messing up their drawing. We decided that it would also be useful to compare the activity at the Smart Board with that at a regular whiteboard to find out whether there would be particular differences in body moves and gesture and speech coordination. Hence, the pairs were mixed up to use these two interfaces, with some undertaking a session at a whiteboard and later moving to a Smart Board, and some vice versa.

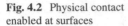

Fig. 4.2 Physical contact
enabled at surfaces

Preliminary analyses revealed that the participants' commitment, politeness and attention to each became reduced at the SmartBoard, in marked contrast to those sketching on a regular whiteboard. Furthermore, the quality of the resulting design was lower when using the SmartBoard. (Borchers et al. 2002; Gill et al. op. cit.).

With the whiteboard, (e.g. Fig. 4.2) we found similar behavioural alignments to the Body Moves identified in the landscape architect study e.g., the body move *ack* for acknowledging (see Figs. 4.2 and 4.3). The touch sensitive SmartBoard brought out 'touch' more as a salient feature of such behavioural alignment. Body fields of people touch when they engage with each other. In the case of paper and the conventional whiteboard, participants are not directly touching each other in the common sense of this term but in the sense of 'contact' with their persons through materials (touching the surface with pens and fingers and hands) and through movement. Touch is part of implicit knowledge (Reiner 2003). In her studies, Reiner investigates how a touch language is acquired by surgeons, through their experience of linking patterns of touch with interpretations in a non-symbolic manner.

In the case of the landscape architects (Fig. 4.3) who are standing at the drawing-table, the junior architect standing to the left (B) has his hand on the drawing surface and is holding a pen (in this case, he is holding a position or idea). The senior architect (A) moves in and makes a design suggestion, pointing to another particular place on the drawing, and as he does so, B lights his pen down to acknowledge his suggestion which he also does in speech ("yeh"). The contact on the surface allows for their simultaneous act. Notice that A's non-drawing hand is also touching the surface.

In the next example (Fig. 4.4), a pair of students are sketching at a regular whiteboard. Person (E) is standing back, watching and talking, and person (F) is drawing on the whiteboard. (F) has his body positioned to accommodate (E) by slightly opening it, slanted to the right, to share the engagement space with (E). At some point, (E) looks to the left of (F) to an area on the whiteboard and moves towards it. He picks up

Fig. 4.3 Body move *ack*

Fig. 4.4 A silent parallel shift

Fig. 4.5 C waiting for D to end his turn

another felt pen and begins to draw as well. As (E) touches the surface, (F) shifts his body and alters his posture so that it is now open slanted to the left, and increases contact with (E). Both are now acting in parallel. This shift occurs in silence.

In an example of activity at a SmartBoard (Fig. 4.5) C is standing back from it whilst D is drawing. He looks and moves to a position on the SmartBoard to the right of D. He leans into the surface but cannot draw because he has to first wait for D to end his turn.

Fig. 4.6 Allowing D to move into the zone of action

Fig. 4.7 A disturbance on the SmartBoard

In Fig. 4.6, D, without looking up, speaks, and his utterance causes C to turn his body back to look at him. As he cannot yet act, C moves back from the surface and waits, and as he is doing so, he breathes in deeply in frustration. C notices, pauses his drawing, turns to look at him and moves back from the zone of action, allowing D to move into it.

Once C is acting, i.e., drawing, D continues with his drawing on the Smart-Board (see Fig. 4.7). The result is a disturbance on the board, and a jagged line cuts across from D's touch point to C's, causing them both surprise and laughter. D momentarily forgot that you cannot touch the surface at the same time. This need to move whilst another is moving is not a conscious one; it is a form of synchrony called *entrainment*.

In Figs. 4.6 and 4.7 we see an attempt to act causing frustration for the person needing to act, until his need is noticed at which point the turn to act is offered to C by D. It is significant that C recognises D's need to act when he signals this need by moving his body away from the SmartBoard creating an awareness of distance in their situation, and that C responds to this with speech and his body, and further, that they forget that the surface is limited in affording their need to move together on it. In contrast, the whiteboard (see Figs. 4.4 and 4.2) permitted a more fluid movement around and on the surface and there is no turn-taking required on one person's part to permit the other person to act.

4.7.1 Autonomy and Visibility

When a designer at the SmartBoard does not easily give the turn to the other one, we see various strategies to force it. These include, moving close to the board and inside the visual locus of the drawing space in a quick motion, or moving back and forth, or reaching for a pen, or looking at the pen, or simply reaching out and asking for the pen the other person is currently using, or just moving right in front of the body of the person currently drawing, thereby forcing them back, and taking a pen from the pen holder. As either person can act at the whiteboard, there is no need for such strategies when drawing on it. These comparative surfaces give rise to differing strategies for *managing 'autonomous' behaviour.* If one considers the engagement space, at the SmartBoard participants may perform body moves such as *take-turn*, where the body field of the person drawing on it is disturbed by the other person's body field entering their's, and a reconfiguration of the engagement space is required. In contrast, at the whiteboard, body moves such as *attempt contact* and *focus* and *ack* (acknowledging) may be used to increase contact.

Being able to move with each other may prevent or repair breakdown in a communication situation. The single touch SmartBoard made those actions that are invisible when acting at a whiteboard, visible. Winograd and Flores (1986) speak of how 'structure' in communication 'becomes visible only when there is some kind of breakdown' (p. 68). Acts of rubbing something out whilst another is drawing, checking something by pointing on it, or touching the surface with a finger or hand to think about an idea, etc. are activities one takes for granted whilst sketching together on paper or a whiteboard. When all these aspects are inhibited or have to be negotiated, our natural rhythms of moving together that would normally be invisible i.e. not something we are consciously aware of doing, is made visible to us in their absence, and we have difficult in finding that fluidity. The single touch SmartBoard's unintended emphasis on autonomous action presented difficulties for the participants to have a tacit awareness of their state of contact in their engagement space.

4.7.2 Summary

The PCM and the other Body Moves as well as all related rhythmic and synchronous collective activity (not coded in the study of the landscape architects), were inhibited at the surface of the SmartBoard, and this lead to strictly sequential turn-taking behaviour. This in turn resulted in a lack of shared attention, withdrawal from the commitment to engage, or produced strategies to force the other person to give up their position at the surface. The participants who started off sketching together at the SmartBoard and were later asked to sketch at the whiteboard, reported that they felt more free, more relaxed, breathed better, and in general enjoyed the experience at the whiteboard much more. Those who moved to the SmartBoard after the drawing at the whiteboard, reported a more tense and awkward experience. Not only was there a marked difference in their emotional experiences, there was also a marked difference in the quality of their designs, with those produced at the SmartBoard being of lower quality than those produced at the Whiteboard.

In Gill et al. (2000), the parallel coordinated move had been mentioned in the work on Body Moves, however it was not developed in that discussion as it did not fit the sequential feedback model. Intuitively I felt that they were part of the same family. This study (Gill 2002; Gill and Borchers 2004) revealed that the Parallel Coordinated Move and the Body Moves share some rhythmic quality and that this is the thread that binds them, rather than, as we had earlier assumed, the frame of feedback or action-reaction.

4.8   Reflections

The discussion in this chapter has continued an investigation of tacit knowing as a personal act of knowing by considering: *I can only see how you see if we share the experience in the same physical space*. It explores the role of the body in mediating experience.

The discussion has taken the example of a mismatch in aesthetic judgements between an apprentice landscape architect located in the company's office in Wales and his mentor and other landscape architects located in the company's main office in the North of England. The mismatch was in seeing colours. His mentor's belief, based on experience, was that the only way the apprentice could come to see colours with him and his team was to colour with them in the same physical space, and that no form of technology, however seamless, could achieve this as this is a matter of lacking and needing experience. Hence, in this example of colouring in maps, they brought the apprentice to their main base in the North of England to re-colour all the maps with them.

What is it about being in the same physical space that enables one to see with others? Sociological studies of scientific knowledge and practice (for example, Collins 1982; Shapin 1994; Goodwin 1997) show how scientific knowledge is learnt, acquired, and articulated as a social process. Goodwin's study of how geophysicists judge when material fibres in a reaction vat are jet black, shows how this is an embodied process. Geochemists use their bodies as 'media that experience the material' being worked, such that understanding the meaning of the utterance 'jet black' requires 'co-participation' in physically working with the fibres.

How does the body mediate experience in 'co-participation'? The study of the two landscape architects sketching gives some insight into this (Gill et al. 2000). A three and a half minute video film of them is punctuated with movements, rather like bodies bouncing off each other, or one pulling the other, in swift action-reaction. One of these movements had a different structure; it was simultaneous. All these 'collective' moments of behavioural alignment have a rhythmic quality. These collective moments are considered as 'dialogue acts' that are *composite across the bodies and voices* of the participants involved, rather than being composite signals of the body and voice of one individual interacting with the composite signal of the body and voice of another. It is further proposed that body moves may be serving to maintain engagement and allowing for the possibility for us to reach a heightened level of engagement experienced in simultaneous rhythmic movement (body and/or voice), as described here in the Parallel Coordinated Move. In every culture we have the 'greeting', an act of simultaneous synchrony which Condon describes as being essential for us to be social beings; the greeting allows us time to achieve simultaneous synchrony together as we engage. When we are unable to achieve this with others, we become isolated and depressed and angry (Condon 1970). We saw the beginnings of this when we blocked the ability of both participants from touching the surface of the SmartBoard together during their collaborative sketching, which resulted in some rather un-collaborative behaviour. Within music therapy, the simultaneous rhythmic moment is called a 'pivotal moment'.[7] For it to occur just once in a 1 h session is an achievement of contact between the therapist and their client: the pivotal moment releases positive emotion.

It is proposed that dialogue acts in which the body fields may intersect, overlap, and touch, allow one person to 'see' with the other. Here one moves from a situation of distance, of *seeing-as*, which requires interpretation, to one of *seeing* with the other. Tilghman terms the state of seeing-as, 'mediated understanding'. Once you have the skill to see, you can understand without interpretation, and just perform. Transposing this to the situation of dialogue itself and out of the context of its discussion on the acquisition of expertise, we could say that the transition from seeing-as to seeing occurs in the spontaneity of rhythmic alignment, where there is understanding (seeing) yet *it is mediated* within our movement.

In the architects example, where the Parallel Coordinated Move flows into the acceptance of the apprentice's idea by the senior architect (Fig. 4.3), there is *mediation of knowledge* that bears a qualitative similarity to that between the mediator and the expert in Chap. 3: "Mediation is not an individual's action (be this a gesture or/ and an utterance), but a collective moment between the mediator and the expert (i.e. two or more persons), and once the expert recognizes the mediator in his/her response, the whole group also understands that the source of the problem has been identified" (Chap. 3). In the architecture study we know that the mediation of the problem, of the difference between the apprentice's proposal and the senior architect's idea, has occurred in the Parallel Coordinated Move, and that the senior architect recognises this and accepts that the apprentice has a valid proposal. The apprentice in turn, is aware that he has been heard and acknowledges this, evident in his body as he stands back up and relaxes his shoulders and breathes. As with the case of the mediator-expert in Chap. 3, mediation is not of an individual's body movement and voice but lies within a collective act, whereby the expert recognises the apprentice's idea as he moves with it, evident in his response of accepting it.

Collective acts are sensory and affective, extending outside the skin membrane. The idea of an *engagement space* or composite body field of engagement allows the spatial, sensory, temporal, and affective dimensions of coordinated activity to

---

[7] Conversation with Helen Odell-Miller, Professor and practitioner of Music Therapy at ARU, during Touching Sound project meetings. A brief description of Touching Sound is given in Chap. 1.

become part of a consideration of what is dialogue. Movement and touch are being thought of as part of a continuum, rather than as distinct. Engagement is a variable space as bodies are constantly negotiating and reforming their fields and their degrees of commitment to the situation (i.e. relation with the other person(s)).[8]

Within this picture of dialogue, placing a pane of glass between two people would fragment their Engagement Space. This goes some way to explain why the video conference seemed to have reduced the bandwidth of communication for my Japanese colleague (Chap. 1) to that of 'words' and 'grammatical fluency' which lies at the transactional level of communicating information. In our face-to-face everyday communications, sharing a physical space allows us to experience *social uncertainty* and enables us to manage it (Cross 2012). When the bandwidth of this complexity is reduced there seems to be a gap in communication at the relational level[9] that makes it difficult to 'make sense' of what is 'said'. The *interface* did not *mediate* the communication. The kinds of cues that the junior landscape architect was missing when he tried to colour in the maps, using the explicit representations of the skilled practices of his colleagues which they had sent to guide him, are of the same kind that my colleague in Japan drew upon in order to be with another person when he speaks and thinks with him or her. It is these other cues that are critical for gaining 'experience' of the other and building 'tacit knowing' and 'trust'.

On the matter of the body and tacit knowledge, this work questions the separation of the somatic from the relational and the collective made by Collins (2013). His categories of tacit knowledge (see Chap. 1) are weighed for their strengths and weaknesses according to whether, in various conditions, the body can be made explicit. In his framework, the somatic and the relational may be made explicit, but the collective may not as this is culture and culture is about ways of ways of behaving with social responsibility. However, it is mistaken to separate the functions of the body for any context of human perception and action from the wholeness of how we grasp and comprehend the world around us, be this material, intellectual, and emotional, as from the moment we are born, this is shaped in our interactions with others. When Polanyi famously says, 'we know more than we can tell', he is referring to our neural processes. We perceive and are attending to what we perceive from our awareness of our neural processes. Our brain is body. Polanyi collapsed the historical dualistic construct between mind and the body. In the collective act of the body move and the parallel coordinated move, the somatic, the relational and the collective categories of Collins are collapsed in this personal act of knowing where the body mediates experience of knowing how, knowing that, and knowing when.

---

[8] This is explored further in the next, and last, chapter in the example of the T-Garden (Sha and Gill 2005), which is a multi-sensory responsive, and topological, media environment.

[9] Cross (2012) considers the primacy of the relational level in musical interaction in contrast to the primacy of the transactional level in speech interaction. The relational level is akin to how we connect when making music together, where the concept of a sender and receiver is not applicable, as participants are such at the very same time. The expression 'relational' is used by researchers working on the design of interactive robots (Breazeal and Picard 2006) and interactive technologies, where 'relational interaction' is concerned with relationships.

References

Allwood, J., Nivre, J., & Ahlsen, E. (1991). *On the semantics and pragmatics of linguistic feedback* (Tech. Rep. No. 64). Gothenburg Papers. Theoretical Linguistics. Goteborg University.

Bavelas, J. B. (1994). Gestures as part of speech: Methodological implications. *Research on Language and Social Interaction, 27*(3), 201–221.

Bavelas, J. B., Gerwing, J. S., Sutton, C., & Prevost, D. (2008). Gesturing on the telephone: Independent effects of dialogue and visibility. *Journal of Memory and Language, 58*, 495–520.

Borchers, J., Gill, S., & To, T. (2002). *Multiple large-scale displays for collocated team work: Study and recommendations*. Technical Report. Stanford University.

Breazeal, C., & Picard, R. W. (2006). The role of emotion-inspired abilities in relational robots. In R. Parasumaran & M. Rizzo (Eds.), *Neuroergenomics: The brain at work*. Oxford: Oxford University Press.

Carletta, J., Isard, A., Isard, S., Doherty-Sneddon, G., & Anderson, A. (1997). The reliability of a dialogue structure coding system. *Association for Computational Linguistics, 23*(1), 13–31.

Clark, H. H. (1996). *Using language*. Cambridge: Cambridge University Press.

Clark, H. H., & Brennan, S. E. (1991). Grounding in communication. In B. Resnick, J. M. Levine, & S. D. Teasley (Eds.), *Perspectives on socially shared cognition* (pp. 127–149). Washington, DC: American Psychological Association Books.

Clark, H. H., & Schaefer, E. F. (1989). Contributing to discourse. *Cognitive Science, 13*, 259–294.

Collins, H. M. (Ed.) (1982). *The sociology of scientific knowledge: A sourcebook*. Bath: Bath University Press.

Collins, H. H. (2013). *Tacit and explicit knowledge*. Chicago: University of Chicago Press.

Condon, W. S. (1970). *Radio interview*. Boston University Radio. http://www.edu-cyberpg.com/Literacy/WhatresearchCondon.asp

Condon, W. S., & Ogston, W. D. (1966). Sound film analysis of normal and pathological behavior patterns. *Journal Nervous and Mental Diseases, 143*(4), 338–347.

Condon, W. S., & Sander, L. W. (1974). Neonate movement is synchronized with adult speech. Integrated participation and language acquisition. *Science, 183*, 99.

Cross, I. (2012). Music and communication in music psychology. *Psychology of Music, 42*(6), 809–819.

Edelsky, C. (1981). Who's got the floor? *Language in Society, 10*(3), 383–421.

Efron, D. (1941). *Gesture and environment*. New York: Kings Crown Press. Republished as Gesture, Race and Culture, Mouton, 1972.

Engle, R. A. (1998). Not channels but composite signals: Speech, gesture, diagrams and object demonstrations are integrated in multimodal explanations. In *Proceedings of the 20th annual conference of the cognitive science society* (pp. 321–327), USA.

Furuyama, N. (2000). Gestural interaction between the instructor and the learner in origami instruction. In D. McNeill (Ed.), *Language and gesture: Window into thought and action*. Cambridge: Cambridge University Press.

Gill, S. P. (1995). *Dialogue and tacit knowledge for knowledge*. Transfer. Ph.D. Thesis, Cambridge: University of Cambridge.

Gill, S. P. (1997). Aesthetic design: Dialogue and learning. A case study of landscape architecture. *AI & SOCIETY, 9*, 273–285.

Gill, S. P. (2002). *The parallel coordinated move: Case of a conceptual drawing task*. Published Working Paper: Helsinki: CKIR. ISBN.

Gill, S. P. (2004). Body moves and tacit knowing. In B. Gorayska & J. L. Mey (Eds.), *Cognition and technology*. Amsterdam: John Benjamin.

Gill, S. P. (2007). Musicality in the human system interface. *AI & Society, 21*(4), 567–605.

Gill, S. P., & Borchers, J. (2004). Knowledge in co-action: Social intelligence in collaborative design activity. *AI & SOCIETY, 17*(3), 322–339.

Gill, S. P., & Kawamori, M. (2002). Coordination of gestures in a non face-to-face setting. In M. Rector, I. Poggi, & N. Trigo (Eds.), *Gestures, meaning and use*. Porto: Fundacao Fernando Pessoa.

Gill, S. P., Kawamori, M., Katagiri, Y., & Shimojima, A. (2000). The role of body moves in dialogue. *RASK, 12*, 89–114.

Goodwin, C. (1997). The black of black: Colour categories as situated practice. In L. B. Resnick, S. Roger, P. Clotilde, & B. Barbara (Eds.), *Discourse, tools and reasoning: Essays on situated cognition* (pp. 111–140). New York: Springer.

Guimbretiere, F., Stone, M., & Winograd, T. (2001). *Stick it on the wall: A metaphor for interaction with large displays*. Submitted to Computer Graphics (SIGGRAPH 2001 Proceedings).

Hayashi, R. (1991). Floor structure of English and Japanese conversation. *Pragmatics, 16*(1), 1–30.

Hood, B. (2012). *The self illusion. Why there is no you inside your head*. New York: Oxford University Press.

Hood, B. (2014). *The domesticated brain. Pelican introduction*. London: Pelican.

Johannessen, K. (1988). Rule following and tacit knowledge. *AI & SOCIETY, 2*(4), 287–301. Springer.

Kawamori, M., Kawabata, T., & Shimazu, A. (1998). Discourse markers in spontaneous dialogue: A corpus based study of Japanese and English. In *Proceedings of 17th international conference on computational linguistics*. (COLING-ACL'98).

Kendon, A. (1970). Movement coordination in social interaction: Some examples described. *Acta Psychologica, 32*, 100–125.

Kendon, A. (1990). *Conducting interaction*. Cambridge: Cambridge University Press.

Kita, S. (1993). Language and thought interface: A study of spontaneous gestures and Japanese mimetics. PhD thesis. Chicago: University of Chicago.

London, J. (2004). *Hearing in time: Psychological aspects of musical meter*. Oxford: Oxford University Press.

Malloch, S., & Trevarthen, C. (Eds.). (2009). *Musicality: Exploring the basis of human companionship*. Oxford: Oxford University Press.

McNeill, D. (1992). *Hand and mind*. Chicago: University of Chicago Press.

McNeill, D., Cassell, J., & McCullough, K. E. (1994). Communicative effects of speech-mismatched gestures. *Research on Language and Social Interaction, 27*(3), 223–237.

Meierkord, C. (2000). Interpreting successful lingua franca interaction. An analysis of non-native-/non-native small talk conversations in English. Linguistik Online 5, 1/00.

Mey, J. (2000). *Pragmatics. An introduction*. 2nd Edition. Oxford: Blackwell.

Polanyi, M. (1962). *Personal knowledge: Towards a post critical philosophy*. London: Routledge and Kegan Paul (Reprint of 1958 version with corrections).

Polanyi, M. (1966). *The tacit dimension*. New York: Doubleday. 1983 Reprinted.

Reiner, M. (2003). Seeing through touch: The role of haptic information in visualizing models and modeling. *Science and Education, 3*, 73–84.

Reiner, M. (2009). Sensory cues, visualization and physics learning. *International Journal of Science Education, 3*(3), 343–364.

Sha, X. W., & Gill, S. P. (2005). *Gesture and response in field-based performance*. The ACM proceedings of creativity and cognition. In E. A. Edmonds, L. Candy, P. Brown, T. T. Hewett, & J. Jefferies (Eds.), *Proceedings of the 5th conference on creativity & cognition*, London, pp. 205–209, 12–15 Apr 2005. New York: ACM Press.

Shapin. (1994). *A social history of truth. Civility and science in seventeenth-century England*. Chicago: University of Chicago Press.

Shimojima, A., Katagiri, Y., & Koiso, H. (1997). Scorekeeping for conversation-construction. In *Proceedings of the Munich workshop on semantics and a pragmatics of dialogue*.

Streeck, J. (1993). Gesture as communication I: It's coordination with gaze and speech. *Communication Monographs, 60*, 275–299.

Tilghman, B. R. (1988). Seeing and seeing-as. *AI & SOCIETY, 2*(4), 303–319.

Traum, D. T. (1994). A computational theory of grounding in natural language conversation. PhD thesis. Rochester: University of Rochester.

Winograd, T., & Flores, C. F. (1986). *Understanding computers and cognition: A new foundation for design*. Norwood: Ablex Press.

Wittgenstein, L. (1958). *Philosophical investigations*. Oxford: Blackwell.

Chapter 5
Tacit Engagement: Betwixt and Inbetween

Abstract This chapter brings the discussion from the previous four chapters together and develops it further. Firstly, it summarises what has been learned about the conception of an interactive and mediating interface, irrespective of specific contexts and technologies. The chapter ties together theory and practice across the various contexts to identify the foundational elements of a personal act of knowing within human relations. It looks to the future at what we need to consider as the foundations for human – technology relations for developing the relational interface, extending this discussion with fundamental philosophical and artistic questions being raised by the arts/performance arts about the relational in performance and human connectivity. A theoretical introduction is followed by a discussion of eight projects of artistic and design research, in which a new scientific paradigm is explored. The result is the formulation of the concept of 'tacit engagement'.

5.1   Introduction: The Relational Interface

This book explores whether the concept of the *interface* can be located in *dialogue*, *performance*, and the *tacit dimension of knowledge* within the human system, and thereby expand possibilities for what it could then mean as technology. For this to be possible, I ask what would we need for an interface to support how we relate to each other, in particular, what Polanyi (1966) called our *personal act of knowing*.

The discussion is set against a background of historical concepts of data, efficiency, utility, and automation, which have permeated the idea of the interface. This is facing challenges, for example, with the problems of bottlenecks of vast quantities of data and how to relate them (expert systems, data bases, big data), and how to support our relations with each other and share and enable us to impart knowledge and skills when we are distributed in space via various mediating interfaces (e.g. Facebook, Skype, video conferences, and other forms of tangible and interactive interfaces). Yet, what does it mean to mediate? What is the difference in the processes of mediation when we are engaged in embodied co-present interaction, and when we are communicating via digital means? What then is the relation between mediation and interface?

The measurement of time and human skilled action in the design of automata and for maximum utility in the workplace has been part of a belief in societal

© Springer International Publishing Switzerland 2015
S.P. Gill, *Tacit Engagement*, DOI 10.1007/978-3-319-21620-1_5

progress (Schaffer 1990), and instrumental in the evolution of the concept of the interface. In the twentieth and twenty-first century the idea that computational artificial agents can replace humans, for example, as companions for the elderly, and will be more effective than humans, for example, as a culturally adaptable teacher or an anonymous therapist, continues this belief. The examples just mentioned are of projects where the intentions are for the social good and to improve people's lives. Yet, as with all *naturoids* (Negrotti 2012) where one reduces the complexity of the natural object, there is the argument that reproduction takes on its own complexity and the further it is improved and developed upon, the further removed it is from its natural counterpart, and our relationships with such technologies will affect our relationships with them and each other and nature in ways that are beyond prediction (Negrotti op. cit.).

This relates to a problem that is often spoken of, of the sum of the parts failing to make the whole. Polanyi in discussion with Carl Rogers states, "There are limits for making something more explicit than it has been, and the mere effort of going in that direction may be destructive. The problem arises in analyzing and trying to put together explicitly a thing which has been broken down into parts. The tragic thing about it is, analyzing and putting together is the most powerful way of getting truth. I mean our whole biology almost exists in analyzing and putting things together. So that we are in difficulty because nobody can tell us whether what we have spilt up can be put together again or not; and if we build up a culture recklessly on the assumption that only things are valid which can be broken into parts – and that putting together will take care of itself – we may be quite mistaken, and all kinds of things may follow." (Kirschenbaum and Henderson 1989, Polanyi in conversation on the topic of "Knowledge or Science?" p. 164). The arts (this includes the performance arts) also investigate truth, for example, in the case of dance (Noh, Ikuta 1988) they do break movements into parts and in creating the whole they discover this possibility by immersing their whole person and making a movement part of their self. In this newly established self where the parts have become whole, trust and truth are established between dancers and with the audience. In art, *authenticity* creates trust between performer/artist and the performer and the audience/viewer. Truth lies in a personal act of knowing which is *relational*. This is distinct from truth acquired through data and logic.

The paradigm of data (of parts) and utility gives primacy to *transactional information* over that which is *relational*. The concepts relational and transactional have been adapted from a comparison made between music and language (Cross (2012), where music is necessarily relational (rhythm, pitch, melodic) and language is primarily transactional (semantics and grammar).[1] In the project Touching Sound,[2] to create an interface to support cooperative musical behavior, this comparison made it clear that a conceptual shift from the transactional towards the relational in

---

[1] This concept of the relational although related, differs from that of 'relational interaction' (e.g. Breazeal and Picard 2009) where it denotes the relationships between people.

[2] http://rhoadley.net/research/touching/index.php. See also Aaron et al. (2013).

human-computer interaction needs to be drawn for the case of musical interaction. The primacy of the transactional permeates the analysis of human interaction and human cognition and the design of virtual agents, intelligent interactive technologies, gesture interfaces, tele-communication, etc. It can be argued that without the balance of the relational (tacit, personal, experiential, ethical, aesthetic), a focus on the transactional in any domain may lead to inflexible systems that are less likely to be able to handle the unexpected and breakdowns.

Technologies of data and utility presume to represent and provide certainty and in the case of expertise this can cause experienced professionals to lose confidence in their ability to doubt (Goranzon 1988, 1992) and thereby in their confidence to make judgements, as the ability to doubt is fundamental to our capacity to judge with confidence. As a result, workers are not encouraged to judge but to accept what output the computer provides them with and may potentially lose their critical capacities over time. The certainty of data abstracted from our experience has implications for a range of interactive technologies that represent human behaviours, including gesture and emotion, and ideas about how we think. These implications have been addressed within a rich discussion on human skill (Goranzon op. cit.; Rosenbrock 1988, 1990, 1996; Cooley 1987, 2007; Rauner et al. 1988; Smith 1992; Gill 1996; Schaffer op. cit., Winograd and Flores 1986). Putting technology aside, such abstraction can lead to serious errors in judgment, as in the case of the pediatrician who administered a fatal dose of 15 mg instead of .15 mg to a baby despite being warned by the experienced nurse that this was incorrect (Cooley 2007). A problem of abstract data, of the explicit, is a notion of *the one best way* (Cooley 1987), and this can affect what is perceived as relevant information or pathways for decision-making (Gill 1995). Abstract ideas of relevance and decision making processes cannot completely capture the complexity of decision making in every day life, including professional practices (Chap. 4), and this leads to designs of decision-making technologies that, in turn, impact on the ways we think about solving problems and making judgements.

In the discussion in this book, I have extended the relational-transactional comparison between music and language to an analysis of mediation and the tacit dimension in human interaction. It is mistaken to believe that knowledge is either tacit or explicit, rather the explicit always has a tacit dimension (Rosenbrock 1988; Wittgenstein 1958), and the tacit can be shared in silence with someone who understands us very well, where you become one, a state of I Thou (Buber 1923), or where you share the same background of knowledge where the utterance of a seeming 'explicit representation' says it all. It is not always the case that a narrative style will convey information in a clearly understandable way, in fact, it may sometimes fail to do so. What is clear is that we can better understand what makes for success if we consider how knowledge is performed in our daily lives with others, i.e. knowledge as skilled embodied performance. It is proposed that the key to success is the process of mediation which is a collective act between the participants engaged in it: in the case of an expert and an apprentice architect (see Chap. 4), mediation is not of an individual's body movement and voice but lies within a collective act, whereby the expert recognises the apprentice's idea as he moves with it, evident in his response of accepting it. In another example of a design team of 'experts' (Chap. 4)

"Mediation is not an individual's action (be this a gesture or/and an utterance), but a collective moment between the mediator and the expert (i.e. two or more persons), and once the expert recognizes the mediator in his/her response, the whole group also understands that the source of the problem has been identified." At any time in a meeting, any person can become a mediator and for any mediator, there will be an expert who recognizes they have mediated something that the expert can do something about. It is often thought that experts identify the source of problems in which they have expertise, however, it is often what I call a 'mediator' who identifies the key to a problem, but it is only the expert who can recognize the key and solve the problem. In the collective moment of mediation, we express our 'know how', that we 'know that', and critically, that we 'know when', simultaneously. Hence abstracting the complexity of the 'personal act of knowing' from ourselves is to presume such abstraction represents how we make decisions but fails to do so.

The concept of intersubjectivity (Husserl 1931) is sometimes considered for developing systems that are more 'friendly', more 'understanding', more empathetic. This is a concept based on the projection of the self, of placing ourselves in the other's shoes and understanding how we would react were we him/her. Concepts of sympathy and empathy tend to be rooted in this *identity transference* (Hall 1976) that assumes or necessitates a sameness of culture. This is natural to assume, as we move with the rhythms of our cultures in learning the dance of life with others around us (Hall 1983), and we fail to be sympathetic or empathetic when someone does not behave as we expect them to and we are offended. The problem with identifying transference is that we may fail to see that the problem lies within us. This is detrimental to developing relations and is highly problematic in the cross-cultural situation. Hall suggests that we need to make culture (our own) explicit so that we can know where we are misunderstanding, i.e. to make ourselves conscious of our own cultural behaviours, and that failure to do so will lead to serious breakdowns in cross-cultural collaborations. In a sense, we need to become apprentices in the cross-cultural situation we seek to become skilled in (Collins 2013).

In conclusion, it is arguable that any interface that seeks to engage with our personal act of knowing needs to be able to afford us our relational dimension in balance with transaction. There is now a slow but growing shift from some thinkers towards the relational, both from within the field of human computer interaction with discussions on action versus cognition (Dourish 2004; 'Tangible Media, MIT Media Lab[3]) and most notably from the convergences of the arts (Vesna 2012, Nevejan 2007), performance arts (e.g. dance, Boddington 2012; dance and music, Fluxustree (2009–2010[4]) and humanities and science (Sha 2013) with digital technology. Some of the most reflective work on the balance between the relational and transactional is coming from artists joining hands with scientists and technologists to find alternative ways to investigate the relation between human and the digital and the mediated human, beyond the dominant concepts of technology as a transactional conduit. This is a shift in paradigm towards what I will term the *relational interface*.

---

[3] http://www.media.mit.edu/research/groups/tangible-media

[4] http://rhoadley.net/comp/fluxustree/

5.2   Art and Science: Betwixt and in Between

Some of the innovative work in the convergence of art, science and technology that addresses the balance between the relational and the transactional is shifting the position of the human from the center of a picture of progress to being part of nature and being material, where cosmological qualities of *energy* and *matter* become salient. This reflects an increasing need for meaning in a world that is becoming more explicitly about quantification, objectivity, and utility. This shift is reminiscent of a questioning by writers, artists and philosophers at the turn of the twentieth century, for example, Henri Bergson whose 'process philosophy' of experience and intuition, time, and Creative Evolution (1911) is a poetic expression of human life, value, and purpose. In the turn of the twentieth century Bergson is questioning the rationalistic and utilitarian approach to knowledge as being about causality and objects, by using poetic expression to explore our creative intuition and draw together our life energy and life energy in our environment as a common force of survival and evolution. Remarkably he was awarded the Nobel prize for literature for his work on Creative Evolution in 1924, demonstrating that a synergy of art and science can open alternative ways of thinking and of expressing knowledge that transcend either of their boundaries.

Such thinkers and artists laid the ground for a paradigm shift in philosophy in the twentieth century with the emergence of concepts of intersubjectivity (Husserl 1931), questioning of the idea of 'certainty' (Wittgenstein 1969), and positing the body as the source of knowledge (Merleau Ponty 1945).[5] In the twenty-first century this questioning is re-emerging in a cross-disciplinary dialogue between art and science and technology, where design is a part of this dialogue rather than being the focus of its attention. This is clearly visible in the collaboration between the artist Victoria Vesna and the neuroscientist Grimzewski, where new art and scientific discoveries are made through a natural process of sharing ideas without a clear idea of where the dialogue might take them but trusting it. This way of working together is reflected throughout the projects presented here. The idea of what constitutes an experiment is itself a philosophical project for the scientist and mathematician Sha XinWei, that he explores in dialogue and practice with dancers and choreographers, historians and philosophers of science, artists, and technologists. The shift is towards what may be described as a balance between an aesthetic, ethic, social, and spiritual *purpose*. For example, Caroline Nevejan's work on Witnessed Presence is rooted in Buber's I-Thou (Buber op. cit.) and the international convention of human rights, and her work with artists investigates what happens to ethical behavior and trust as we become less present to each other in distributed space. The projects are also an expression of an ongoing tension between forces that constrain and bound human freedom and those that seek to free the human spirit. We see this in Kristina Andersen's work on intimacy where she asks people to play and imagine and feel magic using every day materials in experiments that engage their emotions, and she does so in order to think about what an

---

[5] See chapter one for a fuller discussion.

interface would need to be like to facilitate this. Maja Kazmanovic and the FOaM lab's moto, 'Grow your own worlds', is inclusive and invites the public, the community, to partake in the lab discussions, and they have created a free space to develop projects that address the contemporary issues facing society.

In all the projects selected for discussion below, developments in science and technology are motivated by and shaped with the arts and the humanities and social sciences, where each inspires the other and together they seek to engage us at a personal level of commitment. That is, they whether intending to or not, are significant for my questions about whether an interface can facilitate the personal act of knowing of the kind that we are able to achieve with another person and that enables us to understand and live in sustainable ways with nature. These projects or 'designs' are not, as Sha would say 'definitive answers', rather they are investigations where the process itself is deeply important.

The structural engineer and designer Cecil Balmond (2002) describes design as an intervention, a 'local forcing move', a 'juxtaposition that stresses rhythm', or 'two or more events mixing to reveal hybrid natures.' There is no hierarchy, only interdependence in this 'template' of the Informal. The *informal* shares qualities with the *tacit in dialogue*, and architects, artists, dancers, choreographers, musicians and researchers and practitioners working at the edges of disciplines may recognize themselves in this realm of emergence. It is no accident that recurring thoughts expressed by those involved in the collaborations of arts with the sciences and the digital world include the following:

In Between
Betwixt and In Between
Betweeness

Hybrid
Transitional
Liminal
Transcendent

Are these the qualities of the tacit, of mediation, in dialogue? What are the salient factors that need to be considered for bridging the relational gap in the interface, and what may be the limits to achieving this? The arts necessarily deal with the relational level of human engagement and hence are essential for any discussion on what it means to be human, on how we engage with each other, and on the technologies that increasingly form part of our everyday lives.

5.3 Art@Science: Eight Projects

I see these projects as having two kinds of emphases, one being the need to develop philosophies or conceptual frameworks and the other, the need for methodologies. Neither of them focus on a product or a specific design as their objective, and arrive at these as grounded outcomes of a process. Sha, Vesna, Kuzmanovic, Nevejan, Ishii, and Balmond are providing us with philosophies and conceptual frameworks, whilst Boddington and Andersen are developing methodologies. Together they represent the spectrum of art, science, social science, performance, and technology, and they share fundamental ideas about how we need to think about the place and purpose of technology in our lives to meet our need for authenticity, trust, coherent identity, a fairer and inclusive society, continuity between being human and being part of nature, and that our embodied awareness is central for any future interface to support these needs.

5.3.1   Betweeness: 'A De-anthropocentrizing Phenomenology' (Topological Media Lab, Sponge)

In the first of these examples, I take the work of Sha Xin-Wei whom I came to know whilst at Stanford University, where I spent 3 years with the Centre for the Study of Language and Information. One day, in 2001, whilst I was working on an experiment with the Interactive Workspaces lab, Terry Winograd (Prof Computer science, Stanford University) walked in for a meeting accompanied by someone, and just as they were walking past, Terry stopped to introduce us saying he thought we might have shared interests and it would be good for us to know of each other. He was right. Xin-Wei and I did meet and the dialogue has never stopped.

Sha currently heads the School of Arts, Media and Engineering of the ASU Herberger Institute for Design and the Arts, and is the Founder and Director of the Topological Media Lab. His work is on the architecture of responsive media spaces that involves the critical study of media arts and sciences. He is concerned with the phenomenology of performance, phenomenology of differential geometry, and technologies of performance. He applies the idea of topology to media, to create what he calls, pliant computational matter, and this involves the study of issues related to gesture and performance, sensors and active fabrics, temporal patterns, computer-mediated interaction, geometrical visualisation, and writing systems. He collaborates with artists, performance artists, philosophers, designers, computer scientists, musicians, actors, historians and philosophers of science, to address these issues, create topological media, and develop performances, and all the while, working on a phenomenology that is not anthropocentric. Technology is part of the philosophical investigation.

He describes his work as lying between art and philosophy, where "*the betweenness is most essential.*" It is in this betweenness that he is developing his 'de-anthropocentrizing phenomenology' and embeds it in a cosmology where materiality is 'inspired from continuity, field, and philosophy of process', based on 'ethico-aesthetic' as well as technoscientific grounds. What does he mean by this? He tells of how he asks his students and colleagues, "why do you do what you do?" which for him is related to the question, "Why do we live?", that in turn concerns 'how we live'. Hence he is asking us about the quality of life rather than its meaning, which is 'more enamored of epistemology'. He avoids framing these questions as phenomenological ones about our 'experience' of life. Instead, reminiscent of Bergson, he is finding "*a poetic way*" to explore ideas about matter and practice, a process philosophy, within the context of contemporary and emerging technologies of performance. Just as Bergson questioned our perception of the world as consisting of objects and asked us to think of it as consisting in matter and continuity, so does Sha. This alters how we can consider how we relate within the world, without ego and with a greater chance of achieving mutual respect for each other, and it requires a rethink of what technology could be about.

Sha approaches the *continuous* as *topological*, and investigates the topology of media and matter by creating installation-events. He draws on studies of science and technology to consider the ethico-aesthetic[6] consequences of this approach to performance and computational media. This leads him to posit technology as a philosophical question to "accommodate value", exploring notions of interaction, responsive media, and performativity. I find it interesting that he is creating a genealogy of topological media that "*produce matters of value* as well as matters of fact": Topology is about the continuous, about proximity and connectedness without "metric quantity", "immeasurably richer than the graphs and networks favored by engineers and their social scientists!" For Sha, topological media is a set of working concepts, a simple set of material and embodied articulations or expressions that allows us to engage in speculative engineering or philosophy as art, and "to slip the leg irons and manacles of grammar, syntax, finite symbol systems, information and informatics, database schemas, rules and procedures. .... [it] permits us to relinquish a priori objects, subjects, and egos and yet constitute value and novelty." For him, the Topological Media Lab is an art practice, deeply informed by practices of engineering, mathematics, and philosophy to support 'experientially rich, improvisational activity'.

Movement and gesture are explored as the 'formation of subjective experience' but posited within what he calls 'substrate matter' rather than in cognition. He is critical of the dominant model of interaction of 'humans and their proxies engaging in an action-reaction ping-pong', where interaction design, "even in its most enlightened mood, has been centered on the human (viz. "human-centered design"), as if we knew what a human was, and where a human being ends and the rest of the world begins." When I asked Xin-Wei about this, he explained that he would rather we be more modest in assuming that we know what a human "is", more modest about any metaphysical or scientific claims about what any entity "is." "I very much respect and desire and participate in talking about human experience, and what humans ought to do with what they take to be other humans, but also, and more profoundly with the rest of the world beyond one's own ego. I just urge us to do that with a lot more humility – to slow down and stammer, as Isabelle Stengers urged so colourfully".

---

[6] Sha refers to Guattari's work, Chaosmosis: an ethico-aesthetic paradigm (1992).

The implications of the action-reaction human-centred design approach is illustrated in this excerpt from his recent book on Poesis and Enchantment in Topological Matter (2013):

A set of pedestrians' or dancers' limbs moving in tandem could form a body, as could a group of voices momentarily syncopated. What we ought not assume, however, is an invariant deterministic mapping from physiological data to metaphor. Although an invariant mapping may be a necessary working notion for neurologists and linguists and engineers, we need not and should not, as poets or as phenomenological experimentalists, assume a discernible deterministic relation between physiological data like heartbeat, galvanic skin response, or breathing rate and macroscopic aspects of a performative event, like emotion, mood, or narrative entity. Pragmatically, what we learn from neurophysiology and the principled scientific study of neural phenomena is that the data are simply too complex and polyvalent to plausibly map to any simple linguistic token of an emotion or some human behavioral state. A smile could correlate with amusement, embarrassment, confusion, or the rictus of death. A spike in the nervous signal of a muscle could correlate with an equally great variety of putative "causes." But beyond such pragmatic concerns, there is a more fundamental conceptual issue. Such a mapping would be merely a trace of the physical other, which is not identical and may have only accidental relation to the embodied phenomenal experience.

This is a critical point for me and relates to the concerns addressed in the other four chapters in this book, that breaking down the body into constituent parts that correlate with particular effects in us or rather our experience, not only presumes cause and effect, but also prescribes to us how we ought to move/vocalise and respond, and in so doing, conditions our behaviour. This is a point to reflect on as we increasingly use gaming technologies that are based on this premise.

His topological approach to design is "a way to imagine and think about living in the world, how to shape experience, a disposition with respect to the world, rather than a methodology or a technology." It is about spontaneous engagement:

… an artistically compelling experience in a responsive environment … should not induce puzzle-solving behavior. The mechanism should be completely obvious, or completely transparent. puzzle solving is a poor substitute for theater or any thick form of life and ferociously reinscribes only cognitive acts, and a particularly reduced set of such acts at that.

To illustrate what he means by 'transparency', Sha pointed me to the Bunraku puppet theatre (see Fig. 5.1.).

The picture (Fig. 5.1) shows an exchange of presents towards the end of the scene. Bunraku puppet theatre presents a complex idea of transparency and visibility; the master puppeteers are visible and their activity is transparent, yet we attend to their mastery and to the puppet which is imbued with life. There is a vast literature on puppets and they play an important part in ancient traditions of story telling, originally as hidden behind screens, as shadow puppets. At some point, some argue with the advent of realism, the puppet and the puppet master become visible. This example is given for reflecting beyond the current discussion on transparency and visibility in the design of computational artifacts, agents, and robots.

The issue of transparency is also debated in interaction design (Dourish op. cit.) for a range of interactive technologies, where the issue is about how far the computation

Fig. 5.1 Transparency: visible-invisible. This picture is from the first scene in the Bunraku play, Musume Kagekiyo Yashima Nikki (written in 1760). The story – "*A procurer of prostitutes tries to sell a teenage girl Itotaki to a brothel, but they complain the girl has no official papers signed by her parents (many children from poor families agree to a period of servitude to make money for their parents, but the parents must give permission) so are reluctant to buy her*" (Photo and description, Bunraku-Japanese-puppet-theatre 2010)

should be transparent to us, and how far it should be invisible. However, this debate may be seen as an evolution of discussions about whether the workings of the automaton (Schaffer op. cit.) should be visible or invisible, now applied to the computation, for example of our every day objects such as the fridge in the kitchen, the kettle, the lights in the house, i.e. smart technologies, etc. In contrast, one could say that the Bunraku theatre presents a different idea, where the transparency of the puppet is about the transparency of ourselves in relation to the puppet and through it. Sha's second point about the problem of puzzle solving hindering spontaneous engagement is shared with other projects presented in this chapter, where spontaneity in engagement is a fundamental element of co-presence, of sharing intimacy, of playing together, etc.

5.3.2   T-Garden: Movement Analysis (Three Experiments)

The T-Garden is a concept that emerged out of a dialogue between two labs, FoAM[7] (lead by Maja Kuzmanovic) and Sponge (lead by Sha Xin-Wei). Kuzmanovic and her colleagues at FoAM (Brussels) sought to explore how the movement of the body could write, and this aligned with Sha and his colleagues' interest in the body and world as continuous matter. After the two labs collaborated in designing the initial T-Garden, FoAM went on to produce further evolutions of the concept over the next few years, and one these was with choreographer and dancer Ghislaine Boddington.

---

[7] http://fo.am/

The T-Garden is like a black box, where light is projected down onto the floor from the ceiling, and where participants moving in this space wear sensors and clothing that is deliberately outside our normal experience. The clothing is of light and unusual textures, and the designs are playful and exaggerated so that one feels one is wearing a disguise, and can be free to imagine themselves as someone or something else for a while. The T-Garden is described as being a 'responsive environment', as body sensors feedback information about the person's movement and properties in the environment such as energy levels, feeding back sounds into the space, and projecting moving colours and textures from overhead. My interest lay in it being a space in which "people can playfully improvise gestures, and collectively or individually create affective or symbolically charged patterns out of fields of varying light, sound, fabric, or body" (Sha and Gill 2005). In 2004, I collaborated with Xin-Wei to apply the work on Body Moves (Chap. 4) to videos of the activity in the T-Garden to find out whether the dynamics of the Engagement Space, particularly salient rhythms, observed in the collaborative sketching activities of architects and between pairs of students, might occur in a T-Garden (Sha et al. op. cit. 2005).

> The idea of an *engagement space* or composite body field of engagement allows the spatial, sensory, temporal, and affective dimensions of coordinated activity to become part of a consideration of what is dialogue. Movement and touch are being thought of as part of a continuum, rather than as distinct. Engagement is a variable space as bodies are constantly negotiating and reforming their fields and their degrees of commitment to the situation (relation with the other person(s)) (see Chap. 4, herein).

It seemed a good fit for our philosophical explorations, myself on the tacit dimension of knowledge, and Sha on art and philosophy, and our shared interest in spontaneity, movement, sensory awareness, and fields, albeit from different disciplinary origins. Perhaps unsurprisingly, we found that salient rhythms do occur within the substrate of the combined activity in the T-Garden, indicating particular resonances as body fields move in response to each other and simultaneously. In later discussion with Kuzmanovic (FoAM) she and I realized that mapping Body Moves to the T-Garden made sense given that the origins of former lay in the movement of the body in drawing, and their inspiration for the T-Garden lay in the movement of the body as 'writing'. I will present some examples from (Sha et al. op. cit.) that span how an individual and a group are coupled with the TGarden environment.

As each person enters the TGarden and moves around in the space, they experience sounds and textures of colours and lines moving on the floor, and they may notice that if they move or gesture in a certain way they get a particular response, and they explore what the relationship between their movements to these responses might be. Whilst each person tries to understand their own relationship to this responsive environment, they find that some of these sounds and visual textures are connecting them to each other. The feeling of being connected within and with the environment is due to its inbuilt idea of a 'characteristic time' of response. If the characteristic time is too long, the environment begins to feel decoupled from the person and if it is too short the environment responds as a simple discrete series of stimulus-response events. With just the right characteristic time of response, the

player imputes a strong sense of *elasticity* to projected, structured light shining on a
hard floor, i.e. the player feels that the environment is actually related to them (concurrent). The TGarden is engineered with low latencies to produce computed media
that the human perceives as *concurrent* with his or her activity, and interprets the
computed response as a *tangible* quality. Concurrency is a crucial aspect of the
TGarden's field-based computationally mediated experience as it enables people to
become coupled with the room and with one another. In the hop-skip example, this
tangible quality derives from the micro-physics of the body intertwined with the
synthesized dynamics of the visual texture and the rhythmic sound. Within the concept of the engagement space, touch and movement are connected and form part of
a spectrum. The T-Garden seemed to make that connection visible.

5.3.2.1   Hop-Skip

This example illustrates how the T-Garden environment responds to the movement of
the person (via information from sensors) and triggers further spontaneous responsive
behaviours, and how the energies of the human and the system feed each other.

In this example, a person is hopping up and down periodically every eight or nine
beats to sound patterns. The strong beats in the musical textures in this Hop-skip
environment elevate the overall excitement in the room. At three beats after the third
hop, the person leaves their position and begins to hop and skip around over the
floor space. During the third hop there is a white flash on the floor (see Fig. 5.2, first
picture). Just following the hop, the flash re-emerges and moves across under the
feet space and shadow of the person (Fig. 5.2, second picture), after which they
begin to hop and skip across the floor (Fig. 5.2, third picture).

This responsive change in the environment cues the response of the person
hopping. Why does the flash re-emerge? The 3D graphics is filled in with a 'texture
map' and this texture of pale light colour is filled by using two rules: (a) it is triggered

Fig. 5.2 Hop skip. A person hops, and a white flash emerges (**a**), moving under the feet (**b**). The
flash echoes the person's hop. In the last picture (**c**), the person hops and skips away with this
visual and sonic echo that has extended and moved around them

by the person's hop (using movement sensors), and (b) it is interpolated such that its echo, the echo of the person's hop, goes on in the echo of the flash. In other words, the texture map is a continuous function of *both* the internal clock of the machine, *as well as* the rich real-time data from the human body's ongoing physical movement. The responsivity in the T-Garden arises from both software dynamics and body dynamics, the intertwining between simulated physics and material physics or body physics.

5.3.2.2   Dancers

In this example, 'TGarden V2 dancers', four professional dancers walk into the space and as they find positions for themselves, the textures and colours on the floor move with them and connect together. Once positioned, the dancers being to warm up in an improvised rehearsal, sensuously moving with sounds and colours. The shifting shapes on the floor occasionally and momentarily detach from a dancer who then reaches out and regains contact. As they move in the space the dancers quickly find resonant connections with each other as *an engagement field*, as we see happening in Fig. 5.3, where you can see the textures on the floor linking all the dancers.

By the end of their performance, they are fully rhythmically coordinated. This is enabled through grounding their coordinations with the environment and each other during discovery and improvisation as seen in Fig. 5.4, where two dancers move freely together for a brief moment in rhythmic synchrony.

Fig. 5.3 Finding connections – dancers discovering how they can connect with each other via the environment

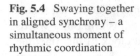

Fig. 5.4 Swaying together
in aligned synchrony – a
simultaneous moment of
rhythmic coordination

5.3.2.3 Slo-mo

This next example, 'Slo-mo', illustrates how the participants' body movement fields
can be altered by objects in their environment. About 41 s into the action, there is a
scene where four dancers converge around the centre of the play space and move
with four large balls. As they do so, there is a change in their rhythmic coordination.
Their dynamics and tempo shift from a smoothly coordinated rhythm to a seem-
ingly staccato random tempo, affected by their individual movement with the balls
and the physical contact between bodies that comes with rolling the balls to each
other. The rhythm alters again as they disperse and *their body fields engage* in
smoother coordinated autonomous choreographies (Fig. 5.5).

A core concept for the TGarden is the 'substrate', which is a way of looking at
the entire room as a continuous distribution of, for example, sound, light, fabrics,
costumes and bodies, and more abstractly, gestures, and fields of speech or attention. Considering the changes in the distribution over time of fields is a dynamic
approach that lends itself to notions such as waves and rhythms. By 'substrate' we
mean the union of all these continuous, time-varying distributions.

In this collaborative analysis of the TGarden, Sha and I applied the concept of the
body field of engagement (Gill et al. 2000) to the activity of players within this
responsive environment. The concept allows for the spatial, sensory, temporal and
affective dimensions of coordinated activity to be considered as part of dialogue. In
applying it to the TGarden, we extended the idea of the engagement space and body
field of engagement from the context of dialogue to include the resonant performance of the environment. This enabled us to consider how players in a TGarden
form tacit awareness in overlapping and autonomous space and gauge elements and
patterns of connectivity, and through this tacit learning, shape the media space and
are concurrently shaped by it.

Fig. 5.5 Slo-mo. Converging on balls – staccato tempo – the objects fragment the flow of movement

5.3.3   'Grow Your Own Worlds': At the Interstices
of Disciplines and Worldviews (FoAM)

The second example is of Maja Kuzmanovic who co-founded the FoAM lab in
Brussels for fostering the development of art-science projects. FoAM has now
become a global network of small 'transdisciplinary labs for speculative culture'. I

first learnt of Maja and met her through Sha Xin-Wei, and have been interested by her approach to exploring the conjunction of art and science and society. Over the years, FoAM has offered a free thinking space to people from a range of backgrounds, including artists, scientists, designers, computer scientists, biotechnologists, anthropologists, etc. It has an inclusive approach to involving the public in their work, and holds a regular weekly event on all manner of thought provoking topics. Kuzmanovic's organic approach to developing research around people and technology won her the Young Global Leader award by the World Economic Forum in 2006. Before creating FoAM she worked in mixed reality interfaces and virtual reality and collaborated with technological arts and has a background in design forecasting and interactive media. Her own interests are in story telling, patabotany, integrative medicine, cultural and personal resilience, speculative culture, and technical-social aspects of food and food systems.

The group FoAM describe themselves as a *cultural laboratory*, '*a generalists' community of practice working at the interstices of contrasting disciplines and worldviews*' consisting of people from arts, science, technology, entrepreneurship, cooking, design and gardening. On visiting their lab I found an open yet grounded exploration of fundamental problems and challenges facing our societies and our planet, and their use of technology as part of this exploration for a balanced future life: 'Guided by our motto "grow your own worlds," we study and prototype possible futures, while remaining firmly rooted in cultural traditions. We speculate about the future by modelling it in artistic experiments that allow alternative perspectives to emerge (e.g. Gaffney and Kuzmanovic 2013). By conducting these experiments in the public sphere, we invite conversations and participation of people from diverse walks of life.'

This public engagement is core to their identity, opening the lab to the public each week and welcoming people with food they have cooked, and food is itself an exploration as it is what gives life, energy, health, well being; it is culturally diverse, has powerful economics, affects the ecology of our planet, as well as being socially bonding (Kuzmanovic et al. 2009). Amongst the various arts-science groups, FoAM directly questions the current and future state of society, for example, in addressing 'climate chaos', 'rampant consumerism', and xenophobia. It describes itself as,

> a haven for people who are unafraid to ask the question: "What If?" and "How could it be otherwise?" Instead of dismissing possible futures because of their improbability, we speculate: What if we see plants as organisational principles for human society? What if lack of fossil fuels turns jet-setting artists into slow cultural pilgrims? What if market capitalism collapsed? By rehearsing for a range of different scenarios, we can cultivate behaviours that make us more resilient to whatever the future holds. This is why we encourage FoAM's activities to explore the breadth of themes and methods – from robotics to permaculture, tinkering to meditation..... FoAM's activities uphold the values of complexity and whole systems thinking, pollinated by the transdisciplinarity of our teams.

They liken themselves to a mass of bubbles (hence the acronym FoAM), a dynamic entity that can change shape and scale as required: 'a transdisciplinary organisation in the morning, a tightly knit family at lunchtime, a learning facility in the afternoon, a loose bunch of philosophers in the evening and a dedicated designers' collective by night.' Most of FoAM's activities occur in their studios which they describe as being hybrids between laboratories, ateliers and living rooms. The studios are designed to encourage a reciprocal exchange of ideas, techniques and experiences, reflecting the group's integrated approach to dialogue where the structure and aesthetics of the physical space itself is part of the process. As FoAM grows as a global distributed network of small labs, its coherent identity is sustained by Kuzmanovic and co-director Nik Gafney making regular visits to each lab. The labs collaborate with people (individuals and organisations) from many sectors: arts and culture, science and technology, academia, policy, business, and civil society. For example, the T-Garden was inspired by FoAM's interest in exploring body movement as writing in a responsive environment, and after the initial T-Garden development with Sha, they continued to evolve the concept with two further designs, one of which is with the London based choreographer Ghislaine Boddington.

The T-Garden is part of their work on responsive environments, which includes the project on transient realities [TRG] (Time's Up and FoAM 2006), that they describe as an exercise in world building:

worlds that you could see, hear, touch and be absorbed in. Worlds aware of your caressing, stepping, talking, twisting or simply moving through. The worlds that would engage with you, as animals would – mimicking your actions, translating them into something that made sense to their internal logic. They are worlds where skin-tight clothing and voluminous architectures communicated with abstract creatures in digital landscapes, in an attempt to stretch your perception of reality. Questioning your certainty of what is commonly understood as 'real'.... For something to be considered real, a continuum of space and time is implied." What they find is that mixed reality is a fragmented field that lacks its own continuum, so a challenge is to create such a continuum to pass seamlessly through it. But their focus is not on the technology, but on the impact of mixed realities at the scale of cities and eco-systems, on 'our urban and biological habitats'. They think aloud about 'origami-like foldable houses for nomadic youth. Buildings with walls acting as cellular membranes. Zoo-morphic subways to make Calabu and Yau smile. Such visions continue to entice us from the periphery and will certainly become a part of our future endeavours. (Time's Up and FoAM op. cit. p. 020)

FoAM seeks to balance art, spirituality, and science, and has a pragmatic character. For example, in their work on *prehearsing* the future, they state there is nothing wrong with representation – "if we had to learn everything we know through direct experience it would take many lifetimes. However, there are some things that remain ungraspable unless we experience them with our own skin. One of these things is the present moment, beginning its life as an unknowable future.

We can try to predict or calculate how we may experience a certain moment, but when it arrives it often differs from our expectations. ... in mindfulness and other meditative practices we learn that our experience of the present moment is largely coloured by our attitudes, grounded in the past and influenced by speculations about the future. We can practice to let go of the past (as we can't change it anyway), but the future is a different thing: we can influence what happens next."

Members of FoAM reflect on how hard it is to say in a nutshell what they are as they will alter their description depending on whom they are speaking with. Yet on meeting them, I came away with a clear identity of people who believe that things can be changed for a better life and a better world and that this can be achieved in collaboration with the various sectors in society and by keeping the dialogue open.

5.3.4   In Between: 'Energy at the Edge of Art and Science'

Once an artist takes on the challenge of making the invisible visible, or the inaudible audible, he/she is almost immediately thrown into the realm of energy at the edge of art and science. The established art world based on visual culture finds it difficult to place this kind of work. The scientific community, used to working in this realm in a reductionist way, finds it hard to comprehend. Yet, the public seems to be drawn to artwork residing "in between," and there seems to be a universal need for a connection to the spiritual realm beyond what established religions offer. Victoria Vesna – Artist (2012)

Victoria Vesna is a creative media artist and Professor at UCLA's department of Design|Media Arts and Director of the Art|Sci Centre at the School of the Arts and California Nanosystems Institute. I met Victoria via her work with the AI&Society Journal, of which she is the North American Editor. She is a creative artist who has a way of exploring issues around technology and society that touch fundamental human experience, such as time, stillness, reflection, well being, beauty. Her projects are art, yet they are also science.

Over the years she has collaborated with scientists from across the spectrum (Physics, Nanotechnology, Biology, Chemistry, Ornithology), and they include Stephen Hawkins. Her work with media (e.g. on concepts of data, virtual, real, body) has focused on interactive artworks that immerse the audience in experiencing the science and the ideas behind a technology, be it an installation, a networked event, or a participatory event. For example in her project NANO, participants can feel what it is like to manipulate atoms one by one and experience nano-scale structures through art-making activities. Vesna describes herself as creating experimental creative research that *resides between* disciplines and technologies. With her installations she explores how communication technologies affect collective behavior and how perceptions of identity shift in relation to scientific innovation, for example, in the projects 'Celullar Trans_actions' and 'n O time network screen saver':

n 0 time is the amount of time that none of us have. n 0 time always grows, especially in a new world of globalized network communication, in which time zones become meaningless and the most important asset is no longer time, but attention. The n 0 time screen saver runs on an idle computer, constantly contributing that computer's amount of wasted time to a central n 0 time database. Screen-saving participants contribute their own n 0 time to either their very own n 0 time bodies, or those of other people. This is called "n 0 time-sharing." The longer you are away from your computer the denser the n 0 time body grows. When a n 0 time body implodes, all participants are notified by the imploading screen saver via email (http://notime.arts.ucla.edu/notime3/).

"Cellular Trans_Actions" performance/talk focuses on issues of real time, physical space interruptions, and the performative aspects of everyday life. With no social protocols established, the constant sounds of interruptions by cell phone use in public spaces have become a daily collective performance. Vesna creates a "ready made" performance by audience members by asking them to leave their cell phones on and feel free to make calls if they feel compelled to communicate with someone at any moment during the talk. They are also given phone numbers of other audience members to break the usual communication in public spaces. The conversations are streamed live to the net and archived. Much is left to chance, depending on the location and the number of audience members who have their phones on.

In her collaboration on 'the realm of energy at the edge of art and science', Vesna and nanoscientist James Gimzewski investigate ideas around the relationship between energy and matter, particularly between body and mind, with their projects on the sounds of bacterial cells (Vesna op. cit.) and their Blue Morph installation at the Integratron. The following illustrates their dialogue process and Vesna's approach to allowing a project to unfold without pre-determining it or its outcome. Their collaboration also illustrates how a dialogue between science and art can lead to discoveries that are both scientific and artistic. In 2002, at the Pico Lab in UCLA, Gimzewski and then PhD student Andrew Pelling discovered that yeast cells oscillate at the nanoscale. Vesna describes how Gimzewski was excited by the initial results and eager to share the data with her but he knew she would not be able to understand the importance by simply looking at their graph:

> Knowing that Pelling was also interested in music, he asked him to output the data into sound files instead and sent me the audio file of live cell vibrations. This was definitely exciting, and through this sound, I could instantly see the importance of this finding. Soon after I asked whether he would "compose" sounds from the yeast cells, and Gimzewski experimented as Pollock would, by throwing scotch on the yeast cells and recording the sound of cell death. I used these sounds in a piece that I called "Cell Ghosts" (Vesna 2004) and Pelling collaborated with Anne Niemetz on a piece called "Dark Side of the Cell" (Niemetz and Pelling 2004), also inspired by these sounds. Not only art was created from this event, but an article on "screaming cells" came out in journal *Nature* (Zandonella 2003), and a scientific paper was produced in which Gimzewski coined a new word for this kind of data amplification of vibrations within a human audible range for research and analysis: "Sonocytology" (Pelling et al. 2004).

The tool with which the cell sounds are extracted is the atomic force microscope (AFM), and Vesna proposes that this could be regarded as a new type of musical instrument. She compares the AFM to a record and a needle that moves across the surface grooves to produce sound—the AFM "touches" a cell with its small tip. The AFM "feels" oscillations taking place at the membrane of a cell and these electrical signals are converted, amplified and distributed by speakers.

The Blue Morph installation is inspired by the sounds of rhythm and silence of the wings of a Blue Morpho butterfly as it develops and emerges from its chrysallis, and the work explores metamorphosis as a spiritual idea. Nanotechnology is changing our perception of life and for Vesna this is symbolic in the Blue Morpho butterfly who's beautiful blue color is not pigment but patterns and structure which is what nanophotonics is centered on studying. Blue Morpho has intrigued scientists for generations because of its subtle optical engineering that manipulated photons. The real surprise of her collaboration with the nanoscientists is in the discovery of the way cellular change takes place in a butterfly, the sounds of metamorphosis. These sounds are not gradual, rather the cellular transformation happens in sudden surges that are broken up with stillness and silence. Then there are the eight pumps or "hearts" that remain constant throughout the changes, pumping the rhythm in the background. During the transformation to emergence each flattened cell of the wing becomes a nanophotonic structure of black protein and space leading to iridescence.

The process of how the project evolved through the connections between people and ideas, and the details that technologies made visible, is beautifully described in Vesna (2012) and summarized here. In short, the work on the yeast cell lead to Grimzewski being approached by a specialist on Butterflies to record the metamorphosis to see what sounds would emerge, and was sent some chrysalis. He did so and sent the recordings to Vesna for ideas on creating a piece from them. In seeing and hearing the metamorphosis, they came to realise that the change is not gradual but 'is a series of intense bursts of energy with a rest period that vibrates in anticipation. (Pelling et al. 2009)". Vesna reflects on how we think about butterflies, for example, 'feeling butterflies in the stomach', and the 'butterfly effect' first proposed by Ray Bradbury in his science fiction "A Sound of Thunder", and later expressed by the meteorologist Lorenz as 'does the flap of a butterfly's wings in Brazil set off a tornado in Texas?" She traces our historical relation to butterflies, depicted in 3500 year old Egyptian hieroglyphics, and the Greek word for butterfly meaning 'soul and/or mind'. The butterfly has signified beauty and 'brought many to ponder the wonder of change and the power of nature'. Vesna believes it is this 'archetypal instinct that moved [her, Pelling, and Grimzewski] to consider this ephemeral and beautiful insect'.

Whilst she was working on these projects with the nanoscientists, Vesna was also intrigued by the symbolic and historical value of a building called the Integraton, a 38-ft-high, 55-ft-diameter, nonmetallic structure designed by Van Tassel as a rejuvenation and time machine (The Integratron 2009). It is located near the Great Rock in California which holds spiritual powers for the Native American Indian. George Van Tassel's Integratron is based on the design of Moses' Tabernacle, the writings of Nikola Tesla, and telepathic design directions that he claims he received from extraterrestrials during meditation. This 16 sided wooden rejuvenation and time machine was conceived and built during a period of interest in 'vibrations, electromagnetic fields and the invisible' realm, an ongoing interest recently re-inspired by a discovery by Japanese scientists that electricity can pass through air. The Integratron was recently re-opened after two decades of renovation, and the website about it describes it as the 'fusion of art, science, and magic'.[8]

Vesna felt that the Integratron would be the ideal space for the Blue Morph installation. As both Vesna and Gimzewski are practitioners of KundaliniYoga, they discussed how to create an environment where people interact by keeping still and/or moving from their centre. They decided to use meteorological balloons as turbans, a jest that became the Alice in Wonderland's 'mad hatter' of the project. People would come and sit in the centre and take turns at wearing this turban whilst experiencing the rhythmic sound of the cellular transformation of the Blue Morpho butterfly's metamorphosis. At the Integraton, the audience brought their own perceptions and interpretations which Vesna and the team allowed to guide them on how to evolve the interaction. What took them by surprise was the ritualistic way people engaged, 'seeing the installation as a place to release… their inner urge for transfor-

---

[8] http://integratron.com/

mation and metamorphosis'. Vesna describes how the audience is the performer when in the centre and the witness when observing others, and 'the artist (herself) and the scientist are on the sidelines.' She describes this as neither art nor science, nor theatre or reality, 'but a scene that is open to interpretation and allows for individualized ritual to take place'.

The experience opened up a new direction for the next phase of Vesna's work with Gimzewski, to look into our neuronal vibrations with our environment, and the rhythm of oscillations in the brain that give rise to consciousness, and how failures in rhythms give rise to brain disorders.

These examples illustrate how art, science and technology can come together and open unexpected investigations about their purposes and function, and how to engage the public in interpreting what these purposes and function might be. Neither is the outcome pre-defined, nor the process pre-determined. The creation, experience, and realisation of the artworks involve the personal act of knowing.

5.3.5 Betweeness: 'Witnessing You: Trust and Truth in a Networked World'

Caroline Nevejan is a deep thinker on digital culture, which she has pioneered since the 1980s. She has been driving the debates around issues of the networked society in the Netherlands through the Paradiso and the WAAG Society in Amsterdam, which she co-founded in 1994 as the Society for Old and New Media. Today, the WAAG has become an independent media lab and a knowledge center with a specific interest in the future of the public domain. She was part of the Doors of Perception network and worked on education and learning research. Over the years she has conducted numerous experiments around distributed performances and networked events. During the last decade she has focused on presence and the design of trust and is now Associate Professor with the Participatory Systems Initiative at the Technical University of Delft.

I had the pleasure of meeting Caroline in Edinburgh in 2003, at a European project proposal meeting on the theme of Presence. We found much in common, and continued a dialogue that eventually led to us working together in 2010 on a journal issue for AI&Society on Witnessed Presence. In reflecting with her on the relationship between rhythm and witnessed presence, we find that witnessed presence necessarily has a rhythmic quality.

In her work on Presence and the Design of Trust (Nevejan 2007), Nevejan has reframed Presence research with her analysis and discussion on what we mean by being present when face to face and when in distributed settings in terms of witnessing and being witnessed. I first saw her present her YUTPA framework in Edinburgh, an acronym for "being with You in Unity of Time, Place and Action". It depicts how four dimensions of *time*, *place*, *action* and *relation* have different values between You and not–You, Now and not–Now, Here and not–Here, Do and not–Do (see Fig. 5.6).

Fig. 5.6 The YUTPA
Framework

- The You/not-You dimension refers to the relationship with the other human being(s) with whom one interacts.
- The Now/not-Now dimension refers to the sharing of the experience of time, synchronous or asynchronous in past or future.
- The Here/not-Here dimension encompasses the sharing of place or not. Depending on how place is defined or experienced this can be geographically small or large, it can also refer to the sense of distance in virtual and online worlds.
- The Do/not-Do dimension refers to the possibility to act as part of or as a result of a social interaction.

The framework posits that trust requires both witnessing and being witnessed, how we do this differs according to the degree of distance one has from the presence of others in 'natural' and in mediated presence via various forms of technology. Critically, the presence of others influences how we 'orchestrate' our own presence. Mediated presence is partial and differs from the whole 'natural' presence that uses all the senses and cognitive and emotional structures in Real Life. We are able to accept the partial presence of another person(s) by balancing the four dimensions (time, space, action, relation) through attribution, synchronization, and adaptation to the partial presence. Differences in time and space, and in how we relate and what possible actions we can take, affect the trade-offs we make for presence and trust. For Nevejan, the distinction between You and not–You, founded in Buber's *I-Thou*, is fundamental to whether we consider mediated communication as mere 'information' or as communication with someone whom we are in a relationship with. "The specific configuration of time, space, action and relation in a certain product or process, in which natural presence, mediated presence and witnessed presence all play a role, enables certain forms of trust and truth to be established while excluding others." I have found Nevejan's concept of witnessed presence to be helpful for understanding how ethics in communication is changing with distributed settings in comparison to how in face to face culture, we have checks on politeness, a subject of much work in Linguistics. We need to consider the nature of witnessing in online interactions, in addition to the discussions on how forms of representation create impolite behavior (such as awareness of how the written word can cause 'flaming' in the online world) and how we project our self onto a virtual environment.

In 2012 she co-lead a European EIT ICT Labs research program on 'Mediating presence' with architect Charlie Gullstrom. This was a cross disciplinary and cross cultural collaboration between Delft University of Technology, KTH Royal Institute of Technology in Stockholm and Lulea University in Sweden. It involved philosophers, artists, designers, computer scientists, architects, crafts designers (e.g. of glass), and social scientists. It was innovative in dealing with both fundamental issues around mediated presence and creating designs for it, simultaneously, in an evolving dialogue. As part of this process, Nevejan designed the collaborative research platform www.being-here.net which extends the concept of a website and what it means to share information and make connections between ideas; in their participation with reflections and ideas, they are responding to a key question, 'what happens when one is witness to the other?'

As part of the being-here research, Nevejan has been working together with 13 artists (Nevejan 2012) to explore today's footprint on the future. The artistic research explores new values for the (meta) design of participatory systems in which people accept responsibility for their words and deeds and negotiate trust and truth in a networked world. The questions they ask are: 'How are trust and truth established in the emerging network society? How do the stories we exchange become part of the experiences we share? Are we in touch with each other, do we witness each other, when time and place are not shared? Witnessing is acquiring new dynamics. Networks are like mirrors to the self and fuel imagination. Love and passion drive engagement. However, engagement in merging realities challenges human dignities to the core.'

The artists' works are an expression of their personal act of knowing which can give insights that scientific methods may not. One of these artists, Anna Carlgren, works with glass, and in her project on 'Looking Glass' she explores how by changing the materiality of glass we can change how we 'look' with it and witness. Angelo Vermeulen creates installations to investigate co-creation and symbiosis between technology, biology, and the social. Karen Lancel's deep and questioning social and artistic experiments explore how public and private space is experienced, and she is investigating how the body is the interface of trust.

5.3.5.1 Example. Intimate Strangers

One of the artists collaborating with Nevejan, Martin Butler, is a performance artist bridging a variety of disciplines. Between film, dance, theatre and visual arts, he explores the new dramatic that information and communication technologies facilitate. His work "Intimate Strangers" (2012) asks, 'How do you create intimacy with strangers? How do you take responsibility for people you don't know? What happens when one person witnesses another? What happens when you witness another? How do you deal with strangers?' He explores these questions through various scenarios – for example, in this project he asks strangers how they deal with strangers. Martin asks 100 people, 50 whom he knows in some way and 50 whom he does not know, two questions:

When would you trust a stranger?
How would you make a stranger trust you?

All 100 people replied to his query and he presents some of their answers:

- Person 1. When I can look him/her in the eyes.. or can read in between his/her lines; When he/she looks me in the eyes, Or when he/she can read in between my lines.
- Person 2. Most of the time. Trust is the base for communication. Trust is always a better first choice. So I trust people from the start... and hope the trust will endure throughout the time.; By trusting the stranger.
- Person 4. Well, it depends on what kind of feeling that person gives me during the first meeting/conversation. Body language, use of words, tone of voice, questions etc. etc.; Just to be myself and to have no alternative motives.
- Person 25. I think everything is in the feeling that I get from that person, the eyes, the smile, the face, what I feel inside... Do I feel good, do I feel repulsion; I will generally trust my feelings, my perceptions. It doesn't have to do with the way the person looks, but more with how I feel when standing in front of him/her.
- Just being myself completely; I don't have to play games, I'm a trustable person. If the other person cannot feel it, too bad!

It is a very interesting exercise to do, and you might like to try this yourselves. One factor that seems to run throughout the responses is that in order to make the other person trust me I need to be authentic, i.e. true to who I am. Likewise in how we trust someone else, are they being honest, truthful, have ulterior motives?

5.3.6 The Future Body and Tele-Intuition (Body-Data)

Ghislaine Boddington's work (Boddington 2012) on telepresence posits the full body as its locus. She explores and questions what happens to somatic knowledge, and thereby our identity, in tele-present interaction with virtual worlds and gaming environments. In the near future younger generations will be working and playing daily in virtual worlds and be communicating extensively with colleagues via telematics and forming new intuitions, that she calls 'tele-intuitions'. Boddington founded the body>data>space in London, which engages the public in what these changes implicate through participatory performances and installations. By engaging the public she seeks to tap into these emerging tele-intuitions and enable these to be creatively used. She approaches this work from her background as a dancer and choreographer. I first met Boddington via ResCen in 2005, a leading performance arts group in the UK based at Middlesex University, and was interested to find a dancer and choreographer working with technology to explore the limits and possibilities of human connection. In 'Woven Bodies, Woven Cultures' (op. cit.) she reflects that "*In terms of the discussions, experiences and writings in the last 15 years re-occurring words such as spiritual, magic, embracing, out of body, extended, disembodied, re-embodiment, transcendence, transformation, shared consciousness all come to mind.*"

At body>data>space, she has been discussing these re-occurring ideas and emerging tele-intuitions with her research group to discuss the multi-identity mode of modern living, of existing in the real and the virtual in many forms, and how it is gradually dissolving boundaries between the real and the virtual. With the evolution of mass interaction on the web through social networks and virtual environments, the opportunity (with web access) to re-present oneself in avatar form in virtual environments today has exploded. With the ease of using online avatar making tools "we have moved into a generation of easy representation of the multiple self through virtual bodies, thereby expanding ourselves into many selves."

She proposes that we recognise and start to engage with the topical and complex issue of the new reflectivity of ourselves on ourselves through the use of the virtual reality, and ultimately our abilities to deal with 'the other' within the virtual, and this means understanding 'identity'. She asks, "How does the telematic 'you' expand and enhance the real 'you'? How do our avatars in the virtual realm reflect on ourselves? What do they teach us about ourselves and how can we use that knowledge to extend our understanding of others?" She reflects on the word avatar being a Sanskrit word, implying re-incarnation. In Hindu philosophy, an avatar (also spelled as avatara) (Sanskrit: avatāra), most commonly refers to the incarnation (bodily manifestation) of a higher being (deva), or the Supreme Being (God) onto planet Earth. The Sanskrit word avatāra literally means 'descent' (avatarati) and usually implies a deliberate descent into lower realms of existence for special purposes.

As with avatar creation, "performative telematics (where you re-present your real self as streamed video data) deals us all with a complex identity card. How have we used this and what has it bought to us all? Travelling through personal space, working with community in distant space and being globally aware at the same time is an intricate place for the body/mind to inhabit and to orientate itself within. Your baseline somatic knowledge knows that you are encapsulating a new you, even though it is you."

She asked her research group, 'What was it like for you in your first experiences in telematic space? What were your feelings and thoughts? Does it still feel the same for you now?' Their responses revealed that telematic experience has shifted the way we exist in the real world today, the way we make relationships and the way we understand the concept of 'presence'.

She gives an example of telematics experience, where young Portuguese artists treat the projection screens in different locations as transparent walls of an unknown fluid, through which they could transport themselves from one space to another. This is in contrast to treating the projection screens as separate image canvases that need to be mixed to enable interaction. In both aesthetics and intent, a very special set of work emerged where they passed objects and gestures through virtual space to each other in a fluid and watery way. This illustrates the physical experience of the body and its reliance on what she calls 'the interface of the mind' and kinetic responses.

Many of the artists whom Boddington has researched see the full bodied telematic space as having the potential to allow a wider representational say in the debates of today's world. To make full use of 'the strong emergent dynamic of a porous network of highly active clusters of interaction is essential to the ways of being in the twenty-first century', and she believes that making this a full bodied physical interface could make a key difference in the world.

Speedier data transfer is allowing more and more people to use video as well as text and voice, from home web cams to office environments, yet this is not often approached through the use of the full body. On the projection of the self onto the virtual, she cites the choreographer Yacov Sharir who works in live performance with virtual avatars that react to his movements within the performance space. Wearable devices used on his performers allow them to generate cyber human counter-parts in real time. These are projected around the performers, creating what he describes as being 'an environment of mutual co-existence'. 'Following many years of this shared performance space, experience, and practice with several computerised cyber human characters, I have continually been experiencing/noticing the presence of a shared energy field in performance much similar to the energy shared between two physical human bodies as they interact in traditional dance partnering work, and as practiced in dance contact improvisation principles. Like in Contact Improvisation, the success of such physical, virtual and spiritual interaction 'necessitates mutual support and trust' (Joe Edelman), which is to say that there are many levels by which we are interacting over and beyond the range of our ability, experience, inhibition and electronic connection.' (Yacov Sharir speaking about the Second Life Internet-based virtual world).

Second life was launched in 2003 to enable its 'users', called Residents, to interact with each other through moving avatars, providing a social network service combined with general aspects of a 'metaverse'. Residents can explore, meet other Residents, socialise, participate in individual and group activities, create and trade items (virtual property) and services from one another. This is a *user-defined world* where the characters created by people 'teleport' from location to location to meet each other and interact. Dance is a large part of this world with many objects to touch enabling your avatar to dance in multiple ways. Boddington describes her first few hours in Second Life as exhausting: 'I hit a dance-enabling object, had a wild time, but did not know how to stop dancing! I emerged feeling I had been clubbing for hours. The physical effect on my real body of the virtual dance of my avatar body stunned me.' Her experience was shared by choreographer Cosmin Manulescu: 'I felt very strange looking to my body flying over virtual spaces. Later somebody taught me how my body can also 'dance' with other virtual bodies. I started to experience different types of dance such as salsa, tango, hip-hop (…) I was dancing and looking at my own body moving at the same time. I had very different sensations from dancing on real stage and in real life. But still it is a powerful sensation. It was real because I knew somebody else was there together with me, we were chatting, exchanging words about the experience. It was unreal because I was just alone in front of my computer.' (Cosmin Manulescu)

Boddington believes that as the flow between real life and the virtual is dissolving in 'hyper existence', the key to full and reciprocal interconnectedness is that it is a full bodied and creative experience. She believes that the role of the artist is to ensure creativity is enabled in these environments. 'And yet what happens when your avatar can make its own avatar (…) or when one has a real space encounter with ones own avatars?'

Boddington's work throws up questions about what is reciprocity, and as we evolve tele-intuitions are we as artists and researchers clear on what is actually changing? How do we gauge this? In 'excited atoms' (Staines 2010) findings from a questionnaire from artists around the globe working on telematics, presents mixed views with some disillusioned about telepresence being able to overcome distributed space and consider it to be failing in real interconnectedness. Boddington's approach is pragmatic, reflective, and positive, that we need to improve things and support the social, creative, and intuitive dimension of our ways of connecting with others, and that the wholeness of bodily connectivity is central to this goal.

5.3.7   Faraway: Intimacy

I first came across the Faraway project by Kristina Andersen and her colleagues at their presentation of it at a V2 event in Rotterdam in 2004. It has remained in my thoughts as their work touches fundamental issues of how we can sense how we are relating with someone else.

Kristina Andersen is based at STEIM (Studio for Electro-Instrumental Music), in Amsterdam. She works with electronics and reclaimed materials to create unusual devices and experience, whilst exploring how we can allow each other to imagine our possible (technological) futures through the making of exploratory objects. I find her approach refreshing, as she begins by asking what the purpose of an artefact might be, and that it must be intuitive, magical. She sees making objects as a method of both thinking about and imagining ideas, teasing out the new and unexpected from the everyday and the mundane. The results are experimental prototypes of "technological matter" that is understood through physical and tactile interaction with the object itself, hence working with ideas is a process of becoming.

This is illustrated well in the project Faraway (Andersen et al. 2002) which explores intimacy in communication, in particular emotional closeness and physical distance. Andersen and her team's aim was to identity new directions and ways of thinking for the design of physical interactive applications that increase our sense of presence of people we love but are separated from by distance. They believe that the objective of mediated communication is to *feel each other's presence.*

Telecommunications is used by loved ones to 'express a wish to be together' more than for any actual exchange of verbal content.

The team describe the focus of Faraway to be on 'high meaning and low bandwidth', and by low bandwidth they seem to mean the degree of complex information being represented. The project is not focused around creating design products but rather on defining a design space and design methodology for developing applications for distant communication applications. The team ask three core questions: How do people communicate with their loved ones? How can this communication be improved? What can interaction design do to increase the perception of distance in affectionate relationships? They investigate: (a) how can we sense the presence of someone in an object?; (b) In distance communication, body messages are lost. Is it possible to use them as substitutes, surrogates or placebo for physical presence?

Andersen et al. draw on Shannon and Weaver's (1949) model of transmission of information, Umberto Eco's (1976) and Jakobsens' (1960) semiotics, to consider the intersection between technical choices and meaning creation, and this is their definition of interaction design. Their approach to the problem is to substitute 'me' and 'you' for 'sender' and 'receiver' (Shannon and Weaver's model) and for 'addresser' and 'addressee' (Jakobsen's model). This is an interesting take on these models.

Another core idea is 'emotional space', which is 'exclusive; only two people inhabit it.' Hence their design framework is 'communicating presence in the emotional space'. They use 'If-only' games to suspend disbelief and take people beyond the reality of current communication to imagine new possibilities.

In 2004 I saw their presentation of one of their Faraway project experiments, called Blush. This game was about 'are you my distant one?' Some players were asked to produce messages for a 'Distant One', and others were given these messages and told they came from their loved one. There were eight players. Four were given white smocks and painting materials and asked to imagine they were communicating with a 'Distant One' (someone they love or feel close to) by painting gestures on this 'magical medium'. The other four players were asked to wear these painted smocks and imagine what their loved one is trying to convey to them. Other experiments included soundscapes and objects. After each experiment, all the players were given questionnaires, which revealed that in general, players who produced messages were happy to express themselves, but players who wore the smocks (and sounds and objects) and received the message had a mixed response, with half of them questioning the identity of a 'distant one'. For example, in response to the question, 'How did you feel wearing Distant One's expression?', one of the players who wore a painted smock replied, 'Good for the first 30 min; then I discovered that was not my Distant One.'

Andersen and the team used a 'scientific method' approach in their experiments, yet were able to use the qualities of the method that supported their investigation within a human life experience context. Andersen's approach is to always question what the purpose of an artefact might be, and that whatever we create must work with our natural intuitions. Most importantly, any interface needs to capture our imagination and immediately hold our attention, and a key ingredient is magic. She humourously and seriously says that she tests all her designs on young children, because they will be bored if it is not easy to understand and if you cannot inspire their wonder, then you have failed. This echoes Sha's call for the obvious or the transparent, as puzzle solving '*reinscribes only cognitive acts, and a particularly reduced set of such acts at that.*'

5.3.8 In Between: Tangible Digital – Radical Atoms and Materiality

Hiroshi Ishii is director of the MIT Media Lab, and his works, such as Transform,[9] conjure up the words, magical, aesthetic, sensory, and organic. Although his projects do not all deal directly with human engagement with others, what interests me is that he explores aspects of our immediate relation with the world and each other in a way which engages the imagination and makes one want to experience. His work is inspired by a problem of how to get beyond the limitations of the computer interface as most of us know it, i.e. a visual interface, and move beyond the keyboard and pen and predefined gesture functions, in order to find ways to seamlessly engage with 'data' and each other. To meet this challenge he reconceives the idea of interface and the digital, not as a screen for a virtual world fronting invisible or visible data, but as tangible bits that we can directly manipulate, and do so together with another person.

In 2012, Hiroshi Ishii and the MIT media lab took things further and proposed that an interface be reconceived as computationally transformed material where dynamic changes in the forms and appearance of materials would be 'as reconfigurable as pixels on a screen' by being 'bidrectionally coupled' with an underlying digital model of 'bits', i.e. dynamic changes in the physical form (materiality) would be reflected in digital states in real time, and vice versa. Such materials could alter their shape, 'conform to constraints' (be manageable and controlled), and 'inform users of their affordances'. The vision is that in human-material interaction, the digital has a physical manifestation allowing us to directly interact with it and manipulate it. Their work, Transform, is an example of this vision called 'radical atoms.'

Transform fuses technology and 'design' transforming still furniture into a dynamic machine driven by a stream of energy and data. By bringing together the aesthetics of furniture and the aesthetics of motion, it draws our attention to the aesthetics of the complexity of the machine, rather than to the complexity itself. There are over a thousand motors (driving pins) to control with a computer, and this complexity disappears in the beauty of the motion. Kinetic energy of viewers, captured by a sensor, drives the wave motion represented by the dynamics pins.

The Lab's recent project on telepresence (Leithinger et al. 2014) involves participants either directly touching and pushing down physical pins, or moving their hands and arms over a screen, to drive the movement of objects by manipulating them using the pins or the pins themselves become the object to manipulate, rather

---

[9] http://tangible.media.mit.edu/project/transform/

than the furniture as in Transform. In order to manipulate objects via movement over a screen, there is a representation of body parts, e.g. the hand and the arm, and this draws on robotics work for manipulating distant objects.

Although Ishii's work does not directly deal with human to human relations, it does explore how our bodies connect via tangible data and can shape the interface and what it means to interface.

5.3.9 Hybrid- the Informal

In this last example, I have drawn on architecture, and in particular the work of Cecil Balmond as his ideas about the 'informal' in design bear a relation to how I think about tacit engagement in human life. His idea of the informal is that it is the essential nature of 'structure', a re-examination of space as rhythm, of syncopation, and he speaks of being 'out of phase', and of a dynamic, a movement. The informal moves architecture beyond a conception of structure as reduction and regulation. In applying the informal to design, he reconceives it as 'intervention' which is a 'local forcing move', a 'juxtaposition that stresses rhythm', or 'two or more events mixing to reveal hybrid natures.' There is no hierarchy, only interdependence. This is the 'template' of the Informal.

In his asking about how to find the dynamic in a building, he reflects on patterns and beauty, and finds the 'answer lies in configuration': We are made of patterns, random and regular, physical and emotional, and in probing the archetype of patterns we may find the element of beauty. Beauty may lie in 'processes of engagement and *be more abstract* than the aesthetic of objecthood'. This resonates with my work on the aesthetics of the empathetic knowledge mediator and the aesthetics of being in the flow with another living being. The informal necessarily allows for the emergence of 'structure', as something spontaneous, just as the architects who were sketching together in Chap. 4.

In the informal, there is structural framing in the punctuation of space which is a syncopation rather than the dull metronomic beat of post and beam, again like human interaction. There is also a layer of ambiguity over structure which makes for richer experience. Balmond's conception of the informal shares much in common with my conception of the tacit in dialogue.

5.4 Conclusion

In conclusion, I would like to leave us with some reflections and questions. In Chap. 1, I proposed that although technologies may have altered in shape and form, the essential concept of the interface whether invisible, available, or backgrounded, seems to have remained unchanged. The convergence of the arts, performance arts, with science and technology explores how our understanding of science, and our relationship with the world and others can be experienced as aesthetic, emotional, trusting, sensory, and imaginary, but is their use of computation and conception of interface fundamentally different?

Sha's topological media 'is an approach to design, *a way to imagine and think about living in the world*, how to shape experience, a disposition with respect to the world, rather than a methodology or a technology." Kuzmanovic's encouragement to grow your own worlds is creating a community of nodes of practice *working at the interstices of contrasting disciplines*. Vesna opens us to the realization that there is a *realm of energy* at the edge of art and science that draws the public to artwork that resides "inbetween" that is neither art not science, nor theatre or reality, but something *open to interpretation*. Nevejan makes us aware that trust and ethics requires both *witnessing and being witnessed*, where the presence of others influences how we 'orchestrate' our own presence in a *spectrum of closeness (I-You) to distance (I-It)*. Ishii seeks to break free from the limitations of the interface to directly *manipulate data by bodily realizing it* and thereby connect with others via bodily touch and movement.

Dancing with a computationally produced shadow reflects how in seeking to make the interface more 'human' we define this in terms of action. Action becomes computed empirical time. However, transparency and immediacy in natural life do not equate to quantified time. Sha's discussion of 'transparency' and Andersen's reflection on 'immediacy' are not simply about action. We can feel time suspended, we can feel it is slow, or too fast, etc. (Einstein's 'theory of relativity'). Empirical and computational time is not experiential time, and a focus on an action paradigm can lose sight of this. This can affect our own conceptions of our self. For example, dancing with computational shadows that are derived from our movement data and to then think we are learning something about this 'other self' of ours, is to perceive and redefine ourselves according to data abstracted from our *person*, something we need to be careful about.

In a discussion with the psychologist Carl Rogers about whether 'science can lead to truth about man?", Polanyi speaks of how in academia, 'in a very characteristic way, the use of the term "scientific" as an appreciation of what can and what cannot be done, [is being] applied in a way which is absolutely destructive ... . And if this is at all characteristic of our culture, our culture is in serious danger'. (ref 1984 op. cit. p. 173) Whilst some may agree and some disagree, there is no doubt that this 'scientific' approach will not enable my colleague in Japan (re. Chap. 1) to share what is tacit in dialogue, and will be unable to bridge the relational gap in distributed interaction (Chap. 1). In our relations with others, as with art and performance art, authenticity makes for trust, and truth lies in a personal act of knowing the authentic is such, experienced and felt in the situation (as with the players who wore the painted smocks in Andersen's Blush game and felt that the person was someone they knew or not).

The projects described here do question what matters, and in doing so, they are creating novel ideas and designs for both what an interface means and whether it is a relevant concept for the relationship between the digital and the non digital world, and for how we might engage with and via the digital at a level that allows us our own personal acts of knowing. They seem to extend ways of doing science and ways of doing art in a cross cultural dialogue with self reflection and conscious awareness of their assumptions. This is a markedly different approach from the 'scientific' one.

As is often said, technology is here to stay, but focusing on the technology seems to limit us culturally. What is the relation between mediation and interface? It has been shown and proposed (Chap. 4) that mediation is not an individual's action (be this a gesture and/or utterance) as a go between of two parties or a conduit between two nodes, but a collective moment between two or more persons, where one recognizes the other in his/her response. In the collective moment we 'know how', 'know that' and 'know when' simultaneously. Can an interface facilitate this? Can a virtual agent or an avatar achieve this with us?

There is a belief that if an interface can facilitate intersubjectivity in human relations this will solve the problems facing the interface. However, the problem of intersubjectivity is that we assume and judge others according to our own 'self', so what if the problem of a difference of opinion or a misunderstanding lies with our assumption and not with the other? How can we realize our cultural assumptions in a distributed setting?

Technologies of data and utility, where a person becomes a user, presume to represent and provide certainty. Just as the expert loses confidence in doubting and making judgements with human certainty ('this feels right', 'intuition', 'skill', 'cultural logic') when using a knowledge based system, might we lose our bodily awareness of grasping and making sense of behavior when interacting with computated representations of behavior, such as the abstraction of gesture and movement from culture?

Tacit engagement involves a structure of mediation, which is a collective moment that involves being consciously aware of the other from the other's perspective and recognizing oneself in that situation simultaneously in a personal act of knowing. Polanyi said all knowing is the same as that of seeing a problem in a personal act of knowing. For an interface to mediate, it needs to afford this process of tacit engagement.

References

Aaron, S., Barnard, P., Cross, I., Gill, S. P., Himberg, T., Hoadley, R., Odell-Miller, H., & Toulson, R. (2013). Touching sound: Vulnerability and synchronicity. In *Proceedings of the CHI2013 workshop on designing for and with vulnerable people.*

Andersen, K., Jacobs, M., & Polazzi, L. (2002). *Faraway.* Interaction Design Institute Ivrea.

Balmond, C. (2002). *Informal.* Munich: Prestel Verlag.

Bergson. (1911). *Creative evolution* (trans: Mitchell, A.). New York: Dover.

Boddington, G. (2012). Woven bodies, woven cultures. In S. Broadhurst & J. Machon (Eds.), *Identify, performance and technology: Practices of empowerment, embodiment and technicity.* New York: Palgrave Macmillan.

Breazeal, C., & Picard, R. (2009). The role of emotion-inspired abilities in relational robots. In P. Parasuraman & M. Rizzo (Eds.), *Neuroergonomics: The brain at work.* Oxford: Oxford University Press.

Buber, M. (1923). *I and thou* (trans: Smith, R. G.) (1958) New York: Charles Scribner's Sons.

Bunraku-Japanese-puppet-theatre. (2010). https://rakugoleon.wordpress.com/2010/11/04/day-19-文楽-bunraku-japanese-puppet-theatre/. Accessed on 20 Apr 2015.

Butler, M. (2012). Intimate strangers. In C. Nevejan (Ed.), *Witnessing you. On trust and truth in a networked world. Participatory Systems Initiative* (pp. 199–242). Delft: Delft University of Technology.

Collins, H. H. (2013). *Tacit and explicit knowledge*. Chicago: University of Chicago Press.

Cooley, M. J. E. (1987). *Architect or bee? The human price of technology*. London: Hogarth Press.

Cooley, M. J. E. (2007). From judgement to calculation. *AI & Society, 21*(4), 395–409.

Cross, I. (2012). Music and communication in music psychology. *Psychology of Music, 42*(6), 809–819.

Dourish, P. (2004). Where the action is. The foundations of embodied interaction. MIT Press (First paperback edition).

Eco, U. (1976). *A theory of semiotics*. Bloomington: Indiana University Press.

Fluxustree. (2009–2010). http://rhoadley.net/comp/fluxustree/ Automatic music for sculpture, dancer(s), instrument ('cello) and computer.

Gaffney, N., & Kuzmanovic, M. (2013). Borrowed scenery: Cultivating an alternate reality. http://libarynth.org/parn/borrowed_scenery_cultivating_an_alternate_reality

Gill, S. P. (1995). *Dialogue and tacit knowledge for knowledge transfer*. PhD dissertation, University of Cambridge.

Gill, K. S. (1996). *Human machine symbiosis*. London: Springer.

Gill, S. P., Kawamori, M., Katagiri, Y., & Shimojima, A. (2000). The role of body moves in dialogue. *RASK, 12*, 89–114.

Göranzon, B. (1988). The practice of the use of computers. A paradoxical encounter between different traditions of knowledge. In B. Göranzon & I. Josefson (Eds.), *Knowledge, skill and artificial intelligence* (pp. 9–18). London: Springer.

Goranzon. (1992). The practical intellect: Computers and skill. In K. S. Gill (Ed.), *Artificial intelligence and society series*. London: Springer.

Guattari, F. (1992). *Chaosmosis: An ethico-aesthetic paradigm*. Bloomington: Indiana University Press.

Hall, E. T. (1976). *The dance of life*. New York: Anchor Books.

Hall, E. T. (1983). *Dance of life: The other dimension of time, anchor books*.

Husserl. (1931). Cartesian meditations, a translation of meditations cartesiennes, D. Cairns. Dordrecht: Kluwer, 1988.

Ikuta. (1988). The role of "craft language" in learning "waza". *AI & Society, 4*, 137–146.

Jakobsen, R. (1960). Closing statement: Linguistics and poetics. In T. A. Seboek (Ed.), *Style in language* (pp. 350–377). Cambridge, MA: MIT Press.

Kirschenbaum, H., & Henderson, V. L. (Eds.). (1989). *Carl Rogers: Dialogues*. Boston: Houghton Mifflin Company.

Kuzmanovic, M., Engelen, S., & Chipperfield, A. (2009). *Open sauces*. Brussels: FoAM.

Leithinger, D., Follme, S., Olwal, A., & Ishii, H. (2014). Physical telepresence: Shape capture and display for embodied, computer mediated collaboration. In *Proceedings of UIST'14*, ACM.

Merleau-Ponty, M. (1945/1962). *Phenomenology of perception* (trans: Smith, C.). London: Routledge and Kegan Paul.

Negrotti, M. (2012). *The reality of the artificial: Nature, technology and naturoids* (Studies in applied philosophy, epistemology and rational ethics). London: Springer.

Nevejan, C. (2007). Presence and the design of trust. PhD dissertation, University of Amsterdam.

Nevejan, C. (2012). *Witnessing you. On trust and truth in a networked world. Participatory systems initiative*. Delft: Delft University of Technology.

Niemetz, A., & Pelling, A. (2004). Dark side of the cell. http://www.darksideofcell.info/

Pelling, A. E., Schati, S., Gralla, E., Velentine, J., & Gimzewski, J. K. (2004). Local nanomechanical motion of the cell wall of Sacharomyces cereusiae. *Science, 305*, 1147. doi:10.1126/science.1097640.

Pelling, A. E., Wilkinson, P. R., Stringer, R., & Gimzewski, J. K. (2009). Dynamic mechanical oscillations during metamorphosis of the monacrh butterfly. *Journal of the Royal Society Interface, 6*, 29–37.

Polanyi, M. (1966). *The tacit dimension*. New York: Doubleday. 1983 Reprint.

Rauner, F., Rasmussen, L. B., & Corbett, M. (1988). The social shaping of technology. *AI & Society, 2*, 47–62. Springer.

Rosenbrock, H. (1988). Engineering as an art. *AI & Society, 2*(4), 315–320.

Rosenbrock, H. H. (1990). *Machines with a purpose*. Oxford: Oxford University Press.

Rosenbrock, H. (1996). Rosenbrock's account of causality and purpose: A compilation of Howard Rosenbrock's works by Satinder Gill. In K. S. Gill (Ed.), *Human machine symbiosis: The foundation of human-centred system design*. London: Springer.

Schaffer, S. (1990). Enlightened automata. In W. Clark, J. Golinski, & S. Schaffer (Eds.), *The sciences in enlightened Europe*. Chicago: Chicago University Press.

Sha, X. W. (2013). *Poiesis and enchantment in topological matter*. Cambridge, MA: MIT Press.

Sha, X. W., & Gill, S. P. (2005). Gesture and response in field-based performance'. In *The ACM proceedings of creativity and cognition 2005*, Goldsmiths College, London.

Shannon, C., & Weaver, W. (1949). *The mathematical theory of communication*. Urbana: University of Illinois Press.

Smith, D. (1992). The psychology of apprenticeship. In B. Göranzon & M. Florin (Eds.), *Skill and education: Reflection and experience* (pp. 83–100). London: Springer-Verlag.

Staines, J. (2010). Excited atoms: An exploration of virtual mobility in the contemporary performing arts. An OTM mobility information dossier. http://on-the-move.org/library/article/13882/otm-excited-atoms-exploration-of-virtual-mobility/

Up, T., & FoAM. (2006). *TRG: On transient realities and their generators*. Brussels: FoAM.

Vesna, V. (2004). *Cell ghosts*. Premiered at the crash and flow exhibition held at the former Seodaermun prison in Seoul. Documentation: http://vv.arts.ucla.edu/projects/04-05/cell/installation.html

Vesna, V. (2012). Vibration matters: Collective blue morph effect. *AI & Society, 27*, 319–323.

Winograd, T., & Flores, F. (1986). *Understanding computers and cognition. A new foundation for design*. Norwood: Ablex Corporation.

Wittgenstein, L. (1958). *Philosophical investigations* (trans: Anscombe, G. E. M.). Oxford: Basil Blackwell.

Wittgenstein, L. (1969). *On certainty* (trans: Paul, D. & Anscombe, G. E. M.). Oxford: Oxford University Press.

Zandonella, C. (2003). Dying cells dragged screaming under the microscope. *Nature, 43*, 105–107.

Printed in the United States
By Bookmasters